The Almoravids and the Meanings of Jihad

The Almoravids and the Meanings of Jihad

RONALD A. MESSIER

PRAEGER

AN IMPRINT OF ABC-CLIO, LLC
Santa Barbara, California • Denver, Colorado • Oxford, England

Copyright 2010 by Ronald A. Messier

All rights reserved. No part of this publication may be reproduced, stored in a retrieval system, or transmitted, in any form or by any means, electronic, mechanical, photocopying, recording, or otherwise, except for the inclusion of brief quotations in a review, without prior permission in writing from the publisher.

Library of Congress Cataloging-in-Publication Data

Messier, Ronald A.
 The Almoravids and the meanings of jihad / Ronald A. Messier.
   p. cm.
 Includes bibliographical references and index.
   ISBN 978–0–313–38589–6 (hard copy : alk. paper) — ISBN 978–0–313–38590–2 (ebook)
 1. Almoravides. 2. Africa, North—History—647–1517. 3. Spain—History—711–1516. 4. Islam—Africa, West—History. 5. Yasin, ʾAbd Allah ibn, d. 1059. 6. Jihad. I. Title.
 DT199.M47   2010
 961′.022—dc22   2010017831

ISBN: 978–0–313–38589–6
EISBN: 978–0–313–38590–2

14 13 12 11 10   1 2 3 4 5

This book is also available on the World Wide Web as an eBook.
Visit www.abc-clio.com for details.

Praeger
An Imprint of ABC-CLIO, LLC

ABC-CLIO, LLC
130 Cremona Drive, P.O. Box 1911
Santa Barbara, California 93116-1911

This book is printed on acid-free paper ∞

Manufactured in the United States of America

For Emily, Anne, and Frank

Contents

Acknowledgments	ix
Introduction	xi
Notes on Dates and Transliteration	xxiii
Chapter 1: Islamic Reformism Comes to West Africa, Eleventh Century C.E.	1
Chapter 2: Gateway of the Sahara	21
Chapter 3: From Aghmat to Marrakech	35
Chapter 4: The Second Founding of Fez	43
Chapter 5: The Urban Nomad	53
Chapter 6: War in the Makhzan	61
Chapter 7: Jihad in Andalusia	69
Chapter 8: The Statesman	85
Chapter 9: A War of Sieges with the Taifa Kings	93
Chapter 10: The Almoravids Confront El Cid	111
Chapter 11: Ali Ibn Yusuf Sets His House in Order	121
Chapter 12: Ali Ibn Yusuf Faces Muslim and Christian Challengers	133
Chapter 13: Voices of Dissent	145

Chapter 14: The Center Cannot Hold	161
Chapter 15: The Almoravids and Ibn Khaldun	173
Main Characters	179
Glossary	183
Commentary on Sources	189
Bibliography	223
Index	235

Acknowledgments

There are always many people involved in writing a book, other than the author himself. There are many such people who have assisted me either directly or indirectly to whom I will be unable to give personal acknowledgement. To all those who are not named in the following pages, I extend my sincere appreciation.

I first came into contact with the Almoravids as a graduate student at the University of Michigan doing research for my Ph.D. dissertation on the circulation of gold currency in the medieval Mediterranean World. My guiding light in that early exposure to the Almoravids was my mentor and advisor, Professor Andrew S. Ehrenkreutz, whose wisdom and sharp, red pencil have had a lasting influence.

Two faculty research grants and one non-instructional assignment (sabbatical) at Middle Tennessee State University allowed me to begin the intensive research necessary for this work. For that assistance, I am most grateful.

To colleagues and friends (Dr. Wilfrid Rollman, Dr. Kenneth Perkins, Dr. June McCash, Dr. Allen Hibbard, Dr. William Caferro, and Dr. John Vile) and to my daughter, Dr. Samantha Messier, all of whom have read all or parts of the manuscript, I express my thanks for their thoughtful comments and encouragement. I especially thank Dr. John Paul Montgomery, who not only read, but carefully edited an early draft of the manuscript. He helped me find a particular voice with which to tell this story and taught me to listen to how writing sounds in addition to how it reads. I thank Dr. Tom Nolan for his generous production of the maps, Mike Summers for his sketches of two of the main characters, and Simintaj Soroushazari for the beautiful photograph on the cover.

The archaeological research at Sijilmasa and Aghmat is an indispensable part of this story. That work was facilitated by numerous grants from the Aghmat Foundation, the U.S. Ambassador's Fund for Cultural Development (U.S. Department of State), the American Institute for Maghrib Studies, Earthwatch, the Max Van Berchem Foundation, Middle Tennessee State University, the Moroccan-American Commission for Educational and Cultural Exchange (Fulbright), the National Geographic Society, and the Social Science Research Council. For all of that assistance, I am most grateful. This archaeological research could not have been done without the collaboration of my research associates Mohamed Alama, Nancy Benco, Stephen Brown, Mohamed Choukri, Said Ennahid, Larbi Erbati, Aaron Fogel, Naima Keddane, Azdine Kerra, James Knudstad, Dale Lightfoot, Montaser Loukili, Neil MacKenzie, Tarik Madani, Samantha Messier (once again), James Miller, John Runkle, and Tony Wilkinson, as well as numerous students, volunteers, and local day laborers; and especially Abdallah Fili, who began working with me as a student in 1993 and continues to be my associate to this day. Three of my students, Julie Coco, Choukri Heddouchi, Pongracz Sennyey, and Sykes Wilford, did work on some aspect of Almoravid and/or Sijilmasa history. Our long conversations shaped my own understanding of Almoravid history. Their insights have found their way into this story. For all of that assistance, collaboration, and friendship, I am most grateful.

I owe a special debt of gratitude to former U.S. Ambassador Frederick Vreeland and Mrs. Vanessa Vreeland for initiating the Aghmat project, for their continued support, and for inviting me to live in their beautiful home in Marrakech for my ongoing archaeological support.

Finally, I thank my family: my stepdaughter Missy, who worked at Sijilmasa during our first season; my son Ben, who offers unqualified friendship; and most especially, my wife, Emily, who has lived with the Almoravids almost as long as I have and has had to listen to me tell their story more than anyone should have to. For her patience, partnership, love, and never-ending support, I am eternally grateful. She is my Zaynab.

Introduction

The account that follows is a true story. It is the story of the Almoravids, a Berber dynasty that emerged from the western Sahara desert in the mid-eleventh century to rule practically all of the land from the Senegal River in West Africa to the Ebro River in Spain. The principal characters are colorful, powerful, charismatic, cunning, and totally dedicated to achieving their goals. There is the succession of *Amirs*: Abu Bakr Ibn Umar, the desert warrior who muddied his hands in the construction of Marrakech but then returned to the desert to extend the Saharan confederation, to fight his final battle and die at the hands of a blind bowman; Yusuf Ibn Tashfin, the Saharan who was more adapted to the urban environment, a disciplined ascetic, a soldier who conquered Morocco and half of Spain and a statesman who set up a government to rule it all; Ali Ibn Yusuf, who, except for the fact that he was not reared in the desert, was every bit his father's son and who brought African and Andalusian cultures together in an unprecedented ferment; Tashfin Ibn Ali, young and feisty, whose life was cut too short in the rising tide of opposition.

There is Zaynab, wife of two *Amirs*; she was not a Saharan, but she ruled like a desert matriarch. There are caravaneers who carried untold treasures in gold and opened routes for teachers and warriors of the faith. There are desert warriors who carried the sword from the sands of the Sahara to the Mediterranean Sea—the likes of Mazdali, who mended potentially fatal rifts within the ruling family; Syr Ibn Abu Bakr, who fought against El Cid and lost; Reverter the Christian, the outsider who became an Almoravid and was feared by their enemies; and Abu Bakr Ibn Tifilwit, whose generosity won the *Amir*'s favor and who was then seduced by the pleasures of courtly life. There are poets who praised the deeds of heroes and chided some for growing soft. There are legists, who used the rigid precepts of Malikite law to impose their will.

At the center of them all is the legacy of a fiery preacher, Abd Allah Ibn Yasin, who came from the *Dar al-Murabitin* (the house of those who are bound together in the way of God) and instilled in the Almoravids a strict sense of moral reform and ignited the spark of holy war. He was more a mirror reflection of Ibn Tumart, that preacher from the High Atlas who was the Almoravids' downfall, than any of them were likely to admit. All are ghosts of a fallen dynasty.

The minor characters are no less colorful and no less significant to the story. They are the people of the desert tribes bound to each other with a powerful sense of tribal solidarity: the farmers in the oases, valleys. and plains, who possessed the skills to prevail on the earth to bring forth a rich variety of foods; the herders, who alternately used the land to graze their livestock; and the inhabitants of the cities, the merchants, craftsmen, teachers, and students.

The stage upon which the characters acted might seem picturesque and strikingly exotic to those of us who see it for the first time. But as we envision the vast horizons of the Sahara or the tall, snow-covered peaks of the High Atlas, as we stroll vicariously through the streets of places such as medieval Fez, Marrakech, Sijilmasa, Aghmat, and Seville, we should know that many of our characters were newcomers to the scene as well and might have found the stage equally picturesque and exotic. When the people of the desert stood for the first time on the northern tip of Africa, peering across the straits of Gibraltar, they too strained to imagine the riches of medieval Andalusia.

There is the wider world with which the Almoravids interacted: the Christian kingdoms of Iberia, imbued with the European spirit of crusade; the Muslim heartland, bracing itself for the Christian onslaught as it struggled with political fragmentation; the Italian city-states, anxious to do business with any place that offered profit; and the African kingdoms south of the Sahara, carefully guarding the West African gold trade that provided the Almoravids with a source for much of its wealth.

The Almoravids were camel drivers from the western Sahara desert who came forth in the mid-eleventh century to build one of the richest, most powerful empires in the history of western Islam. Before they were Almoravids, they were nomads who roamed the western Sahara desert in what is today Mauritania. They lived close to nature, earning their living by raising camels, sheep, and goats and by giving safe passage for a price to caravans who passed through their desert land. They were steadfast in their effort to survive in the harsh environment of the desert, swift and mobile, and brave in the face of adversity. Out of necessity, at first, they had an aversion to luxury. They were hardy warriors. They demonstrated a sense of moral righteousness that took the form of loyalty toward the tribe and confederation, the blood vendetta being a cornerstone in tribal solidarity. They were Muslim, but they knew little of the teachings of Allah. They became Almoravids when one of their tribal chiefs returned home from a pilgrimage to Mecca and brought with him a fiery preacher to teach them, a scholar from a school in southwestern Morocco called *Dar* (house) *al-Murabitin* (of those who are bound together); "Almoravids" is an Anglicization of *al-Murabitin*.

As people of the desert, the Almoravids understood the need for cooperation between the townsmen and farmers of the oasis. They worked out a system of alternating usage of the land and the trade of goods that it produced. Under the date palms of the oasis, farmers would cultivate winter grains, a variety of vegetables, and spring wheat. Then, after a number of years of this kind of cultivation, they would give way on the land to the desert nomads, allowing them to pasture their livestock. The nomads traded products of their beasts for goods available in the towns. In time, the breakdown of this kind of cooperation in the area around the oasis city of Sijilmasa, located on the northern edge of the Sahara desert in southeastern Morocco, invited the Almoravids to take the city and restore the balance. When the people of Sijilmasa petitioned the Almoravids to rescue them from their tyrannical rulers of the Bani Wanudin tribe, the Almoravids obliged and moved to the city. They expelled the Bani Wanudin and moved into the garrison themselves. The following year, the Almoravids conquered Audaghust on the southern edge of the desert. It, like Sijilmasa, was a port city on the edge of the great desert "sea." Both ports were key to the gold trade from West Africa to the Mediterranean world, which provided the Almoravids with the wealth they needed to build an empire.

It took the Almoravids about 20 years to subdue the rest of Morocco and western Algeria, what the Arabs call *al-Maghrib al-Aqsa*, or simply *al-Maghrib*. The conquests beyond the Atlas Mountains were not steady as an advancing front. They were more like a rising of the tide, with waves rolling in and then washing back, gaining ground and then losing ground, making only slight progress with each successive wave. They controlled the countryside first by isolating the urban fortresses and forcing them into submission. Ruling the empire involved controlling the major cities, the surrounding farmland whose produce they needed, and the routes connecting the whole system. But there were areas, especially in the mountains, that were always just beyond their control.

City life appealed to the Almoravids—once it became accessible. It provided the wealth and security they needed to rule an empire. Within a few years of their conquests in Morocco, the Almoravids set to building the imperial city of Marrakech. At first, it looked little different from the nomadic camps in which the Almoravids lived in the desert. But during the second generation of its existence, it took on much of the appearance of the imperial city for which it is known, adorned with architectural masterpieces largely inspired from those the Almoravids had seen and admired in the cities they conquered in Andalusia.

Islam was vital to the Almoravids' rise to power. The chief of the Sanhaja confederation brought a fiery reformist preacher to the Sahara to instruct his tribesmen, who were pious but ignorant of the law. The teacher was a disciple of the *Dar al-Murabitin* in southwest Morocco. The particular *madhhab* or legal interpretation followed by the *Dar al-Murabitin* was Malikite Islam. It was fundamentalist at least in the sense that it was based on a strict, literal interpretation of scripture. On a practical level, it meant total acceptance of Malikite religious scholars who looked back nostalgically at a mythical simplicity in the faraway Arabian desert. It was puritanical and reformist in that it rejected alcohol, music, womanizing, or compromise of any type with the infidel (most broadly defined). When the Malikite preacher won a party of tribesmen over to his particular version of Islam and offered his religious endorsement to a particular candidate as the new chief for the confederation, religious ideology became the force that drove the Almoravids to victory against all odds.

The mission of the new religious movement was jihad, which eventually came to mean holy war. At first, jihad was a struggle to attain and uphold a "true" understanding of Islam. Then it involved fighting against the desert tribesmen, nonbelievers who obstructed the spreading of this puritanical, reformist Islam in the western Sahara desert. Shortly thereafter, it meant defeating the regimes of bad Muslims and imposing their own royal authority, as they did in Sijilmasa. Finally, it brought the Almoravids to Spain to wage war against Christian infidels. Each new meaning of jihad did not replace an earlier one but was added to a cumulatively evolving concept.

When the Muslim city of Toledo fell to the Christian King Alfonso VI of Castile, the inhabitants found their new master to be even less tolerant than they had ever dreamed. The prospect of *reconquista* forced the Muslim kings of Andalusia to invite the Almoravids to their shores. The Almoravids were reluctant to come, but once there were even more reluctant to leave. Andalusia was a wealthy land. Its wealth was based on the introduction of new crops and agricultural technology described by two mid-tenth century writers, the Muslim Ibn Hawqal and the Christian Recemund. Andalusia was a consumer of raw materials and a producer of fine industrial goods. It was the western end of the east-west axis of trans-Mediterranean trade. All in all, it was a considerable prize for a dynasty from the western Sahara. The Almoravids rescued the Taifa kings and made Andalusia part of their empire. For the first time, southern Spain and the Maghrib were under the same regime. The Almoravids brought political stability and economic prosperity to both, although some say that the veiled Sanhaja killed "high culture" in Spain. To the extent that Andalusian high culture resulted from the interaction of Muslim, Jewish, and Christian minds, perhaps they did; the latter two communities had less freedom under the Almoravids. Muslim poets fled Andalusia and came to the Maghrib, but they were not a happy lot. They were exiles, political opponents of the Andalusian *faqih*s (legal scholars). Their verse had an edge as sharp as that of Dante, the political exile of his beloved Florence. But the very fact that the Andalusian poets could come to the Maghrib and continue writing, even critical verse, shows that the Almoravid hierarchy at the very top was anything but anti-intellectual. They were patrons of Andalusian artists and poets and brought them home to adorn the courts of North Africa. To that extent, they fostered a degree of cultural unity between the Maghrib and Andalusia that was unprecedented.

 The Almoravid's jihad in Spain mirrors a vital chapter of any comprehensive account of the Crusades. The monastery of Cluny spearheaded a reform movement in western Christendom comparable to the reform movement of the Almoravids. The Cluniac movement certainly added fervor to the Crusades in the East, but it was involved in Spain as well. Christian church leaders urged French knights to carry the crusade to Spain. Pope Gelasius II granted crusade indulgences to all who joined. The frontier between Muslim and Christian Iberia is the venue where Christian heroes like Roland and El Cid became legend. It is where the concepts of pilgrimage, crusade, and *reconquista* merged. The *reconquista*, the Iberian Christian effort to expel the Muslim conquerors, began immediately after the Muslim conquests in the early eighth century. It picked up in intensity in the late eleventh century after the conquest of

Toledo, at a time when pilgrimages to Christian shrines in Spain were on the rise. A specific link between the three concepts is the Abbey of Cluny, which provided the church with Crusading popes, organized pilgrimages to Santiago de Compostela, and encouraged the Christian kings in Northern Spain to "re-conquer" Andalusia. The king of Castile supported the monastery with contributions in gold. Among the ironies of it all, the gold came from West Africa through Almoravid territory. Muslim kings in Andalusia used the gold to pay tribute to Christian kings and soldiers of fortune, thus financing the *reconquista*. The Almoravids severely rebuked such payments of tribute and, as much as they could, cut it off. The Almoravid jihad in Spain was both a reaction to and stimulus for a Crusading spirit among Christians.

In the end, holding on to Andalusia cost more than the Almoravids could afford. Their credibility depended on sustaining a jihad against the enemy. It also depended on upholding their policy of no non-Koranic taxes. Unfortunately, these two ideological cornerstones of the regime were incompatible. Whether or not the Almoravids lost sight of their religious ideology toward the end of their reign is debatable and may even be beside the point. The fact is that their religious ideology was challenged by another Islamic reformer, in another tribal confederation, trying to establish a new dynasty buttressed by a new religious ideology. Its adherents were called *al-Muwahiddin* or Almohads, "those who profess the oneness of God." The theology of the new regime was more mystical than that of the Almoravids. It condemned the Almoravids as polytheists, claiming that their scriptural literalism made a god out of scripture. On a popular level, the new preacher promised little different than the Almoravids. He vowed to restore the community and equality of believers and promised to suppress wine, women, and song. He pledged to collect no non-Koranic taxes. The vitality of the new zealot held promise for the masses who were disappointed that all of their expectations of the Almoravids had not been fulfilled.

These are the broad outlines of the story. Yet how are we to understand its patterns? The story of the Almoravids, at least in broad terms, fits the paradigm that the famous fourteenth century Arab historian Ibn Khaldun developed to explain the rise and fall of royal dynasties. According to Ibn Khaldun, dynasties originate among desert tribes. The desert breeds those qualities that a ruler needs, the virtues of discipline and endurance, courage and combat, temperance and loyalty, the virtues for which Yahya Ibn Umar and his brother Abu Bakr were chosen to be the first commanders of the Almoravids. The tribe provides both the need for royal authority and its base of authority. Tribal solidarity, what the Arabs call *asabiya*, provides for various interactions within the group. Sometimes those interactions are competitive, and royal authority is needed to restrain individual action that is at odds with the group as a whole. Royal authority, during its first generation, relies on the tribe for protection and shares its glory with the tribe. Tribal solidarity is preserved.

The second generation moves from the desert to the city, from privation to luxury and plenty. Since the second generation had direct contact with the first, and with the desert, it retains many of its virtues. Royalty, at this point, moves beyond its struggle for basic needs toward maturity. It seeks sedentary or urban existence, luxury and ease, and the security of city walls. In this phase of Almoravid development, the ruler Yusuf Ibn Tashfin built the walled city of Marrakech. The wealth of this urban civilization and the power of the dynasty peak simultaneously. The dynasty claims glory for itself, and the vigor of tribal solidarity is strained.

The third generation—among the Almoravids, that of Ali Ibn Yusuf—has no contact with the desert. It has forgotten desert life and toughness as if they never existed. It knows only the luxury and ease of city life, which corrupt the desert virtues and contribute to the dynasty's decline. The nomadic virtues of hardiness and courage wane, and the dynasty moves toward senility. The desire for luxury and ease exceeds the resources. The regime goes beyond itself to meet its desires. It then narrows its base in hopes of holding on to what it has. The royal dynasty becomes vulnerable to peripheral rival forces from within as well as to challengers from without. Those challengers will destroy the dynasty and establish a new regime. Thus, in three generations, the dynasty has come and gone. *Asabiya* is lost. Ibn Khaldun explains the decline of dynasty in terms of this loss. The narrative that follows, however, demonstrates the opposite. The Almoravids were trapped by *asabiya*; they were ultimately unable fully to make the transition from desert to urban life.

The polarity between city and desert is crucial to Ibn Khaldun's paradigm of the rise and fall of dynasties, including the Almoravids. Noble qualities develop in the desert and are corrupted in the city. There are two reasons that dynasties establish themselves in cities. First, because of the concentration of commercial activity and accumulation of wealth, the regime can more easily secure the resources it needs to support itself. The wealth of the Almoravids poured forth from the official mints in more than 30 cities in North Africa and Spain. The volume of coinage struck in the name of the dynasty was small at first; but shortly before the dynasty's collapse, the volume peaked at a level that rivaled any other regime in the Mediterranean world.

The second reason that dynasties reside in cities is that cities provide defense. The Almoravids built a protective shell around themselves in the form of city walls. Much of their story takes place in the streets of Seville and Cordoba and Valencia, in Sijilmasa, Aghmat, Fez, and Marrakech. Although Almoravid armies were almost invincible in open combat, most of their campaigns involved extended sieges of major cities. They demonstrated their skill in military architecture when they built a new wall around the city of Fez and when they fortified their capital in Marrakech that kept out their enemies for more than 20 years. The regime finally collapsed when the walls of Marrakech were breached.

The story of the Almoravids vents another important tension in North African and Andalusian history: Arab versus Berber. Ibn Khaldun distinguishes Berbers by the language they speak, referring to an ancient legendary king, a contemporary of Moses, who gave them the name Berbers when he heard their jargon and asked what that *barbara* was. Modern scholars still distinguish Berbers from Arabs by the language they speak, but there is also a certain amount of cultural baggage that is relevant to the story. Berbers, says Ibn Khaldun, lack "taste," which he defines as "the tongue's possession of the *habit* of eloquence," or "the conformity of speech to the meaning intended"—in other words, language. Since the language of culture and authority in the Islamic world, and most importantly the word of God himself in the Holy Koran, is Arabic, and Berbers did not speak Arabic as a native language, they lacked taste, and Arabs looked at them disparagingly for that.

Not only did Berbers lack taste, but there was something inherently rebellious about them. The conquest of North Africa by the Arabs was one of the longest and bloodiest episodes in the extraordinary expansion of Islam. Another early Arab historian, Ibn Abi Zayd, says that the Berbers of North Africa revolted 12 times before they accepted Islam. Ibn Khaldun says that even after the Muslim religion had been established among them, "they went on revolting and seceding, and they adopted dissident (Kharijite) religious opinions." He adds that that is what is meant by the statement that Ifriqiya (the medieval name for what is now Tunisia and eastern Algeria) divides the hearts of its inhabitants. The statement is a play on words connecting Ifriqiya with the Arabic root *f-r-q*, "to divide."

Introduction

The antagonism between Berber and Arab was there from the time of the Arab conquest. Arabs and Berbers brought it with them to Spain when they crossed the Straits. Ibn Khaldun correctly observes that when the Arabs in Spain were no longer ruled by the Arab dynasty of the Umayyads, and the Almoravid Berbers became their rulers, the Arabs "detested this domination. Their oppression weighed heavily upon them, and their hearts were full of hate and indignation against the new rulers." It was as much fear as hate. The residents of Andalusian cities were terrorized by the Almoravid militia, cloaked in their dark robes and veils that hid all but their eyes. Fear turned to resentment when the regime went back on its promise of good government, of tax reform, and security against the Christian invaders. Resentment reached that critical point where another ideologue, perhaps any ideologue, could succeed in offering a better alternative. That alternative was offered by the Almohad preacher Ibn Tumart, whose base of operation was the High Atlas Mountains, just south of Marrakech, a region that was always just beyond the control of the Almoravids.

Land controlled by the central government would be called *bilad al-makhzan*; land just beyond that control would be called *bilad as-siba*, the "lawless land," reflecting an age-old theme of Maghribi political life. Land that a dynasty controls, says Ibn Khaldun, is that land which is occupied by members of the tribe or people who support the tribe. Beyond those borders, the dynasty cannot control, especially if they contain several tribes with a strong *asabiya* of their own. One modern scholar, David M. Hart, says that the difference between the *bilad al-makhzan* and the *bilad as-siba* is essentially one of payment or withholding of taxes. Ibn Khaldun agrees. At first, dynasties collect large tax revenues from small tax assessments. Assessments are small because the regime imposes only those taxes stipulated by the religious law. People are less resistant to paying these taxes. In fact, small assessments encourage economic activity, which expands the tax base. Later on, regimes raise taxes to meet the higher costs of satisfying their desire for luxuries and protection. The Almoravids conform to the pattern. They came to power on a platform of "no non-Koranic taxes," a policy that made them popular, at least for a while, among all who paid taxes. The regime fell increasingly in disfavor when it went back on its promise.

The rise and fall of the Almoravids, like that of so many other dynasties, fits Ibn Khaldun's paradigm so well that it gives the fourteenth century historian the stature that he has as one of the greatest historians of all times. But if Ibn Khaldun's observations are correct, his explanations might be lacking. Explaining the cycle as *natural* or as inevitable might be too fatalistic, or explaining the move from desert to city in a Muslim world as a shift from virtue to corruption might be too moralistic. Finding a more assuring explanation for the rise and fall of the Almoravids, then, is one of the tasks of the following story.

Not a single detail in the story is fiction. The story comes from contemporary sources: medieval Arabic chronicles, writings of early Arabic travelers and geographers, and contemporary literary sources. For example, when I describe the enchantress Zaynab as "exceptionally beautiful, with a smooth olive complexion . . . " that is the consensus of several medieval writers. In some cases, the narrative mentions certain events but provides no details. The events are important enough to include in the story, but the details are not included because the chroniclers provided none. Here, the narrator begs the reader's patience. The pace of the story will quickly resume. The dialogue that appears in the narrative is translated from the medieval chronicles, which is admittedly risky. We know that early Arab chroniclers tend to be overly dramatic; they exaggerate facts of historical events and qualities of historical personalities. One should be cautious to accept what each of them says individually as historical "truth." The medieval sources present perceptions of truth of writers who were convinced of the heroism and moral righteousness of their leaders, people who had enough charisma to create a strong sense of Moroccan/Muslim self-awareness; or, they had a particular ax to grind. How these writers felt about the people and events about which they wrote is also an important part of the story and must be included in the inventory of "facts" upon which this account is based.

For each chapter, there is a commentary on the sources; these form an integral part of the story. They are intended to answer the question, "How do we know that?" They describe the medieval Arabic sources from where the story comes and offer analytical commentaries on those sources. In some cases, they offer competing versions of the story that would have interrupted the flow of the narrative.

As in any story, there is conflicting evidence and potentially several differing interpretations of a given event or sequence of events, personality, motive, cause, or result. In the account that follows, the narrator's goal to present *one* coherent version has forced me to choose one interpretation above another, the one that, in view of the entire inventory of information at my disposal, seems to be most logical, or which best fits the narrative. As a historian, I have tried to *understand* the evidence that I have accumulated and to extrapolate as much of the story as possible from that evidence. For example, there is confusion as to when the city of Marrakech was built by the Almoravids. Two accepted dates, each appearing in a medieval chronicle, are a full decade apart. Until 20 years ago, most historians believed that Marrakech was founded in C.E. 1060. But since then, new evidence, and in my judgment the bulk of the evidence, suggests that it was built in C.E. 1070. That is the date that appears in this narrative. But that creates another chronological problem placing Yusuf Ibn Tashfin's campaign against the Zanata, culminating with the conquest of Fez, before the founding of Marrakech rather than after it as it appears in most of the medieval narratives. My explanation is that the final conquest of Fez is actually sandwiched between the establishment of Marrakech as a fortified camp sometime in the late 1060s and the beginning of the actual building of the city in 1070–1071. Placed here in the chronology, the conquest of Fez would have contributed to the level of prestige that Yusuf Ibn Tashfin is said to have had when he replaced his cousin Abu Bakr in Marrakech at the time of its founding.

New interpretations are based not so much on *new* texts as on rereading all of the textual evidence largely in light of new numismatic and archaeological research, including recent excavations under my direction of the medieval cities of Sijilmasa and Aghmat. The new reading has led to important new interpretations: the impact of the Almoravids on the urban development of Sijilmasa and Aghmat, the importance of their role in the African gold trade, their alleged intellectual repressiveness, and their initial success in winning the support of the masses but their ultimate failure to hold it. Finally, the story calls into question the validity of Ibn Khaldun's paradigm on the rise and fall of empires.

Woven into the story are descriptive vignettes of the Almoravid world: the state of disunity in the Maghrib on the eve of the birth of the movement; the Malikite center in Qayrawan that provided the ideology, the kingdom of Ghana that provided the wealth to launch the movement; the city of Sijilmasa that served as a springboard for the movement into North Africa; the city of Aghmat that served as the Almoravid capital for a little over a decade; the cities of Fez and Marrakech, Andalusia under the Taifa kings and later under the Almoravids themselves; Christian Europe that mounted a crusade against the Almoravids as part of their larger Crusade against the world of Islam; that "larger world of Islam" to whom the Almoravids sent reinforcements for the counter crusade; the caliphate, far away in Baghdad, whose sanction the Almoravids sought. These are views of the Almoravids' world as they would have known it.

The net result is the first comprehensive English language narrative history of the Almoravids accessible to the nonspecialist. It portrays the Almoravids as reactive to external stimuli, as opportunistic, as taking advantage of opportunities for conquest more than being motivated by a visionary ideology. They were able to take advantage of the anarchic conditions of the western Sahara, where short periods of unity were interspersed within periods of fierce rivalry and fighting among the tribes of the Sanhaja. They exploited the political instability among the tribes of the Zanata, which Ibn Yasin observed in Morocco as he returned to the Sahara from Andalusia, and they seized upon the plea of the *Muluk al-Tawa'if* to defend Andalusia against the Christian *reconquista* and extended their empire across the straits of Gibraltar. They did, of course, develop from the start an ideology of spreading Malikite Islam, of waging jihad first against "bad Muslims" and later against the Christians in Andalusia. But that ideology was more of a justification for their actions. On the other hand, that ideology did limit their choice of opportunities to exploit. They expanded northward into Spain rather than eastward into the territory of the Sanhaja of Ifriqiya. When it became impossible for them to fulfill the demands of their ideology, which asked them to sustain a two-front war against the Christians in Iberia and the Almohads in Morocco, they were no longer able to maintain the support of their subjects. The ideology that justified their opportunism became their downfall.

Notes on Dates and Transliteration

Dates for events in the narrative are given as *Hijra* (Muslim Calendar, A.H.) date/(Common Era [C.E.] date). Dates for sources are given only as Common Era dates. Medieval authors are referenced with dates for their death (d.) or dates in which their work was written (wr.) in the Common Era. A bibliography with complete bibliographic reference to all works consulted is included.

Transliterations of Arabic words into Latin script have been simplified. For example, the *ta marbuta* (h), silent "t" does not appear at the end of words. The initial *hamza* (') and *'ayn* (') are omitted as are dots below and above consonants. Words that are commonly seen in an Anglicized form, such as Koran and vizier, appear in that form and are not italicized. Names of recent authors are written as the authors render their own names in Latin script. Place names that are still used today are rendered as they are in the country where they are located, for example, Fez rather than *Fas* and Marrakech rather than *Marrakush*. The word *Amir* is uppercase when referring to the Almoravid ruler. It is lowercase when it refers to a commander or regional governor. The plural of Arabic words are rendered by adding a nonitalicized "s" at the end of the word, as in, *faqih*s rather than the Arabic plural *fuqaha*. The one exception is *ulama* (plural of *alim*), since it appears more often in plural form than singular, at least in this work.

CHAPTER 1

Islamic Reformism Comes to West Africa, Eleventh Century C.E.

The pilgrims had been traveling for a long while by the time they arrived in the city of Qayrawan, in Ifriqiya, in what is known today as Tunisia. Yahya Ibn Ibrahim, the great chief of the Sanhaja confederation of tribes in the western Sahara, had made the pilgrimage to the holy city of Mecca along with other Sanhaja chiefs. After three years of journeying, he was now returning home. His commitment to Islam was much greater than his understanding of it. The year was 430/1038.

Before leaving Qayrawan to continue his journey home, Ibn Ibrahim sought to hear the sermons of the famous teacher Abu Imran al-Fasi. What Ibn Ibrahim had learned about Islam throughout his pilgrimage, confirmed here in Qayrawan, alarmed him—what he had known as Islam differed from what he had seen in the great centers of learning that he had visited. Islam was a way of life based on what was revealed to the prophet Muhammad some 400 years earlier. The ruler of the Islamic world was Muhammad's successor, the caliph in Baghdad. But now Ibn Ibrahim learned that here in the Maghrib region, sectarianism had set in: religion had become polarized between Sunni and Shi'ite partisans. The unity of the caliphate had been shattered by the birth of two other rival caliphates, the Umayyads of Andalusia, who were Sunni, and the Fatimids of Ifriqiya, who were Shi'ite. The Maghrib had become the battlefield in which the competition between the two rivals played itself out. But it was not religion that pushed these regimes to seek to dominate; it was money.

Of the two competitors, the Umayyads were the first to become established in the West. The founders of the dynasty had fled to

West Africa in C.E. Eleventh Century. (© Thomas Nolan. Used by permission)

Andalusia at the time of the Abbasid Revolution during the second century A.H. (eighth century C.E.), which had put the caliph in power in Baghdad. For a long time, the Umayyads had been profiting from the gold coming from West Africa across the Sahara. When the Fatimids became firmly established 150 years later, they tried, with some success, to seize this trade for themselves. Both protagonists used intermediaries and formed alliances with Berber tribes in the Maghrib who were Kharijite Muslims, adding a third divisive element. For the most part, the Umayyads allied with tribes of the Zanata confederation in the western and central Maghrib, and the Fatimids aligned with Sanhaja Berbers in the East. But it was not always that clear cut; individual tribes switched their allegiances from time to time, depending on which protagonist offered more advantages or presented more of a threat to their own survival. Fatimid and Umayyad rulers both increased their ideological appeal by declaring themselves to be caliph, first the Fatimid in 297/910, and then the Umayyad in 317/929.

When the Fatimids shifted the nucleus of their state and moved from Ifriqiya to Egypt in C.E. 969, they left the Bani Ziri of the eastern Sanhaja confederation to rule the eastern Maghrib in their stead. The Umayyads relied on their Zanata vassals, especially the Bani Maghrawa, to maintain their interests in the western and central Maghrib. After the Umayyad dynasty collapsed in Andalusia, the Zanata became free agents.

The politics of all of this was very confusing to Yahya Ibn Ibrahim, and well beyond his interest. But the sectarian divisions were alarming and had religious implications that would impact him and also his people. The teacher he had sought out in Qayrawan, Abu Imran al-Fasi, was originally from Fez, as his name suggests. Abu Imran was expelled from Fez for criticizing the "injustice" of the rulers, the Bani Maghrawa. The Maghrawa of Fez were Kharijite Muslims—heretics, according to Abu Imran.

After fleeing from Fez and before settling in Qayrawan, Abu Imran had studied with some of the great scholars of Muslim law in the East, where he developed a conservative theology and radical political theory. Abu Imran saw the caliph in Baghdad as the sole legitimate authority to whom all Muslims owed allegiance. He longed for a way to transcend tribal disunity and the rising sectarianism in the Maghrib. One of his teachers in Baghdad, a scholar of Asharite theology, saw Asharism as a potential ideological foundation for the Seljuk Turks to outflank the Fatimids in the East. If Asharism could provide the basis for anti-Fatimid propaganda in the East, why could not Malikism do the same here in the West?

Qayrawan had been the center for Malikite Muslim law since the middle of the ninth century. Like other schools of Sunni Islam, Malikism bases its doctrine on the Koran and on the *sunna*, the traditions of the Prophet and his companions. But the Malikites exclude the traditions of Ali, who, according to Shi'ite Muslims, was the first successor to Muhammad and the true *imam*. Malikite law was uncompromising in its acceptance of the consensus of the religious scholars (*ulama*) of Medina above all others. They sometimes relied on the legal opinions of their own theologians, more so than on *hadith*, the traditions of the Prophet. Malikites were intolerant toward Shi'ites, whom they viewed as disturbers of public order and agents of corruption.

In the eleventh century, Malikite scholars in Qayrawan had become increasingly assertive in public life and openly critical of the Zirid representatives of the Shi'ite Fatimids. Some suspect that they even contributed to provoking riots directed against the Shi'ites and to increasing pressure for the Zirids to break from the Fatimids. If Malikism was an effective arm against Shi'ites, they supposed, why not against Kharijites, as well?

Abu Imran al-Fasi questioned his visitor, Yahya Ibn Ibrahim, quite thoroughly. He asked the chief all about his confederation in the western Sahara. He asked about the size of the population and the scope of the chief's influence there. Finally, Abu Imran asked what school of law they followed. It was as if he were sizing up this tribal chief from the desert as a potential agent in spreading Malikism to defeat heresy.

Yahya Ibn Ibrahim spoke a Berber dialect; his knowledge of Arabic was very limited. He spoke to Abu Imran through an interpreter, Jawhar Ibn Sakkun, a jurist from Ibn Ibrahim's own tribe, who was well versed in Arabic. He answered the Malikite scholar honestly. Ibn Ibrahim explained that Islam had come to his world with the traders a little over a century earlier. At first, his people took on material aspects of Islamic culture, features such as the wearing of Islamic amulets, ornaments, and dress and the acquisition of food and household habits. Then, they adopted some elements, including ritual prayer and other religious obligations. That is why Yahya Ibn Ibrahim and other Saharan chiefs were now making this pilgrimage. The teachers that they had were not moved to piety, nor were they learned in the law.

Abu Imran was moved by the Sanhaja chief's sense of nobility, his honesty, and his innocence, but he expressed shock at the Saharan's shallow understanding of the faith. Ibn Ibrahim then implored Abu Imran to send a disciple back to the western desert to teach his people.

Abu Imran could not recommend a teacher from Qayrawan. Rather, he sent Ibn Ibrahim with a letter addressed to a former student, Wajjaj Ibn Zalwi, asking him in turn to send a teacher to the Sanhaja of the western Sahara. Ibn Zalwi was originally from the northwestern region of the Sahara known as Sus al-Aqsa, in the southwest in today's Morocco. After studying Malikite law with the great master in Qayrawan, Ibn Zalwi had returned to Sus al-Aqsa and founded a school of his own for students of science and reciters of the Koran. Berbers in the area came to him to be blessed and to ask him to pray for rain. He called the school the *Dar al-Murabitin*, which means "the house of those who were bound together in the cause of God." Naturally, the *Dar al-Murabitin* was steeped in the teaching of Malikite law.

Ibn Zalwi sent one of his students, Abd Allah Ibn Yasin, to preach to the nomadic tribes in the desert. Ibn Yasin, also from Sus al-Aqsa, was a disciple whose piety, blamelessness, learning, and diplomacy led Ibn Zalwi to hold him in the highest regard. Ibn Yasin had studied for seven years in Cordoba, across the Straits of Gibraltar, and then returned to join the school of the Susi saint and rainmaker. As Ibn Yasin traveled through the Maghrib, he noted the lack of unity among the confederation of the Zanata Berber tribes: The heretical Barghwata were entrenched in the plains along the Atlantic coast. The Maghrawa, whom Abu Imran had taught his disciples to despise, held the commercial cities of Aghmat and Sijilmasa, as well as the city of Fez. The Bani Ifran controlled the Mediterranean coast, including the two important port cities of Tangier and Ceuta. Ibn Yasin might have seen an opportunity in this internal division, but for now he accepted the mission bestowed upon him by his master, and he became convinced that it was his duty and within his power to bring the tribes of the great western desert under the teachings of the *Dar al-Murabitin*. Those teachings included the obligation to strive (*jahada*—the root word for *jihad*—in Arabic) for truth and the suppression of injustice. It would soon include the specific injunction against illegal, that is, nonKoranic, taxes and even holy war. The task that lay ahead for Ibn Yasin was far more complex than he could have foreseen.

In the deep Sahara, more than 20 days' journey over the curve of the horizon to the south, Ibn Yasin found a harsh terrain, strange customs, and a warlike people who had known victories of their own. The Sanhaja was a confederation of Berber tribes, formed to maximize their control over the western Sahara and to ensure their own mutual protection. There were some 70 tribes among the Sanhaja, the three main tribes being the Bani Gudala, the Bani Lamtuna, and the Bani Massufa. They were desert nomads, pastoralists who lived off their herds. Their wealth was measured in the number of their sheep, goats, and camels. These tribes roamed the western desert, seeking new pasturage of small, thorny bushes sparsely scattered across the vast space. The search for pasturage was not random. The tribes followed a natural cycle that would bring them back to a particular spot when the pasturage was renewed. Their skill as cameleers gave them tremendous mobility. A single tribe wandered over the territory, which they claimed as their domain, extending for a distance of two months' traveling from the horizon, where the sun rose, to where it set and for a distance the same in length between the Maghrib and *Bilad al-Sudan*, the Land of the Blacks.

The homes of these nomads were the tents that they carried with them—huge, natural-colored blankets made from the hair of their animals, supported by sticks, the tallest in the middle with shorter ones around the periphery, making a series of peaks in the roof of graduated height. Each tent was divided into two sections by a suspended blanket. In the front section, the herders sat and shielded themselves from the scorching sun in the heat of the day. The back "room" provided the sleeping quarters, which held the heat of the day through most of the night. As the tribe moved from site to site, they dismantled and reset the tents in the same, almost ritual-like way. Every precious possession was carefully packed and unpacked in its own special place.

To protect themselves from the sun and the blowing sands, the Sanhaja clothed themselves in cloaks of wool, dyed dark blue with indigo. They wrapped their heads with a cloth forming a turban, with part of it covering their forehead. Another cloth wrapped around their face, forming a veil which hung from above the bridge of the nose, down across the chest. No one had ever seen the face of any of these Sanhaja, except for the whites of the eyes peering through the narrow slit between the turban and the veil. The wearing of the veil was a strict custom passed on from father to son among the descendants of the patriarch Himyar of the Bani Lamtuna. The practice stems from a particular incident in a story that was told over and over again. A group of Lamtuna tribesmen donned the veil to disguise themselves as women, as the approaching enemy had expected to find only women in the tents. The women had left the camp disguised as men. When the enemy came, the men fell upon them with their swords and killed them. Since that time, the Bani Lamtuna have kept the veil in order to preserve the *baraka*, the blessing of God, which brought them victory. It was well known that the wearing of the veil was the distinct privilege of the Sanhaja male elite.

The Sanhaja knew nothing about tilling the land. Their nourishment came from the milk and meat of their herds. They ate no bread unless a passing caravan gave it to them or provided them with flour. The desert tribesmen served as guides to caravans passing through their territory in the trade between the Maghrib and the Land of the Blacks. It was indeed dangerous to travel through the Sahara, impossible without the cooperation of the desert tribes. At a place called Awkazant, for example, where there were shallow wells of water, bandits waited in ambush to attack caravans. They selected this spot because they knew that all travelers had to stop here for their water supply. The Sanhaja sold protection to the caravans passing through their territory. During the reign of Yahya Ibn Ibrahim, they levied

Abd Allah Ibn Yasin was the preacher who came from the *Dar al-Murabitin* to preach Malikite Islam to the Sanhaja tribes in the western Sahara. (© Michael Summers. Used by permission.)

dues, as they had done for at least 200 years, on every camel load of merchandise that passed.

Among this Saharan confederation, Ibn Yasin settled and preached first among the Bani Gudala, the tribe of Yahya Ibn Ibrahim. He found that most of the Sanhaja tribesmen were ignorant of the law of Islam, and their faith amounted to no more than the testimony that "there is no God but God," and that "Muhammad is the prophet of God." They knew no other tenets of Islam other than those two. He became their *imam*, the man who would lead them in prayer and teach them the law.

A group of 70 religious leaders from the Bani Gudala gathered around their new teacher to learn everything he had to teach. From the start, he imposed a strict enforcement of the laws of Islam, as he understood them, with a sternness that the Bani Gudala had not known. He applied the laws to suit the conditions he saw among the Sanhaja. For instance, taking booty on a desert raid was standard practice. But Ibn Yasin forbade the taking of booty among the faithful. If he allowed it on occasion, it was only because he identified the victims as infidels.

Even though the Sanhaja were mostly monogamous, concubines were tolerated and divorce was easy. Ibn Yasin reminded them of the Koranic injunctions limiting a man to four legal wives. Still, in his own life, Ibn Yasin had several marriages and subsequent divorce. We are told that whenever he heard of a beautiful woman, he asked for her hand in marriage, but he never paid more than four *dinar*s as a bride price. (*Dinar*s were gold coins, each worth approximately half a month's salary for a skilled craftsman.)

Ibn Yasin's piety led him to be intolerant toward those who shirked their religious duties. He could be harsh and unforgiving, almost to the point of seeming cruel. Even when a man joined the cause and repented for his past misdeeds, the master would say to him, "You have committed many sins in your heart, so you must be punished as stipulated by the law, and so purified from your transgressions." Ibn Yasin's interpretation of the law required 100 lashes for an adulterer, 80 lashes for a slanderer, and the same for a drunkard; and sometimes the number was even more.

Since the Bani Gudala were not well-instructed Muslims, it was important that they prayed behind an *imam* who could instruct them. According to the *Muwatta*, the book of Malikite law that was a basic text in Ibn Yasin's schooling, the believer must follow the *imam* exactly. He ordered that those who failed to attend the Friday prayer receive 20 lashes, and for those who omitted one prostration (*rak'a*) during prayer, 5 lashes. He compelled everybody to pray the noon prayer four times before the public recitation of that prayer on Friday. Indeed, he applied this rule to all the other prayers. He explained to a new convert, "In your past life you have omitted prayers many times, so you must make up for it." If anyone raised his voice in the mosque, he was given the number of lashes thought suitable by the person Ibn Yasin had appointed to administer the beating. Allegedly, people were so fearful of being punished that they came to the mosque and went as quickly as possible and even prayed without having performed the ritual ablutions.

Ibn Yasin did not consider himself above the law, that is, the law as he saw it. According to one story, a Gudala tribesman called a certain merchant to appear before the court over which Ibn Yasin presided. In one of his replies to the plaintiff, the merchant said, "God forbid that it should be!" Ibn Yasin ordered that the merchant be flogged, saying, "He has blasphemed; he has used a scandalous expression, so the most severe punishment must be inflicted!" Among the audience was a man from Qayrawan who asked Ibn Yasin, "What do you find wrong in what he said? God himself, great and powerful is he, has used these words in His Book." The man reminded Ibn Yasin of the case of the women who cut their hands, as related in the story of Joseph in the Koran, who had said, "God forbid! This is not a man, this is none other than some gracious angel!" Ibn Yasin refrained from flogging the man.

Sometimes Ibn Yasin resorted to armed warfare to proselytize. He convinced the Bani Gudala that the Bani Lamtuna were polytheists, so that when he unleashed his followers against their opponents he allowed them to take booty. The Bani Gudala fought against other tribes as well. Their power grew as Ibn Yasin's teaching of Islam spread among them.

More and more, the people of the Sanhaja considered Ibn Yasin to be a man of great *baraka*, a man to whom God had given special powers. They told stories about miracles that he performed. They said that on one of his travels Ibn Yasin and his companions were out in the heat of the day and were taken with great thirst. The companions complained to Ibn Yasin, who said to them, "Let us hope that God may deliver us from our plight." After they had traveled for some time, he said, "Dig in front of me." They dug, and they quickly found water. They watered their animals and then quenched their own thirst with water as fresh and sweet as they had ever tasted. Another time, at the end of a day's travel, Ibn Yasin stopped at the side of a pool of water which was full of frogs croaking incessantly. As soon as Ibn Yasin stood at the pool's edge, not another croak was heard from them. The Sanhaja had told similar stories about other Saharan "saints."

Ibn Yasin dwelt among the Sanhaja nomads, but he never really felt a part of them. He refrained from eating meat from their flocks and from drinking of their milk. He ate only the wild game hunted in the desert. The holy man and teacher ordered the construction of a town the Sanhaja called Arat-n-anna, in which no building was to be higher than any other. Ibn Yasin taught them that in the eyes of God, all men are equal, a concept that was new and difficult for the nobility of these Sanhaja tribes to accept.

Some 10 years passed, and the Bani Gudala remained loyal to Ibn Yasin's teaching up until the death of Yahya Ibn Ibrahim, the chief of the Bani Gudala and great chief of the Sanhaja confederation. The new chief of the confederation was to be picked according to customary tribal election. Solidarity (in Arabic, *asabiya*) was strong within the Sanhaja, but it was even stronger at the level of the tribe, often leading to intertribal conflict, and sometimes even war. Each tribe had its favorite candidate. The front-runners campaigned. They visited tribal elders, religious leaders, family, and friends. They bestowed favors wherever they could. Then the prominent tribesmen of the Sanhaja assembled, and after much discussion and debate of the strength, wisdom, generosity, and the baraka of each, they reached a consensus. They picked Yahya Ibn Umar, chief of the Bani Lamtuna. It was not unusual for the leadership to change from one tribe to another because among the desert tribes succession was matrilineal; it was custom to choose sisters' sons to succeed as chiefs. Yahya Ibn Umar's mother was a member of Gudala nobility who had married a Lamtuna. His Lamtuna heritage was important. His tribesmen told stories, true or false, of ancestors who had come from Yemen to dominate the Sahara, especially the one called Italukan Ibn Talakatin, who ruled over the entire desert until he was 80 years old. The Bani Lamtuna had come to be a caste of nobility among the tribes of the Sahara.

Abd Allah Ibn Yasin endorsed this succession of power from the Bani Gudala to the Bani Lamtuna. In making this choice, he placed the future of his mission from that time on into the hands of the Bani Lamtuna, and their prestige became his.

Yahya Ibn Umar welcomed Ibn Yasin warmly. He and his family and all of his people were now ready to accept the teachings of this holy man from the Sus. *Amir* (commander) is the title that Ibn Yasin gave to Ibn Umar. He taught his new commander the discipline needed to lead the Almoravids to victory. One day, Ibn Yasin said to Ibn Umar, "*Amir*, you deserve to be punished!" Ibn Umar asked what he had done to merit this. Ibn Yasin, the story goes, answered, "I will not tell you until I have inflicted the punishment." "I am ready to obey you," said the *Amir*, as he uncovered his bare skin. Ibn Yasin flogged him many times and then explained, "I have whipped you because you fight in the midst of battle and expose yourself to the gravest danger; that is your mistake. An *amir* should not be thus exposed to danger. On the contrary, he is supposed to encourage the combatants. The life of a commander is the life of the whole army; his death is its loss."

The Gudala nobility were angered by the election of Ibn Umar. Tradition notwithstanding, supremacy among the tribes was a jealously guarded prize. They had put forth their own candidate to succeed as great chief, and they had failed. Some of the nobility of the Bani Gudala conspired with Jawhar Ibn Sakkun, the same jurist who had served as translator for Ibn Ibrahim in Qayrawan and who had helped bring Ibn Yasin to the Bani Gudala to begin with. It was easy enough to turn the people against Ibn Yasin. Ibn Sakkun pointed to the harshness with which Ibn Yasin enforced the laws of Islam. He stirred up the nobility by pointing to Ibn Yasin's egalitarian views, which countered their tribal custom. The conspirators managed to sow enough distrust that the Bani Gudala no longer sought Ibn Yasin's legal opinions, counsel, or judgment. They deposed him from his position as director of the treasury, as collector of tribute and taxes. When a mob looted his house and destroyed it, Ibn Yasin fled the community, fearing for his life.

He went back to Sus al-Aqsa, where his teacher, Wajjaj Ibn Zalwi, offered solace and advice. The master of the *Dar al-Murabitin* sent a message back to the Bani Gudala, rebuking them severely. He informed the chiefs of the desert tribes that whosoever was in dispute with Ibn Yasin was in dispute with the whole community and would be excluded from the body of true believers.

The teacher told his student that his mission in the desert was far from finished, and that he must remain among the Sanhaja. Ibn Yasin retreated with seven faithful companions to an isolated spot, shrouded in legend, and established a *ribat*, a fortified monastery. He clearly intended this place of refuge, and those who came to it, to be a bulwark against those who refused to accept the teachings of *Dar al-Murabitin*.

When Ibn Yasin returned to the desert, he sought vengeance against the Bani Gudala who had opposed him. He issued a *fatwa*, a legal ruling, condemning Ibn Sakkun and the other Gudala rebels for obstructing his preaching of the true faith. He accordingly had them all killed.

He turned his attention next to teaching the Koran and the *sunna*. By now, Ibn Yasin, like Muslim scholars elsewhere, viewed the *sunna* to mean the prophet Muhammad's way of doing things based on traditions going back to the Prophet and to his companions. It included the ritual ablutions, prayer, almsgiving, and the other duties taught by the Prophet. For Ibn Yasin, the *sunna* was a buttress for his own authority.

The *imam* began to preach to his people, exhorting them to *strive* to do good deeds, to seek paradise, and shun the fire of hell and the wrath of God. This was the root meaning of what the prophet Muhammad had described as the greater jihad. He steered them from evil and talked of God's rewards. He called his followers *al-Murabitun* (Almoravids). He said to them, "Almoravids, you are many; you are the chiefs of your tribes and the heads of your clans. The Almighty has reformed you and guided you on the straight path. You must thank Him for His blessings by exhorting men to do good and to shun evil and by striving in the cause of God."

Not everyone listened. When Ibn Yasin passed through the land of the Bani Massufa, he found them raiding each other, looting their property, killing the men and taking their women, and failing to follow the authority of any *imam*. Ibn Yasin reproached them for this. But the *shaykhs* of the Bani Massufa claimed that they did believe in God and in his prophet, Muhammad, yet they were not willing to submit to the authority of anyone outside of their own tribe.

Then Ibn Yasin called the Almoravids to what the prophet Muhammad described as the lesser jihad (holy war) against those tribes who refused to follow the religion of Islam as he taught it, even after he beckoned them to the true faith. They warred against the Bani Lamta and confiscated one-third of their possessions. Ibn Yasin told the Bani Lamta that taking one-third of their possessions purified the two-thirds that they were allowed to keep. The Bani Lamta found it best to join the movement. In accordance to the law of the Koran, the Bani Lamtuna divided the spoils of victory, four-fifths among the combatants and one-fifth for the commander. This was the first time the practice occurred among the Bani Lamtuna. Indeed, this was the first of a series of jihads that the Almoravids would fight against the "infidels," holy wars that would subdue the tribes of the western desert. Most of the tribes answered his call, joined his movement, and pledged themselves to follow the sunna, the path of the true faith under his direction. He collected alms (*zakat*) and tithes (*ushr*) and established a treasury from which he began to provide his warriors with mounts and weapons.

The Almoravid warriors learned new tactics under their new *Amir*, Ibn Umar, and their *imam*, Ibn Yasin. They abandoned the attack and withdrawal style of warfare that was typical among the Berbers of the desert. Now, they placed their camels and pack animals in line formation behind the ranks of charging warriors. During intervals between charges, the mounted warriors used this steady rear formation as a shelter to fall back upon when they were attacked in turn. A sufficient number of camels were needed for such a line of defense. Horses were much too skittish.

The Almoravids learned to fight in tight infantry ranks. The first line of combatants was armed with long spears and tall, broad shields made of the skin of the *lamt*, a large African oryx. They would soon become famous for these shields. The front line formed a barrier to protect the lines of soldiers in the rear, each one of whom was armed with several javelins which were hurled with such accuracy that they hardly ever missed their mark. About one-third of the Almoravid army was cavalry, taking full advantage of the Lamtuna skills as horsemen and cameleers. This provided an element of swiftness to their attack. A standard-bearer marched in the forefront of the first rank and signaled with his flag to coordinate the whole maneuver.

Why the change in tactics? Because the Koran says, "Truly God loves those who fight in His cause in battle array, as if they were a solid cemented structure." The prophet Muhammad fought that way, and so did his first four successors, the *Khulafa' al-Rashidun*. Modeling themselves on such a lofty series of precedents added to the moral resolve of these new warriors of the faith, even though fighting in this way led to numerous casualties. In one battle, the Almoravids lost as much as half of their army. But the Almoravids were not afraid to die. They preferred death to retreat, as they considered it a sin to flee from the enemy.

With this newly acquired and divinely inspired military might, they set out to conquer the world. In the year 446/1054 the Almoravids raided the town of Sijilmasa. That was the principal port on the northern edge of the desert for the traffic coming across the Sahara from the Land of the Blacks. The *ulama* of Sijilmasa and of the Draa, the fertile valley to the west, gathered and wrote to Ibn Yasin and to the *shaykh*s of the Almoravids, urging them to come and free them from the oppression of the rule of the Bani Maghrawa. They told Ibn Yasin of the injustice, contempt, and tyranny suffered by men of science and religion, as well as by the community of faithful Muslims at the hands of their *amir*, Mas'ud bin Wanudin.

The Maghrawa rulers of Sijilmasa were, in fact, upsetting the balance between the farmers of the oasis and the nomads who lived in the desert to the south. In earlier times, the Sanhaja Berbers wandered freely with their herds in the whole region around Sijilmasa. These nomads were permitted to use the land as pasturage and were granted authorized access to the cultivated lands and watering places for camels, sheep, and goats. They traded with the farmers of the oasis some of the wool and hides of their animals for foodstuffs grown among the date palms.

The tribes of the desert supplied the many thousands of camels needed to carry the cargo, and they provided protection to the caravans making the long journey across the Sahara. Thus a delicate balance of

This *dinar* was struck in the name of Mas'ud bin Wanudin, the last ruler of Sijilmasa as an independent city-state before the Almoravids conquered it. (© Steve Album, Rare Coins, Photographer Michael Barry. Used by permission.)

resources and services was established and maintained between the urban rulers of Sijilmasa and the nomads of the surrounding plains.

Some 75 years earlier, the Maghrawa had become the vassals of the Umayyad caliphs of Cordoba. They controlled the local economy as well as the long-distance trade and sent much of the profits to the distant Andalusian capital. The Maghrawa were now independent of the Umayyads. They restricted the pasturage rights of the Sanhaja Berbers to the south of the city, they collected from the region taxes that were not in accordance with the Koran, and they struck both gold and silver coins in the mint, boldly bearing the name of the new ruler "al-imam Abd Allah Mas'ud."

When the letter from Sijilmasa reached Ibn Yasin, he gathered the Almoravid leaders, read the letter to them, and asked their counsel. They said, "Oh learned *shaykh*, this is an obligation on you and on us. Let us be off with God's blessing!" Ibn Yasin ordered them to wage jihad—to bring reform, to be sure, but also to gain other profits from this wealthy caravan city.

The Almoravids came with an army numbering 30,000 warriors mounted on camels. On the outskirts of Sijilmasa, they fell upon a herd of 50,000 camels belonging to the Bani Maghrawa. The numbers from contemporary accounts are probably exaggerated but nonetheless must have been extraordinarily large. The ruler of the city, Mas'ud Ibn Wannudin, came out to confront them and to defend this valuable stock. He was killed, and his army was cut to pieces. The Almoravids confiscated the Maghrawa's riding animals and their weapons. Again, Ibn Yasin distributed a fifth of the booty among the religious leaders of Sijilmasa and divided the rest among the Almoravids.

With victory well in hand, the Almoravids entered the city. Ibn Yasin ordered the execution of the rest of the Maghrawa rulers. He destroyed their musical instruments and burned down the shops where wine was sold. Shortly after the battle, the Almoravids returned to the desert. They were not willing, however, to risk losing the advantage that they had just achieved, nor were they confident that the residents of Sijilmasa would remain as gracious hosts. They established a garrison in the city and placed it under the command of a Lamtuna tribesman.

The Almoravids conspicuously strengthened their forces with the weapons and camels they captured from the rulers of Sijilmasa. Their increased strength allowed them within the same year, 446/1054, to turn their energy against the city of Awdaghust 1,000 miles away on the opposite edge of the Sahara, in a region the Arabs called *sahil* (shore), marking the boundary of the ocean of sand to the north. Awdaghust was a large town, the capital of a prosperous country, the main port corresponding to Sijilmasa, and the port from which gold was shipped across the desert. There were busy markets, and many date palms and henna trees so large that they looked like olive trees. The architecture was typically mud brick, but quite ornate. The city was inhabited by Berbers of the Zanata confederation and Arab merchants from the north. The people were rich, and they owned many slaves.

The Almoravids attacked Awdaghust and ravaged it with a harshness that they had not shown before. They sacked and pillaged—and, it is said, they violated the women. They declared everything that they took there to be legitimate booty, even though the population was Muslim. The Almoravids justified their behavior by saying that the people recognized the authority of the pagan king of the Sudan, who was called Ghana.

Ghana was not only one of the titles of the king. It was the name by which the kingdom was known to outsiders, as well as the name of its capital city. The kingdom included most of the land between the Niger and Senegal Rivers. Most of its inhabitants were Soninke people, that is, Blacks who were speakers of the Soninke language. Even though the stories that the Arabs told of Ghana far exceeded the reality, they described the capital as consisting of two large towns, six miles apart.

The main town had many Muslim inhabitants. It had several mosques, including a Friday mosque just off the main square near the center. There were many prayer leaders, muezzins, paid reciters of the Koran, jurists, and men learned in the law of Islam. Water from the many sweet wells in the town provided drink and irrigation for the gardens of vegetables. The other town was where the king of Ghana lived, in a palace with many domes that rose above the enclosure that surrounded it, like the defensive wall of a city. Although the king was not a Muslim, there was a mosque not far from the hall where he held court for those Muslims who came on diplomatic missions. These visitors were dazzled by the amount of gold displayed at the court: the king was adorned with jewelry of gold, protected by body guards bearing shields and swords decorated with gold, and dogs were wearing collars of gold!

Indeed, Ghana had become synonymous with the source of gold. Traders had been coming to Ghana for hundreds of years seeking this precious metal. The gold was weighed in units called *solidi* from a time when merchants supplied the ancient Romans with gold. Ghana had been the main source for gold in the Maghrib and the western Mediterranean ever since. Successful trans-Saharan trade depended on a certain amount of cooperation between the Berbers of Awdaghust and the Soninke of Ghana. In times shortly before the Almoravids, Ghana had expanded to include Awdaghust in its kingdom, as it had other city states whose lesser kings were also seen at the court of the king of Ghana. In this savannah to the south of the great desert, agricultural settlements had grown into commercial cities, cities into states, and states into an empire.

Awdaghust is as far south as the Almoravids went during the time of Ibn Yasin. Of course, as long as they controlled Awdaghust and all of the routes across the desert to Sijilmasa, they did not really have to go any farther to monopolize the transportation of gold across the desert. Perhaps Abd Allah Ibn Yasin sensed this opportunity to fuse the ports of Awdaghust and Sijilmasa into a more cohesive religio/politico-economic system. In any case, the profits of this cartel would finance the Almoravids' future expansion.

Still, it was not going to be that easy. Trouble broke out once again in Sijilmasa within a year after the Almoravids had taken it. The residents of the city turned against the Almoravids who were garrisoned there, supposedly while they were praying in the mosque, and massacred many of them. Ibn Yasin began to plan a second expedition against the city of the Maghrawa.

The timing could not have been worse; it seemed as if the whole of the Sahara was in rebellion! The Bani Gudala chose this moment to break away from the Sanhaja confederation. This open revolt of the Bani Gudala is linked with their rejection of Ibn Yasin; but it could also have something to do with their desire to seek their own fortune, now, along the salt routes to Awlil on the coast of the Atlantic. Regardless, it forced the Almoravids to split their forces.

Ibn Yasin went north with a small detachment of Almoravid warriors. He added to his army as he went, recruiting tribesmen from the Bani Sarta and the Bani Tarja. He joined his forces to those of Abu Bakr Ibn Umar, Yahya's brother, who was already in the region of the Draa to the southwest of Sijilmasa. Yahya Ibn Umar, meanwhile, remained with part of the army in the Adrar, in the heartland of the Bani Lamtuna. He established his base at a place called Jabal Lamtuna. These mountains were surrounded by some 20,000 date palms. There was abundant water and pasturage. Most importantly, the place was easily defensible. He held up in a fortress called Azuggi, which his brother Yannu had built.

The Bani Gudala had amassed a sizable army to march against the Bani Lamtuna, allegedly some 30,000 men. Yahya Ibn Umar had formed an alliance with the Berber chief of Takrur, a principality along the Senegal River and recently converted to Islam, so that his total forces were almost as numerous as those of the Bani Gudala. Yahya Ibn Umar's fatal mistake was to allow the Bani Gudala to draw his army out of the mountains. The two opposing armies met at a place called Tebferilla, neutral ground that lay between the domain of the two tribes. The ensuing battle was a disastrous defeat for the Bani Lamtuna. Much of the Lamtuna army was killed, including the commander, Yahya Ibn Umar. The defeat was so decisive, in fact, that from that time onward, the Almoravids made no further attempts against the Bani Gudala. Legend has it that at the site of this major battle, the voices of those who once called to prayer can still be heard five times a day. The traditional looting of the battlefield did not occur. No sword or shield or other weapon, not a single piece of clothing was taken—a myth, to be sure, but denoting evidence of the reverence paid by the Almoravids to those who fell on this battlefield.

After the dead were buried, Ibn Yasin marched to Tamdult, not far from Sijilmasa, a place well known for mining silver. There was a fortress there with an ample supply of water. It was a good place to regroup and rebuild his army. Ibn Yasin ordered Abu Bakr Ibn Umar to take his brother's place as commander of the Almoravid army. From here, Ibn Yasin and his new commander set out to conquer Sijilmasa for a second time. They were determined to establish control over all of Sijilmasa's dependent provinces, the whole of Sus al-Aqsa, Nul Lamta, and the region of the Draa.

In the town of Tarudant in Sus al-Aqsa, Abu Bakr encountered a community of Shi'ite Muslims, who believed that theirs was the only true interpretation of Islam. The Almoravids fought them, took over the town, and slew many of the Shi'ites. Those who were not killed accepted the teachings of the *Dar al-Murabitin*.

Ibn Yasin sent out his governors to all the districts in Sus al-Aqsa and in Draa, and he commanded them to uphold justice and enforce the laws of the true faith. This became the pattern that the Almoravids would apply in every city that they would conquer. He imposed Malikite Islam, obliged the people to pay alms and tithes, and he abolished all other illegal, that is, non-Koranic, taxes.

The campaign was completed in 448/1056. Ibn Yasin and Abu Bakr established their base in Sijilmasa. Although the residents swore an oath of allegiance to the Almoravids, the new rulers moved into the

The Sijilmasa Citadel, no longer extant, would have been located on this elevation, north of the Grand Mosque. (© MAPS [Moroccan-American Project at Sijilmasa, Ronald Messier, project director]. Used by permission.)

garrison, which was still within the same curtain walls of the city, on the elevated plateau north of the Grand Mosque. But they built another wall to separate the citadel and the *dar al-imara*, the governmental palace, from the rest of the town. It was the custom of the Bani Lamtuna to extend their power by appointing members of their extended family to positions of power. Abu Bakr appointed his cousin Yusuf Ibn Tashfin to command the garrison of Sijilmasa. Ibn Tashfin was a young Lamtuna who had already demonstrated prowess as a warrior and whose family loyalty was beyond question. He commanded a garrison of desert warriors trained in the new military tactics of the Sahara, inspired with the peculiar Malikite reformism of Abd Allah Ibn Yasin, and financed by the gold from Ghana. The citizens of Sijilmasa would endure the austerity of Malikite reformism as long as they enjoyed the increased security and prosperity provided by the new regime.

CHAPTER 2

Gateway of the Sahara

Imagine the day that the great caravan from across the Sahara, from the Land of the Blacks, arrived in Sijilmasa. It was a large, highly organized caravan, in which several merchants traveled together to secure mutual protection at minimum cost and maximum profit. For the traders, Sijilmasa, perched atop a slightly elevated plateau, was the first city of any size that they had seen in at least 20 days. For the people of Sijilmasa, such caravans brought valuable wares, and the cargo was always very heavily guarded.

In the early morning hours, people were already gravitating toward the market. What began as a trickle would soon become an unbroken chain of travelers coming from every direction on every mode of transportation available: many on foot, some on donkey back, a few on camels. It was market day in Sijilmasa. Merchants were beginning to set up their wares. Those who had arrived with the new day were already seeking a sneak preview of the best bargains.

By late morning or mid-day, the market area was full of people, local inhabitants, buyers and sellers from the surrounding villages, and merchants from far away, some from the northern Maghrib, some from Ifriqiya, a few from the Orient, and several from the deep south across the desert. Sijilmasa was not only the most important weekly market site in the oasis but also the port of entry to the Maghrib for caravan routes coming north out of the desert from the western Sudan. It was the border town at the very southern edge of the Maghrib, or the northern edge of the desert, depending on one's perspective.

The city was bounded by two rivers, whose source was fed by many springs. On approaching Sijilmasa, the River Ziz divided into two branches, with the main branch flowing along the western wall of the city and a smaller irrigation canal flowing along the eastern edge. The urban center was perched on an elevated plateau between the two branches.

The *gamanin*, the agricultural zone that surrounded the city, was enclosed by a wall of sun-baked mud. The city itself, long and narrow, stretched along the east bank of the main branch of the river. It was enclosed by much more impressive ramparts made of mud, built on a stone foundation. The walls were thick and protected at intervals with square, slightly tapered towers, some the same height as the walls and others considerably taller. The walls' reddish brown color was intensified by the early morning and late afternoon sunlight. This is not unlike the many *qusur* (sing. *qsar*), or fortified tribal strongholds in the area, except that rather than having just one entrance, Sijilmasa had 12 gates, a tribute to its size and importance—and the many directions from which people approached the city. One gate, for example, was called *Bab al-Sharq*, "Gate of the East"; another was *Bab al-Gharb*, "Gate of the West." The solid, wooden doors, some partially reinforced with iron, stood open but would be closed and heavily guarded during the night.

Bab Rih (Gate of the Wind), also known as Bab Fez, was the northern gate of Sijilmasa. (© MAPS [Moroccan-American Project at Sijilmasa, Ronald Messier, project director]. Used by permission.)

The gate on the north side of the city, called *Bab Fez* because it faced the direction of Fez, was actually a complex of three gates through which traffic passed in succession, having to turn at a right angle between each one. The main gate here, *Bab al-Rih*, "Gate of the Wind," had a graceful, scalloped frame sculpted in mud around the pointed arch and a herringbone pattern above the portal. Inside the gate was a covered patio with arches opening in several directions.

The main axis of the city ran north-south, parallel to the river, connecting a series of villas to the north and south of the city's center. It took the better part of half a day to walk from one end to the other. Most of the city's population lived in the *qsar*, the enclosure that sat on the rise in the very center of the settlement. Along the main street were the houses of the wealthier merchants. From the street, these houses looked rather plain: a solid mud wall, thick enough to insulate the inhabitants from the heat of summer and the cold of winter, and broken only by one door and a few grilled windows. Only the residents and their guests could see the exquisite patterns in mud brick and ceramic tiles, the courtyards and interior fountains. The side streets, unpaved and dusty, were generally quite narrow, and in many cases the houses were built above them, forming dark tunnels.

A small weekly market was near the center of town, in an enclosed square devoid of any buildings, where the merchants set up makeshift stalls. But the main marketplace was located on the west side of the city, outside the main city wall, at a place called *Suq Ben Aqla*. There, the *funduq*s, or caravansaries, consisted of large, square enclosures. Along the inside wall of the four sides were stalls, most of them two stories high, faced by a colonnade of rough brick pillars. At street level they had stables for the pack animals, while on the floors above there were guest rooms. The stalls were also used as warehouses for products brought from afar or purchased in the local market for export to the great desert to the south.

Most of the traders in the great caravan from the south were Berbers from a number of tribes. Originally desert nomads, many of these Berbers became well-established merchants in large trading centers on the northern and southern fringes of the great Sahara. Some became so successful that they ceased making the trans-Saharan trek themselves and instead entrusted their caravans and fortunes to servants and slaves. In much smaller numbers, Arab traders from different parts of the Muslim world managed to break into the business, but they usually did not fare as well as the Berbers.

Most caravans from Awdaghust normally reached Sijilmasa in 40 days. They were plagued by occasional wind storms, some of which blew with such intensity as to create an almost impenetrable screen of sand, threatening to cause the expedition to lose its way. Traders told of how they were saved by a blind guide who rode foremost on his camel and commanded that some sand be given to him at every mile's end. He raised the sand to his nose, and by its smell he could sense the right direction to take. Still another trader told of a thief they had caught, who had climbed down into a well and had cut the ropes of the buckets so that the caravan would not be able to get the water it so desperately needed when it arrived at the watering hole. The thief had planned to hide in the well, and, after the caravaneers had died of thirst, he would climb out and claim their treasures. But a slave of the caravaneers had climbed down into the well and killed the thief.

Those who stood around listening to the storytellers had heard these same stories before. Although they knew that these tales were not true, they liked hearing the stories over and over again as much as the storytellers liked retelling them. Still, all knew that there was a real danger of thieves and of being lost, and that the trek of the caravan was indeed a tremendous risk. The prospect of profit was what made it worth the risk.

The Almoravids now controlled Sijilmasa. They, too, became interested in making profit, and would reduce the risks because they were in a position to protect the routes connecting Sijilmasa with the Land of the Blacks. When traveling from one city to another, and more importantly from one oasis to another across an area as vast and as harsh as the Sahara, it was important for merchants and caravaneers to know in advance how they would be treated when they arrived at their destination. Islam, of course, increased that level of predictability wherever it ruled. But the particular politico-religious system imposed by the Almoravids increased the level of predictability even more.

Each of the merchants of the caravan had 70 to 100 camels, so that in all, there were several thousands of these beasts, each capable of carrying 250 to 300 pounds of merchandise. As the seemingly endless caravan chain gathered in the huge, open space on the west side of the city, the curiosity, if not the anxiety, of the entire city could hardly be contained. The wrapped cargo was heavily guarded as it was unloaded. As were most of the caravans arriving from the south, this one was carrying gold.

Some of the gold was transported in the form of dust, but most of it was transported as refined gold, melted down and then poured into the shape of bricks or bars or in the form of blank coins, which were more convenient to transport. One of the stories the gold traders would tell for a long time to come was of the king from the Land of the blacks who went on a pilgrimage to Mecca, taking with him 100 camels, each of which carried gold in the form of millstones, one on each side of the camel's back.

The traders described how they engaged in the "silent trade" for gold. They would lay down their merchandise and clothing on the banks of the river, they said, and then they would leave. The blacks from farther south then came and placed a quantity of gold that they were willing to pay for the merchandise and left in turn. When the owners of the merchandise returned, if they were satisfied with the amount of gold, they would take it and leave. If not, they retreated to allow the blacks to increase the quantity until both sides were satisfied and the transaction was completed. This was another myth often told in Sijilmasa. The traders and the travelers never really said where the gold was coming from; they did not know. What they did know was that the trek across the desert was well worth their while. They obtained the gold from intermediaries who managed to keep the sources secret. Sometimes they said that it came from the Land of the Blacks or the land south of Sijilmasa. Sometimes they referred to the kingdom of Ghana as the source of the gold. In fact, the kingdom of Ghana served as this intermediary, and the secret location of the source was the basis of the king's power and wealth.

Almost as precious as the gold, a cargo that attracted even more attention was cargo in humankind, the slaves. From the time that traders first started to make the trek across the Sahara on a regular basis, the inhabitants of Ghana and the surrounding states made forays into the region of Lamlam further south to capture slaves. They rode on swift camels through the night to take their prey. They took their captives back to their own country to sell them to the slave traders, who would march them north as part of their caravan.

One can imagine a large crowd gathered in that part of the open market where the slave traders began to exhibit their wares. A large caravan such as this could have 600 slaves or more. Some would be sold here to work in the fields or to shepherd livestock. Others would be used as domestic servants and or become concubines. The most talented became trusted assistants to their masters. It is said that some merchants from the wealthy city of Aghmat to the northwest had even entrusted their caravans to their slaves. Some slaves would become soldiers in the armies of kings. The black female slaves were especially prized and sold for 100 *dinar*s or more. "This one is an especially fine cook," would cry the slave trader. "She specializes in preparing delicious confections such as sugared nuts (*jawzinaqat*), honey doughnuts (*qata'if*), various other kinds of sweetmeats, and other delicacies."

One could see "pretty slave girls with light complexions, sculpted figures, slim waists, round buttocks, wide shoulders, and sexual organs so narrow that each of them could be enjoyed indefinitely as though she were a virgin." One of the merchants from Awdaghust said that he had seen one of these women lying on her side as they did most of the time, rather than sitting on their buttocks. Her infant child played with her, passing under her waist from side to side without her having to draw away from him at all, "because of her ample lower body and the gracefulness of her waist." Still another man exclaimed, "There is not a wealthy man who does not have several girls that he dresses in fine clothes and adorns with jewels to offer them along well-traveled routes." Some of these women were purchased for as much as 1,000 dinars. They were sometimes called *funduqiyya*, since they tended to frequent the *funduq*s (caravansaries).

The caravan merchants had even more rarities from south of the desert to offer—ostrich feathers, beautiful ebony wood, and ivory that would be carefully carved and crafted to make exquisite jewelry boxes, combs, and Koran stands, destined to be sold to the residents of the many fine palaces in the Maghrib and in Andalusia. They had African products to offer in the spice market of Sijilmasa. The strong scent of cinnamon and cloves from Zanzibar overpowered the milder scents of sugar produced in the Sus and saffron and ginger roots from Andalusia. The browns, reds, and yellows of the spices mounded on cloth sacks accented by the bright sun light were as much a stimulus to the eye as were the scents to the nostrils. The local spice merchants doubled as medicine men, and thus sold a variety of medicinal herbs and drugs and, of course, dried animal skins, skulls, and bones to be used as magical fetishes.

The caravaneers would spend the next several days in Sijilmasa. Their pack animals needed an extended rest. There was abundant pasturage in the plains all around Sijilmasa, enough to support the needs of the local population as well as these large caravans. Waters of the River Ziz were supplemented by the many springs and wells in the area to provide drink and to irrigate the fields among the date palms. The irrigation system supported the cultivation of grapes in quantities that far surpassed what could be eaten as fruit. They were made into wine in spite of any Islamic injunction; that is, until the Almoravids came and smashed the shops where wine was being made or sold.

Sijilmasa was renowned for producing a variety of dates, including a particular one called *berni*, which is a deep green color with an especially small nut and an unequaled, mild taste. Under the date palms, residents of the oasis cultivated winter grains, an assortment of vegetables and spring wheat.

After a few years of this kind of production in one area, the farmers withdrew to allow the nomads who wandered in the area to the south to graze their livestock among the date palms. Among the products of such a pastoral life were leather and wool, which the herders sold to the people in the town to support the local industries of tanning and weaving. This local barter was actually a platform for the long-distance trade that made Sijilmasa famous. The townspeople traded their surplus in dates and leather goods and textiles for a variety of industrial products from the north. The benefits of that trade then provided the vast variety of goods from all over the world right there in Sijilmasa.

The tribes of the desert also supplied the many thousands of camels needed to support this long-distance trade. They sold the camels to the caravan to replace those that could not make the return journey. The only reward for these poor beasts making the arduous journey was to be put up for livestock auction, the noisiest place in the whole market. The deep-voiced bellows and growls of the camels along with the lowing of cattle and braying of donkeys combined for an eerie, dissonant symphony and caused a steady crescendo in the voices of the auctioneers, customers, and spectators. The price was especially high for fine Berber horses that were in demand in the royal courts south of the Sahara. Some merchants in the market were willing to offer in exchange for a single horse of exceptional breeding the value of 15 to 20 slaves. The price would obviously be much greater still in the far distant Land of the Blacks, four or five times higher than a fine steed would sell for here.

The merchants from Awdaghust reinvested part of the profits of their trade to buy a vast variety of products of a truly international origin that were available in the market at Sijilmasa. These large caravans attracted goods from all over the Maghrib, from Andalusia, from Ifriqiya, from Egypt, and from points even farther east. The traders purchased manufactured items and foodstuffs that were otherwise simply not available in the Sahara or in the western Sudan.

The skillful merchants from the south carefully examined textiles and manufactured clothes. Local weavers in Sijilmasa produced cloth from the wool bought from sheep herders in the surrounding area.

There was also the fine cotton from Egypt, as well as smooth silks and brocades woven with gold and silver thread from Egypt and from the Yemen. This material was rather expensive and was purchased only by the wealthiest customers.

A wide variety of manufactured products were imported from far and wide. Coptic bronze lamps from Egypt might be found in the market. Some of those were exported to grace the homes of the more affluent in the south. Copper, bronze, and iron utensils—a teapot or spoons made in the Maghrib—were likely to grace the Bedouin tents in the desert. One could admire the colorful enameled pottery from Cordoba or sculpted marble tiles from Almaria, some of which would become tombstones for the elite in towns as far away as along the River Niger.

As more and more scholars and students came to Sijilmasa, books were increasingly in demand in the marketplace. They were painstakingly copied in the great intellectual centers of the north and east, cities like Fez and Cordoba, in Qayrawan and especially in Cairo. Typically, books sold for four or five *dinar*s apiece, almost as much as a fine suit of clothes, and some very rare books sold for 20 *dinar*s or more. Among those who sought them, books were among their most prized possessions and were considered a major part of their wealth. Merchants preparing to head south across the desert were also in the market to buy books. They were relatively easy to transport and would bring a good price in gold in the Islamic cities south of the Sahara.

A particularly colorful and curious stall was that of the merchant who sold pearls and coral, which were imported from Ceuta on the Mediterranean coast. The local craftsmen made beautiful necklaces of pearl, glass, amber, and other semi-precious stones. These were exported to Mali where they were in great demand and where it was said that the coral was used as a form of currency. The jewelers of Sijilmasa even refashioned some of the precious metals that were imported from near and far, including silver bracelets and amulets with deeply incised geometric patterns, and rings of delicate gold filigree.

The traders bought up an ample stock of food staples but did not neglect the more sensitive parts of the palate. They bought locally produced wheat in bulk quantities. The dates produced in the area around Sijilmasa were the very best in the northern Sahara. They selected fruit from the northern Maghrib; they chose almonds, candied fruit, figs, and dried raisins from Malaga and Almaria; they bought pistachios from Gafsa and olive oil imported from Seville and from Sfax.

As soon as a prospective buyer entered the market area, peddlers would elbow him closer to their stalls as they shouted enticing descriptions of their merchandise and gave assurances that theirs were the very best values to be found in the market that day. The bargaining and the bartering would be intense. Surely, many assurances of the finest quality and lowest prices far exceeded reality. But in the end, these experienced traders knew exactly what they were looking for and how much they were obliged, or at least willing, to pay for it. When the shouting and bickering were done, the buyer would tap the palm of the seller with his purse to indicate their mutual satisfaction with the deal. Thus the market ended each day at around dusk, except on Fridays. On this holy day of the week, business halted shortly after mid-day, and the men, local residents and the many visitors, prepared for the public Friday afternoon prayer.

Most of the visitors and many locals went to the *Jami'* Ibn Abd Allah, the Friday mosque. There were three other mosques in town, but the Friday mosque was the famous one. It was well known as a center of learning and the seat of justice for the region. As growth and prosperity had come to Sijilmasa over the last century, so too had come the scholars, *sufi*s (mystics), and students. It was also the only mosque that was large enough to accommodate the large number of the faithful wanting to pray together on Friday afternoon. Those who could not enter the mosque itself prayed in the open square outside.

The *Jami'* Ibn Abd Allah was located just to the east of the main street that ran along the central axis, on the highest elevation of the city. This is the same spot where al-Yasa Ibn Abu 'l-Qasim built the first mosque some 250 years earlier. The new mosque was larger and more richly decorated, with sculpted plaster and a new prayer niche which faced, like most other mosques in the far western Maghrib (as it turns out), incorrectly toward Mecca. Why incorrectly? No one knows for sure. But it had been done that way since the very beginning.

There was a long tradition of religious dissent among the people of Sijilmasa. They, like most Berbers of the Maghrib, had converted in the very early years of Islam to the Kharijite sect. The Kharijite attitude toward the caliphate, the central authority in Islam, was perfectly suited to these Berbers because of their general resistance to any form of centralized authority, especially if it was imposed by foreigners. They rejected the idea of dynastic legitimacy. They felt every believer who was religiously and morally irreproachable should be eligible for the position of caliph or *imam* by the vote of the community "even if he were a black slave." Indeed, if the chroniclers are correct, the first ruler chosen in the year 140/757 in Sijilmasa was Isa Ibn Yazis al-Aswad, a black.

The same rigor that characterizes Kharijism in its conception of the state is found in its ethical principles. It demands purity of conscience and body for acts of worship to be valid. Kharijites push their moral strictness to the point of refusing the title of believer to anyone who has committed heresy. Kharijite extremists say that he who has become an infidel in this way can never reenter the faith and should be killed for his apostasy, along with his wives and children.

The Sufriya branch of the sect which had been dominant in Sijilmasa since the beginning was more lenient on this particular point. In the palace across from the mosque, an inscription from the Koran reads: "On no soul doth God place a burden greater that it can bear. It gets every good that it earns and it suffers every ill that it earns." It still places responsibility on the individual soul, but offers promise of God's forgiveness.

For the last three generations, the people of Sijilmasa were following the orthodoxy of Sunni Islam. The Maghrawa Berbers had imposed orthodoxy on the inhabitants when they conquered Sijilmasa. The local Muslims complained bitterly of the impiety of the Maghrawa rulers. It is precisely those complaints that eventually brought the wrath of the Almoravids down upon the rulers of the city. It was a delegation of

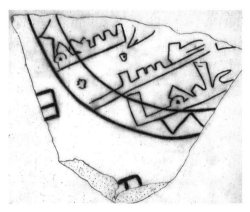

This fragment of wall plaster contains three words from the Koran II: 286, "*wus'aha, kasabat, 'alayha*." The fragment was found in an elite residence at the earliest level of occupation (likely the residence of the ruler) in Sijilmasa. (© MAPS [Moroccan-American Project at Sijilmasa, Ronald Messier, project director]. Used by permission.)

the religious scholarly elite who had gone to Abd Allah Ibn Yasin to persuade him to come to the rescue of the people of Sijilmasa.

The Almoravids came ostensibly as religious reformers. The religion of the new rulers was now the strict Malikite doctrine of the *Dar al-Murabitin*. It banned musical instruments and alcohol. It promised, the reformers said, a religious law that was much closer to that preached by the prophet Muhammad himself. The people of Sijilmasa expected a lot from the new rulers. They sought protection against tyranny; they welcomed tax reduction; they expected prosperity. Beyond that, they went about their daily lives as usual. For many, that included gathering in the mosque to pray on Friday afternoon.

At the loud, resonant tone of the *muezzin*'s call to prayer, the faithful would gather at the mosque. Those who had not the opportunity to perform the ritual ablutions in one of the local baths would quickly wash their hands in symbolic fashion. They would face the *qibla* wall, and, following the direction of the *imam*, the faithful recited the opening *sura* of the Koran, fulfill the proscribed number of *rak'a*—that is, the prayers, bowings, and prostrations—and then make their own special petitions. They would pray for health and well being. They would pray for peace. They would pray for the governor of the city and his sovereign, who was now the Almoravid *Amir*. And the travelers of the caravan would pray for a safe journey home.

Caravans would leave Sijilmasa very early in the morning, long before sunrise. On each of the 40 days in its march back to Awdaghust, it would travel for about three hours until the sun rose above the horizon. Then the camels were relieved of their burdens. Their front legs were tied together, allowing the camels to graze but not to wander very far. Tents were set up to provide shade from the sun's insurmountable heat at mid-day.

Once the sun began to fall in the late afternoon, camp was broken, the camels were loaded once again, and the march continued for another four hours or so, until the time after dusk when the sky was slightly purple, when there was still just enough light to set up camp before the fall of darkness. At this rate the caravan could travel about 18 to 22 miles a day.

The caravan's route depended on two things: water and pasturage. The trail varied several miles in one direction or another, depending upon the preceding years' rainfall to provide sufficient pasturage. But within that variance the caravan moved steadily in the most direct route possible from one watering spot to the next. When the distance to the next one was especially far, the camels could double the day's march for several days, as long as they were given a proportional rest once they reached the watering hole. As they approached, the pace quickened. The tribes who controlled the wells, the watering agents, were well paid in kind for their service from the manufactured goods brought from Sijilmasa, goods that were as scarce and precious in the Sahara as was the water they sold. The camels appeared grateful as they crowded shoulder to shoulder around the mud troughs and drank their seven gallons of water each.

The caravan also sold some of its goods in the desert to pay for protection, the right to cross the territory of the particular tribe that controlled each segment of the route. The protection was a service indispensable for the caravan and provided income and industrial products that were otherwise unavailable to the desert nomads.

All of the caravans stopped in Taghaza, the city of salt, located about 20 days' march south from Sijilmasa. It lay within the territory of the Bani Massufa, one of the tribes of the Sanhaja confederation. Taghaza's rise to predominance in the salt trade coincided with the advance of the Almoravids. Until then, much of the salt exported to the Sudan came from Awlil on the Atlantic coast, within the sphere of the Bani Gudala. When that tribe revolted against the Almoravids, the salt route that they controlled became more isolated from the hegemony that was developing in the central Sahara under Almoravid protection. That hegemony was most conducive to the import-export industry of the caravans that traded gold in the north for manufactured products that they exchanged for salt in the desert, which they in turn traded in the south for more gold—a profitable business indeed!

The traders described Taghaza as the most impressive source of salt in the Sahara. The mines were like quarries of marble. The salt was cut from the "quarries" in square slabs about eight inches thick. If the stories of the traders were true, then all of the buildings, the *qsar*, the walls, the dwellings, were made of salt. The traders sold more than half of their manufactured goods from the north at Taghaza in exchange for this salt, which was very much in demand south of the desert. The merchants exaggerated only slightly when they said that the traders sold the salt for an equal weight of gold. The traders were good storytellers, but the fact of the matter is, salt was very expensive in the south. The caravaneers charged as much as 80 percent of the salt's value to transport it to market in Ghana or in Mali. Soon, the cycle in the trade triangle—manufactured goods for salt for gold—would start again, and the caravan would return to Sijilmasa, which was, after all, on the receiving end of most of the gold that made its way across the Sahara. From Sijilmasa, much of the gold was reexported to ports all over the Mediterranean, but much of it, too, was destined for the mint at Sijilmasa, which had been striking gold coins for many generations for one regime after another.

The first *dinar* to be struck in Sijilmasa in the year 342/953, almost exactly a century before Ibn Yasin's invasion of the city, bears the name *al- Shakir li'llah*, which means "one who gives thanks to God." That was the surname of Muhammad Ibn al-Fath Ibn Maimun Ibn Midrar, a descendant of the founders of the city. His rule in Sijilmasa was the beginning of a period of great prosperity for the city, such prosperity that it attracted many rivals. It became a source of contention between two powerful Muslim caliphates, the Fatimids of Ifriqiya (modern Tunisia) and the Umayyads of Andalusia.

The Fatimids had definite expansionist designs that included plans to increase revenues in North Africa. The lucrative gold trade of Sijilmasa was very much a part of that plan. The Fatimids conducted five major military campaigns against Sijilmasa and finally captured it in C.E. 958. The Fatimid governor levied taxes on caravans going to the Land of the Blacks, in addition to the *zakat*, the land tax, and the customary duties imposed on the buying and selling of camels, sheep, and cattle, as well as customs on all the merchandise destined to or coming from Ifriqiya, Fez, Spain, the Sus, and Aghmat. For the next 20 years, Sijilmasa produced half of the tax revenues of the Fatimid state, and its mint struck as much as a fourth of its official gold coinage. That the Fatimids spent so much time and effort to control Sijilmasa shows not only that it was profitable but also that their efforts did not go unchallenged.

The Umayyads of Cordoba were the Fatimids' chief competitors for control of the lucrative trade center. In 367/977, through a client Berber tribe, the Maghrawa of the Zanata confederation, the Umayyads took Sijilmasa. The name of the Umayyad caliph stamped on the gold coins minted in Sijilmasa showed that they were ultimately in control, but only until C.E. 1016 when the Maghrawa broke from Umayyad control.

The Maghrawa reached out and colonized the region all around Sijilmasa. They occupied the valley of the Draa to the west as well as the valley of the upper Moulouya to the north, the key to the route to Fez. The "state" that they controlled was five days' march long by three days' march wide, at this time one of the largest in the Maghrib. They put the name of their own ruler on the coinage struck in the mint, continued to collect all of the taxes that previous rulers had collected, and they restricted the pasturage rights of the Sanhaja Berbers to the immediate south and west of the city.

The people detested the Muslim orthodoxy that the Maghrawa had brought with them. Foremost among their grievances was the oppressive taxation that was lining the pockets of foreign rulers. The local leadership of the city appealed to the Almoravid *imam*, who had a reputation as a warlord, but a just and holy one.

After the Almoravids' second conquest of the city, a young Lamtuna *amir*, Yusuf Ibn Tashfin, was residing in the *Dar al-Imara*, the administrative palace within the citadel on the northern edge of the city. The wealth of the city would give the Almoravids the will to carry their mission northward still farther. It would also provide the resources that would make it possible.

The new regime took over the *dar al-sikka*, the mint. New *dinar*s were struck in the name of God and his prophet, in the name of the Abassid caliph in Baghdad, and in the name of the Almoravid *Amir*, Abu Bakr Ibn Umar. The new coins also bear an inscription that clearly states: "If anyone desires a religion other than Islam [the Almoravids understood this to be Malikite Islam], never will it be accepted of him; and in the Hereafter, he will be in the ranks of those who have lost." These coins were struck in abundance with gold coming from the Land of the Blacks. They would command a favorable exchange in markets both near and far.

CHAPTER 3
From Aghmat to Marrakech

In the early summer of the year 450/June 1058, the Almoravid army marched across the High Atlas mountains. Abu Bakr led a force of 400 horsemen, 800 cameleers, and 2,000 foot soldiers, in what had become a standard proportion of horsemen to cameleers to foot soldiers in the Almoravid army. The first city they came to in the foothills of the northern slopes of the mountains was the beautiful city of Aghmat, well situated in the lush valley of the Wurika River. The city itself, almost three-quarters of a mile by three-quarters of a mile square, was surrounded by a circuit wall made of adobe. It was situated a little over a mile to the west of the river which supplied water to the city through a series of *seguias*, man-made canals, the main one of which ran alongside the main road diagonally across the center of town.

Aghmat was a wealthy city, comparable in commercial importance to the city of Fez to the north. Contemporaries described it as two separate towns. Aghmat Wurika was the political and commercial center. In earlier times, it served as a regional capital for the Idrissid rulers of Fez, who struck silver coins in Aghmat's mint. Aghmat Haylana was a little over a mile away, where tribesmen of the Bani Masmuda lived and had established markets of their own. The markets of both towns attracted merchants from all over the Maghrib and from as far away as the Orient. Of the city's citizens, contemporaries said, "there are none richer or in easier circumstances than the people of Aghmat." Given the Almoravid objective to control the major trade routes and centers of trade, Aghmat was the logical target for the first Almoravid assault north of the High Atlas.

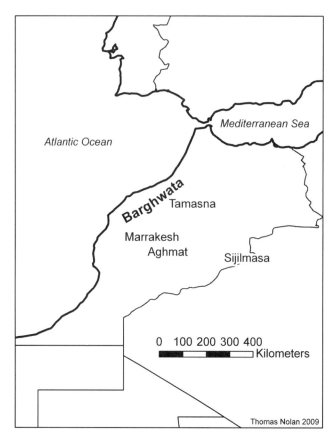

The Western Maghrib. (© Thomas Nolan. Used by permission.)

Abu Bakr camped on the outskirts and besieged the city. When the ruler of Aghmat, Laqut Ibn Yusuf Ibn Ali al-Maghrawi, saw that he had no power to resist, he surrendered the town. Under the cover of night's darkness, he fled to the Tadla region and sought the protection of its overlords, the Bani Yifran. The Almoravids tracked him down and killed him two months later. Aghmat was firmly in Almoravid hands. It would serve as their capital city for the next 13 years.

The eloquence and persuasiveness of Ibn Yasin's preaching paved the way for the campaign north of the mountains. The *imam* who had ignited the Western Sahara with the flame of Malikite Islam arrived at Aghmat on 2 *Jumada al-Ula*, 450/27 June, 1058. Certain *shaykhs* of the tribes of the Masmuda met him at a distance of two days' march from the city. The many tribes in the area were too disunited to offer any resistance against this holy warrior from the Sahara.

Ibn Yasin persuaded the Masmuda Berbers to the south of Aghmat that he would be able to establish unity among them if they submitted to his authority. He met with the chiefs of the Wurika, the Haylana, and the Hazmira and made a tour of the other tribes of the Masmuda and the tribes of the land of Tamasna. He asked them, "Do you not know that any one of you who dies in these *jahiliya* wars is one of the people of the Fire?" By *jahiliya* wars, he meant those fought to combat ignorance of the law. He went on to say, "Fear God, and reject this state of rebellion in which you are, and place over you one who will hold you together. If you will listen to me I will show you sound judgment by which God will put right your affairs. This is the *Amir* of the Lamtuna, a people of asceticism and piety." These tribes had already heard of him and of the lands which God had reformed at his hands. They readily accepted his preaching.

Within six months of his great success in Aghmat, Ibn Yasin directed his religious campaign against the Barghwata, who inhabited the region to the northwest along the coast of the Atlantic. The Barghwata were Muslim, but they were viewed by most as heretics. They clung to many of their earlier customs that did not conform to the true faith. Their opponents accused them of fasting during the month of *Rajab* rather than *Ramadan* and of praying ten times a day rather than five. When they prayed, they moved their heads without prostrating. It was said that they were permitted to marry as many wives as they wanted but were prohibited from marrying their cousins. They could repudiate and take back their wives a thousand times a day if they wished, since women were not protected under their law. Rather than cut the hands of thieves, they killed them. They could not eat the heads of animals or birds. They could neither kill nor eat cocks because these announced the morning prayer; if they did, the penalty was to free a slave.

But considered worst of all of the errors of the Barghwata, they recognized Salih Ibn Tarif as their prophet, and they had their own Koran, in their own Berber language, which had 80 chapters named after Adam, Job, Noah, Moses, Aaron, Asbath, the 12 tribes, the cock, the grasshopper, the camel, and the wonders of the world. In the eyes of Ibn Yasin, they were not Muslim. And that was all the reason he needed to conduct a holy war against them, beyond which they stood in the way of his carrying the vanguard of the *Dar al-Murabitin* farther into the Maghrib.

The campaign that followed against the Barghwata was bloody. The Almoravid army, reportedly 50,000 strong, marched north from

Aghmat into Tamasna. Among those to fall on the battlefield at a place called Kurifala was the *Imam* Ibn Yasin himself. Severely wounded, Ibn Yasin was carried from the field to his camp. The Almoravid chiefs gathered around to hear him speak for the last time. He told them, "Almoravids, you are in the land of your enemies, and I will surely die today. So beware lest you lose courage and lose the day. Be united in defense of the faith, and in defense of your brothers for God's sake. Beware of dissension and envy in seeking the leadership, for God gives his authority to whom he will, and makes his deputy on earth whom he wishes of his slaves. I leave you now, so consider which of you will put forward to exercise authority, and lead your armies, and make raids upon your enemies, and divide the booty among you, and collect your alms and tithes." Ibn Yasin had earlier made clear his choice for a successor, Abu Bakr Ibn Umar, and that was the consensus of the assembled Almoravid chiefs.

Ibn Yasin died on Sunday, 24 *Jumada al-Ula*, 450/8 July, 1059. For a long time to come, people were obedient to him and to the faith that he followed. They recorded and followed his legal rulings and answers to moral questions. People prayed at the tomb that was built at the place where he fell. Likewise, long after his death, the Almoravids would only choose a man to lead them in prayer who had prayed behind Abd Allah Ibn Yasin, even though there might be among them a more meritorious and pious person who had never prayed under his guidance. Ibn Yasin's position as *imam* fell upon Sulayman Ibn Addu, but that role was limited to religious leadership. The Almoravids never fully accepted his authority. Real authority fell upon Abu Bakr as *Amir*.

Blood for blood! That was the law of the land. Vengeance for wrongs done against the tribe or against any member of it was a cornerstone of *asabiya*, and the responsibility of seeking vengeance for the martyrdom of the Almoravid saint at the hands of the Barghwata now fell upon the new *Amir*. The Almoravid chiefs among the Sanhaja accepted his appointment, so his authority was well established, at least in theory. Abu Bakr's first order of business was to "bury the dead." He departed with a detachment of Almoravids, having taken God as his commander in this holy war. The Almoravids killed many Barghwata in this campaign and took many captives. Many Barghwata bore witness to God, according to the doctrine of the victors, some willingly and some under duress. Many others managed to escape into the surrounding countryside. At least for the moment, Abu Bakr had eliminated the Barghwata heresy from the Maghrib. His next task was to consolidate his power.

Abu Bakr was still a nomad. He had grown up in the Sahara among the Lamtuna tribe. As a youngster, he had undoubtedly tended herds of camels and goats. As a young man, he took part in local conflicts over watering and grazing rights or over jurisdiction of caravan routes, and he had observed intertribal politics firsthand. Now in the Maghrib, he lived with his brothers and with his troops in tents on the outskirts of Aghmat. He lived off the booty captured in battle and which he distributed according to the new custom taught by Ibn Yasin, one-fifth to support his tribal government and four-fifths to be distributed to his troops.

From his base in Aghmat, Abu Bakr planned his campaign to extend his control over the rest of the Maghrib. He relieved Yusuf Ibn Tashfin of his duties as governor of Sijilmasa so that the two of them could fight side by side against the Bani Zanata and the Bani Yifran. It soon became clear that the two warriors should separate. Ibn Tashfin would carry his campaign north into the central Maghrib while Abu Bakr tried to hold on to the southern Maghrib as well as their territory in the Sahara.

The key to Abu Bakr's political power in the Maghrib presented herself in 460/1068. She was a woman of extraordinary enchantment. Many local aspiring *shaykhs* sought the hand in marriage of the beautiful Zaynab al-Nafzawiya. She was the daughter of Ishaq al-Hawarri, a merchant from Qayrawan who had settled in the wealthy town of Aghmat. The little girl had grown to full maturity in this lush, green valley abundantly watered by the Wurika River, which flowed heavily and continuously throughout the year from the High Atlas in whose foothills Aghmat was situated. The flowers in the formal gardens were as beautiful and as fragrant as the wild flowers in the surrounding countryside, which was rich with orange and lemon blossoms in the springtime. In such an environment, a child with a keen intelligence, a sense of adventure, limitless ambition, and a father with the means and inclination to provide for her whatever she wanted could attain unlimited power. In a land where women traditionally were not formally educated, Zaynab's father agreed to send her to the mountains to learn from an old woman healer and soothsayer. As a woman, Zaynab would have to exert her political influence by marrying well, and she would do that more than once.

Zaynab was exceptionally beautiful, described as having a smooth, olive complexion, a slim waist, and firm breasts. She had a magnetism about her that led her contemporaries to call her a magician and to say that the *jinn*, those supernatural spirits that perform feats of magic for

Zaynab was the daughter of a merchant in Aghmat; she became the concubine of a tribal chief of the Bani Masmuda; then married to Laqut, the ruler of Aghmat; then married to Abu Bakr; and finally married to Yusuf Ibn Tashfin. (© Michael Summers. Used by permission.)

their summoner, served her. When local men would ask for her hand in marriage, she would say, "No one shall marry me but one who rules the whole Maghrib." She became the concubine of a tribal chief among the Masmuda in the mountains. Then she married Laqut Ibn Yusuf Ibn Ali al-Maghrawi, the ruler of the city in which she was raised. But he was killed by the Almoravids in their conquest of the city just a few years earlier. Now, she was a widow—and betrothed to Abu Bakr.

Zaynab promised to produce much wealth for the Almoravid *Amir*. Legend has it that she took him blindfolded to a nearby secret location. When he opened his eyes, he was greatly astonished at the treasures—gold and silver, pearls and rubies—which he beheld. Zaynab told him, "All this is your wealth and property. God has given it to you by my hand and I now pay it over to you." He had seen the fortune by the light of candles. Then she brought him out from that place blindfolded, just as she had taken him into it, so he knew neither where he had gone in nor where he had come out. His marriage with her took place in the month of *Dhu l- Qa'da*, 460/September, 1068. Whatever other benefits it afforded, the marriage to Zaynab, widow of the former ruler of Aghmat, was a considerable asset to Abu Bakr's power in the Maghrib.

By this time, the local dignitaries of Aghmat were becoming weary of the occupying forces of the Almoravids. The occupation was an obvious drain on the local resources. Shortly after Abu Bakr's marriage, the local *shaykhs* came to him to express their growing displeasure and impatience. Time after time, the *shaykhs* of the Wurika and Haylana tribes came to complain to the *Amir* Abu Bakr, until he finally told them, "Designate a place for us where I may build a city, if God, who is exalted, wills it."

Abu Bakr had another reason for wanting to build his capital somewhere else: Aghmat was too close to the foothills of the High Atlas. The city virtually sat in the middle of a bowl formed by the mountains on three sides, and those mountains were the stronghold of the tribes of the Bani Masmuda, Berbers from the Atlas. Although the Bani Masmuda had sworn allegiance to the Almoravids in Aghmat, the Almoravids remained wary.

The two tribes disagreed about where to build the city; naturally, each tribe requested that it should be built on its own territory and that it should be named after them. Finally the *shaykhs* of the tribes of the Bani Masmuda and others held a meeting and decided to locate the city between the lands of the Bani Haylana and the lands of the Bani Hazmira. The spokesman of the assembly said to the *Amir*, "We have searched for a desert place for you with no living thing except gazelles and ostriches and nothing growing except lotus trees and colocynths." They said that some desired that the city should be on the Tansift River. But the *Amir* refused this choice, saying, "We are people of the desert, and have our flocks with us. It is not suitable for us to live on the river."

The *Amir* rode at the head of his army, accompanied by the *shaykhs* of the tribes. He stopped in the plain of Marrakech. The site was on the west bank of the Issil River, a small river that flowed into the Tansift from the south and separated the lands of the Bani Haylana and the Bani Hazmira. The plain was within a day's march of the fertile Nassif Valley, where food supplies were abundant. It was also 18 miles of flat terrain from the foothills of the High Atlas. Any attack from the mountains would stir up such a cloud of dust as to warn the

Almoravids well in advance of an opposing force's arrival at the gates of their new city.

The open, although somewhat barren site did not impose the restrictions on space that the narrow river valley of the Wurika did. The nomadic encampment of these Saharan warriors was huge, but in no other way different than what they were used to at home. The Bani Lamtuna moved in with their camels and their horses, their sheep and their goats, and their armaments and their treasury. Choosing where to set up a tent seemed spontaneous enough, as brothers and cousins settled in close proximity one to the other. The result was a tent city established according to their own customs in their own land.

Some tribes of the Bani Masmuda also moved to the site with the Almoravids as vassals of Abu Bakr. They were not nomads. While the Bani Lamtuna were content to live in tents, the Bani Masmuda began to build houses out of mud bricks, although many of these were no more permanent than the tents of the Bani Lamtuna. The Bani Masmuda moved in with their women and their children. It was a curious juxtaposition of the semisedentary becoming nomadic and the seminomadic becoming sedentary. The Almoravids hurriedly constructed temporary fortifications around their new encampment. They would not finish the actual walls of the city for several years.

CHAPTER 4
The Second Founding of Fez

It was winter in the year 455/January, 1063. Ibn Yasin had been dead for more than three years, and Abu Bakr was well on his way to consolidating the southern part of the Maghrib. To the north, the central Maghrib offered considerably more resistance. This was the stronghold of the Bani Zanata, a confederation of Berber tribes who would turn out to be the most persistent competitor to the Almoravids between the Middle Atlas Mountains and the Mediterranean. Abu Baker assigned Yusuf Ibn Tashfin to the task. The young commander, cousin and lieutenant to the new *Amir*, devised a strategy to isolate the major cities by controlling the space between them. He would seek to win over the people in the small villages in the countryside and thereby strangle the urban strongholds of his opponents. Ibn Tashfin promised peace to the villages as he brought war against the fortresses that protected them. "Remember the hardships you suffered under the tyranny of the Zanata!," he reminded the people. This strategy was also designed to control the trade routes connecting the major cities. Consequently, the Almoravids' line of march followed the direction of the major trade routes, from the valley of the Ziz River across to the valley of the Moulouya, to the River Sebou into which flowed the River Fez. This route took them to the city of Fez itself.

Fez was a main center of resistance against the Almoravids north of the Middle Atlas. The city is situated about halfway between the Rif Mountains to the north and the Middle Atlas mountains to the south. To the west lie the lush, fertile, rolling plains of the Bani Miknasa, the cities of Meknes and Moulay Idris, and the ancient city of Volubulis. To the east, the distance between the two mountain ranges narrows

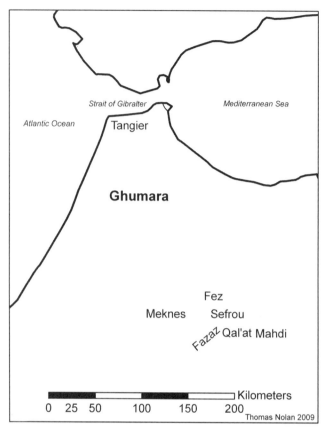

Campaign in the Central Maghrib. (© Thomas Nolan. Used by permission.)

at the Taza Gap that guards the eastern access. Fez is the hub of what the Arabs called *al-Maghrib al-Aqsa*, at the intersection of two great axes of communication and trade, one going from the Atlantic to Ifriqiya and the other from the Mediterranean to the Ziz Valley and so beyond to the Land of the Blacks.

At the same time that Cordoba reached its cultural and intellectual peak under the Umayyads in Andalusia, Fez had become the dominant city in Moroccan trade, culture, religious life, and, at times, politics as well. At the death of its founder Moulay Idris at the end of the eighth century, Fez was little more than a village on the east bank of the river. A generation later, Idris II made the city his capital, and the city began to grow. When civil war drove some 8,000 refugees from Andalusia, Idris II welcomed them. Likewise, he harbored another tide of

The Second Founding of Fez

refugees fleeing revolution in the holy city of Qayrawan in Ifriqiya. The two new communities established a settlement pattern in separate, walled towns on either side of the river bank. Their tradition and highly developed expertise as craftsmen and merchants transformed Fez into an urban center that rivaled their own hometowns. The Qarawiyin Mosque, established in Fez in the ninth century, at first a modest building of only six bays, had grown to become the religious and intellectual center of the Maghrib. Its fame spread beyond the Maghrib, and its university attracted scholars and students from Europe and the Middle East, as well as from all over the Maghrib. Among its students was a Christian scholar from France who had been studying mathematics and astronomy in Spain from C.E. 967 to 970. How long he stayed is unknown, but some time after he returned home, he became Pope Sylvester II.

Like Sijilmasa, Fez had also been a prize highly sought by both the Fatimid and Umayyad dynasties. The Umayyads ultimately won out and brought Malikite law to the Qarawiyin Mosque. Now, in the mid-eleventh century, as the Almoravid armies approached, Fez was firmly under the control of a prominent family of the Maghrawa tribe of Zanata Berbers, who ruled Fez first as clients of the Umayyads. When the Andalusian regime proved incapable of holding on, the Bani Maghrawa began to rule in their own right. On the eve of the Almoravid arrival, the ruling family was plagued by civil war. Caught in the middle were the people of Fez, who were despoiled by rival factions. The Arab authors who trace the history of Fez recount that, for a short time, prosperity gave way to paucity, security to fear, justice to injustice. The last Maghrawa ruler of Fez was Mu'ansir Ibn Ziri, whose subjects supported him only because they feared him. He became a persistent thorn in Ibn Tashfin's side.

The first step in Ibn Tashfin's strategy called for laying siege to the fortress of Ibn Tuli, known as Qal'at al-Mahdi. Located in the valley of Fazaz between Fez and the Middle Atlas Mountains, it was a strategic fortress that controlled the waters of the Sebou River. But Ibn Tashfin soon called off the siege to take advantage of what seemed to him a better offer.

The longtime opponents to the Maghrawa rulers of Fez were the lords of Meknes, a significant city some 40 miles to the west of Fez. The current ruler of Meknes, al-Mahdi Ibn Yusuf al-Jazna'i, offered an alliance to Ibn Tashfin. Al-Jazna'i had already heard of the Almoravid program of religious reform as well as of the might of the Almoravid armies. He had heard that the Almoravid *Amir* preferred to govern newly conquered areas through its own local rulers, provided, of course, that these local rulers remained loyal to the Almoravids. So al-Jazna'i surrendered his city to the Almoravid, only to receive it back again. Ibn Tashfin appointed al-Jazna'i governor of the province of Meknes and ordered him to take up arms against the Maghrawa in Fez. This fit perfectly into Ibn Tashfin's overall strategy of isolating his opponents.

At first, it appeared as if the march on Fez would be easy. Ibn Tashfin's plan was to control the countryside all around Fez. In his line of march, he captured a number of strongholds that were allied to the *amir* of Fez. Considerable force was needed in some villages to persuade the people. In Saddina, for example, Ibn Tashfin entered by force, destroyed the ramparts, and killed more than 4,000 people.

Meanwhile, the elusive *amir* of Fez, Mu'ansir Ibn Ziri, had managed to escape. He fled the city with a large part of his army and took refuge among the Saddina tribesmen in the mountains to the north. Before fleeing, however, he had placed in charge of the garrison a man named Bakkar Ibn Ibrahim, who made a valiant effort to defend the city. Ibn Ibrahim led a sortie against the Almoravids, trying to break their siege, but the attempt failed. The Almoravids captured and killed Ibn Ibrahim. But Fez did not fall, and the Almoravids still could not enter the city.

Ibn Tashfin decided to divert his effort at this point and attack the fortification at Sefrou, some 20 miles south of Fez. He was especially harsh against this last town because it harbored the family of Mas'ud bin Wanudin, the Maghrawa ruler whom the Almoravids had killed eight years earlier when they conquered Sijilmasa. Bin Wanudin's family had escaped from Sijilmasa and had sought refuge here in Sefrou. The Almoravids took Sefrou handily and massacred the refugees from Sijilmasa.

When Ibn Tashfin resumed the siege of Fez, now several months into the campaign, he finally succeeded in entering the city. The inhabitants, accustomed to the oppressive authority of the Maghrawa, were hoping for liberation. Ibn Tashfin had been saying all along that his purpose was to free the people from Maghrawa oppression. He said that he wanted to defeat the rulers, but not to rule over the citizens.

The Almoravid did not quite follow through with his promise. He was not confident enough of the people's loyalty to appoint local self-rule. Rather, he stationed 400 mounted Lamtuna warriors there and appointed one of his own tribesmen to govern Fez. Without abandoning his siege of the fortress of Fazaz to the south of Fez, Ibn Tashfin directed a campaign northward against the Ghumara and marched on to Tangier. His armies were engaged on two different fronts.

Ibn Tashfin took village after village in the region of the Ghumara until he was encamped on the hilltops overlooking Tangier, the very northern tip of Morocco, opposite Andalusia. As Ibn Tashfin was perched on the hilltops overlooking Tangier, surely he may have wondered what was beyond, on the other side of the Straits of Gibraltar. Such curiosity would have to wait. Ibn Tashfin learned that Tangier was in the hands of Suqut al-Barghwati, a slave who had been appointed governor of Tangier by the Hammudid king of Malaga in Spain. Al-Barghwati was a hard, old soldier. He was also allied to Mu'ansir Ibn Ziri, the *amir* of Fez, Ibn Tashfin's most persistent enemy in the Maghrib. Ibn Tashfin exercised some discretion and judged that Ibn Ziri's talent and experience were too much of an obstacle for the moment. Ibn Tashfin reconsidered his plan and temporarily abandoned the idea of marching on Tangier. He returned to the valley of Fazaz and concentrated his efforts on Fez's southern flank.

Ibn Tashfin's control in the Maghrib, at least so far, depended very much upon his personal presence and direction. He had not been gone from Fez for very long when Mu'ansir Ibn Ziri, the Maghrawa ruler of Fez whom Ibn Tashfin had earlier driven from the city, took advantage of Ibn Tashfin's absence to retake his seat of power. Ibn Ziri beseiged the city, promising amnesty to the Lamtuna garrison, but when he entered Fez, he killed the Lamtuna governor that Ibn Tashfin had placed in charge.

Ibn Tashfin was in the Fazaz Valley when news of his loss in Fez reached him. He ordered his ally, al-Jazna'i of Meknes, to join forces with him. The faithful vassal immediately left the town of Wassufa and headed for the Fazaz, but news travels faster than armies in the Maghrib. Ibn Ziri was able to intercept al-Jazna'i and crush the army of his enemy. Al-Jazna'i himself was killed in the battle. Mu'ansir Ibn Ziri sent the head of the victim to Tangier to Suqut al-Barghwati, not so much as a gesture to an ally as a statement to instill fear in the enemy whose spies were quick to report the news to Ibn Tashfin.

Ibn Tashfin was determined to get his revenge. He sent band after band of his Sanhaja warriors to attack and harass those who came to and from the city of Fez. The desert fighters adapted well to this new tactic of siege warfare. Ibn Tashfin tightened Almoravid control of the surrounding countryside and his blockade of Fez so much that food and supplies had become scarce. He planned to starve out the enemy, and Mu'ansir Ibn Ziri could feel the noose tightening.

Ibn Ziri realized that he would have to engage in a head-on battle against the Almoravids or else Fez was going to fall. He had no choice but to face the Almoravids in a direct combat—he decided to fight! He gathered his whole army from his own tribe of Maghrawa and added to it reinforcements from the Bani Yifran, a tribe of the Zanata confederation who occupied the hills and valleys south of Fez. In a last ditch effort that entered the annals of Zanata folklore as an outstanding example of bravery, Mu'ansir Ibn Ziri left the city whose walls were at the same time a source of protection and a prison. He engaged head-on in battle against the Lamtuna warriors and was killed on the battlefield that day, along with many of his followers. The man who had led the Maghrawa in Fez was now the city's martyr.

Still, the Almoravids were unable to enter the walls of Fez. The Zanata in the area were not ready to give up. They quickly rallied around Qasim Ibn Abd al-Rahman, a man of noble descent from nearby Taza who took up Ibn Ziri's struggle. The Zanata cornered the Lamtuna army at the Siffir River and routed them after destroying most of the cavalry in a horrendous battle.

Meanwhile, Ibn Tashfin was still directing the ongoing siege of the fortress of Fazaz. He was totally frustrated at the news of Qasim's victory. All or nothing, it was now time for Ibn Tashfin to take charge of the campaign against Fez himself. He would have to stick to his original strategy of controlling the countryside. To the north and to the east of the city were the mountains, which all too often served as a refuge for the Bani Zanata, just beyond the reach of the Almoravid cavalry. Fighting in the mountains was different than fighting in the desert. But Ibn Tashfin knew that if he wanted to secure his control of Fez, he would have to route the Zanata warlords from these surrounding mountains. The campaign would take the next five years, much longer than he had anticipated.

Ibn Tashfin left Fazaz in the year 456/1064. Within a year, after killing many of his enemy, he had gained control of the territory of the Bani Marasan and the Fandula to the north of Fez. Two years later, he crossed the Sebou River and occupied the territory of the Wargha tribe, managing to reduce the opposition of the tribes in that area. In 460/1067 he penetrated the interior of the mountains of the Rif and at least temporarily subjugated the tribe of the Ghumara. Ibn Tashfin even managed for the first time to occupy the Mediterranean coastline between Ceuta and Tangier. But he could not follow through and take those two important coastal cities. First he had to resolve the matter of Fez.

The Second Founding of Fez

Late in the winter of 462/1070, Yusuf Ibn Tashfin's forces were camped all around the walls of Fez. They no longer feared resistance from the countryside. Finally, on Thursday, 2 *Jumada*, I/18 March, Ibn Tashfin took the city by storm. He entered Fez, sword in hand, and ordered the killing of thousands of tribesmen from among the tribes of the Maghrawa, the Bani Yifran, the Bani Miknasi, and others. It was told that the markets and the streets were strewn with corpses, sometimes stacked one upon another. At the two mosques alone, the Qarawiyin and the Andalusian, more than 3,000 people were killed. The Almoravids had vented their frustrations, and blood flowed among the cobblestone streets of Fez. Those among the enemy who managed to escape the wrath of the Almoravids on that day fled more than 300 miles to the east, to the city of Tlemcen.

Ibn Tashfin was a fierce conqueror, but he was not a harsh ruler. As he conquered, he promised not only leniency but reform to those who submitted to his authority, a promise that was easier to accomplish in the city than in the countryside. He now set about to repairing the damage done to Fez. He rebuked the inhabitants of those neighborhoods that had no mosque and told the people to build one immediately. The very heart of the city under the Almoravids would be the Qarawiyin Mosque. It was already 200 years old when the Almoravids occupied the city. Legend has it that the Qarawiyin was founded by a Tunisian woman who had fled to Fez from Qayrawan in the middle of the ninth century. Ibn Tashfin restored the mosque and made it the main mosque of the city. Here, the *faqih*s, religious legists from around the world, but mainly from the Maghrib and from Andalusia, sat cross-legged and discussed the law of Malikite Islam. Ibn Tashfin would come here to seek their advice.

Fez's most wealthy citizens lived near the Qarawiyin Mosque. Their houses, plain on the outside, opened to lush courtyards, and their gardens were scented by a variety of fruit trees, with apple trees from Tripoli being the most famous in the quarter. The focal point was the fountain fed by a canal of running water.

If the Qarawiyin was the heart of the city, then the marketplace that reached out in every direction from the mosque was its organs of nourishment. Ibn Tashfin repaired and embellished the bazaars and commissioned the building of caravansaries to house the itinerant merchants whom he hoped would come in still larger numbers than before. The market became a labyrinth of narrow alleyways with row upon row of shops. All the minor crafts were to be found here, each one more or less in its own street or quarter. There were a few side streets leading from the city gates to the market, but even they were rarely wider than was absolutely necessary for two laden pack animals to pass each other. The main street leading toward the Qarawiyin Mosque, the street called *Suq Attarin*, "market of the spice merchants," was lined with stall after stall of spices, some locally produced, some imported, but all of them colorful and filling the air with an aroma that unmistakably identified the place.

In the square just outside of the Qarawiyin library, which housed one of the greatest collections of Islamic manuscripts outside of Baghdad, metalworkers hammered away on simple iron cauldrons and ornate brass and copper plates used in weddings and festivals. To the south of the metal workers' district the cloth dyers worked. The colorful wool yarns—the yellows colored with saffron, the blues with indigo, and the reds with henna—were all intensified as the wet skeins dried in the sunlight. On the far northeast side of the city, tanneries produced the fine leather for which Morocco is so famous. Here, too, the aroma unmistakably identified the place. Such foul-smelling and "dirty" industries were customarily restricted to very edge of town.

Ibn Tashfin demolished the wall that separated the quarters of al-Andalus and al-Qarawiyin that had been situated on opposite sides of the river. He built new ramparts around what would be from now on a united city, thereby eliminating the duality that prejudiced the city's development. The endless neighboring feuds over water rights ended. The Almoravids were from the desert and knew all about the efficient collection and distribution of water as well as the need to cooperate in order to maximize the use of such a precious resource.

The engineers constructed open canals that, leading directly from the river, channeled water toward the different quarters. The water then passed through underground conduits made by the potters of Fez, where water circulated by simple gravity as the general slope of the terrain permitted. Canals flushed waste downstream from the city. Only the quarters situated in the southeastern part were somewhat at a disadvantage from this point of view, but they supplemented their water supply from numerous wells. Ibn Tashfin ordered the construction of new baths and mills, both now possible because of the abundance of water, much more than most cities had at this time. There were many public fountains where animals and people could drink without charge. Mosques had the pool and water hall that were indispensable to ritualistic ablutions.

On the west side of the city, on the crest of the plateau that overlooks it, Ibn Tashfin built a citadel, the Qasba Bou Jaloud, where the

Almoravid governor would reside and the garrison would be stationed, both to protect the city and to ensure its loyalty to the new rulers. Building to the west of the city established the direction of future development for a long time to come. In fact, Ibn Tashfin's impact on the city's growth was such that he is often considered to be the second founder of Fez.

Ibn Tashfin spent almost a year in Fez, and he left in the month of *Safar*, 463/November, 1070. This is only about a month or so before his *Amir* Abu Bakr was called from his newly established base in Marrakech to return to the Sahara. Because Ibn Tashfin had been so successful in securing the major cities in the central Maghrib, because he had managed to establish, at least for the moment, Almoravid dominance over the various tribes of the Bani Zanata, Abu Bakr was more confident than ever that his cousin could serve as his lieutenant. He placed Ibn Tashfin in command over all of the Almoravid forces in the whole of the Maghrib and entrusted his cousin with the care of his wife.

CHAPTER 5

The Urban Nomad

Abu Bakr began to establish some permanence in his base camp at Marrakech. In the year 462, on 23 *Rajab*/7 May, 1070, the cornerstone was laid for the *Qasr al-Hajar*, a fortified repository that would provide more security for the Almoravids' storage of arms and treasury. The walls were made of hewn stone and were raised in about three months. The *qasr* measured some 240 yards long and nearly as wide. It was larger than one would expect for any city, but so too were the stores that would be kept there.

Some of the people among the Bani Lamtuna began to build their own houses, each according to his own means, as the Bani Masmuda had done earlier. The first of the Lamtuna to build such a house was Turzin Ibn al-Hasan, who built in the place called Asdal. He built it of sun-dried brick, and it would mark that spot for a long time to come.

With construction of the *qasr* in full swing, one day in 463/1070–71, Abu Bakr was sitting on the wall supervising the work when a messenger rode in on a lathered horse, bringing news of a rebellion against Almoravid authority in the Sahara. He said to Abu Bakr, "May God support the *Amir*. The Bani Gudala have made a raid on your brothers in the desert. They have killed many men and seized property." Abu Bakr answered, "We belong to God and to him we shall return!" The *Amir* sent for the *shaykhs* and elders of Lamtuna and said to them, "The Bani Gudala have made a raid on our brothers and killed them and routed them. I am going to travel there, if God wills, to seek vengeance for them." For nearly 20 years since the Bani Gudala had broken from the confederation at the time of Yahya Ibn Umar's nomination as chief, they threatened the solidarity of the Sanhaja's control over the western Sahara, over the routes that crossed it, and over the profits that the trade in gold and slaves could bring. The Almoravids had already lost the benefits of the rich salt trade of Awlil.

Political and economic reasons aside, the legend is that Abu Bakr heard an old woman of the Sahara crying because she had lost her camel. "Abu Bakr Ibn Umar has done us harm by taking the Maghrib," she cursed. The truth is, Abu Bakr, too, wanted to leave the city and longed to return to the Sahara he had left more than a decade earlier. He could not adjust to what was already too much of an urban life to suit him.

Abu Bakr had asked his local commanders to choose someone to serve as his lieutenant during his absence, but they could not, or at least would not. He then claimed to have had a vision in which God instructed him to appoint his cousin Yusuf Ibn Tashfin, who had already proved himself in battle with the enemy. Ibn Tashfin had distinguished himself as a military commander, conquering the city of Fez and winning several campaigns in the central Maghrib against those Zanata Berbers who had refused to submit. Ibn Tashfin arrived in Marrakech a hero! He greeted his *Amir* and assured him, "I will be your deputy, if God who is great and exalted wills it!"

There was still another personal matter for Abu Bakr to resolve before leaving—how to provide for his lovely wife, Zaynab. He feared that she was too beautiful and much too delicate to endure the hardships of the desert. He told her, "Zaynab, I am going to the Sahara; you are a woman, lovely and frail, and you will not be able to endure the heat. Besides, I cannot go while you are under my protection, for if I die I shall be responsible for you. It would be best if I divorce you." According to the provisions of the law, he renounced her, thus granting her a divorce. Abu Bakr told her that when her period of *idda* was finished, after the number of days that are prescribed by Islamic law before a widowed or divorced woman can remarry, she was to marry Yusuf Ibn Tashfin, his cousin, whom he had appointed as his lieutenant. He then told Ibn Tashfin, "Marry her, for she is a woman who brings good fortune." Zaynab's reply to Abu Bakr was simply, "Your judgment is sound."

Abu Bakr's expedition was carefully planned. With the command of the Almoravids in the Maghrib safely in the hands of his lieutenant, Abu Bakr marched out of Marrakech with a large part of the Almoravid army, accompanied by Yusuf Ibn Tashfin, and crossed the High Atlas Mountains. He spent three days in Sijilmasa making sure that this vital gateway between the Maghrib and his homeland was firmly in the hands of his newly appointed governor, his own son, Ibrahim. Here he made his final preparations for the trek into the desert by assembling more than half of the Lamtuna army and requisitioning the camels necessary to mount his cavalry and to transport the food and equipment obtained in the Sijilmasa market. He left for the Sahara at the beginning of the month *Rabi al-thani* in the year 463/January, 1071.

Yusuf Ibn Tashfin returned to Marrakech with what remained of the Lamtuna warriors and began to consolidate his own authority. When Abu Bakr had announced Ibn Tashfin's appointment, the local *shaykh*s agreed to accept it, they said, because of Yusuf's "reputation," because of what they knew of his religiosity, virtue, bravery, resolution, courage, justice, and sound judgment—all those qualities that constitute *muruwah*, the qualities needed of an *amir*. During his own lifetime, Yusuf Ibn Tashfin would become a hero of folkloristic proportion. He was dark skinned with black, piercing eyes, black hair that was short and curly, and a fuzzy beard. He was not a large man; he was thin, of medium height, but nonetheless a man with an imposing presence. Some suspected that some of the blood that flowed in his veins was from the Land of the Blacks. Ibn Tashfin was a deeply religious man, an ascetic who disdained worldly pleasures and was modest in everything. He dressed only in wool, ate nothing but meat and camel's milk, the staple of the Sanhaja of the Sahara and was able and even more willing to endure any hardship for his faith and for his cause. Yet he would amass more wealth than any other Sanhaja tribal ruler before him.

Ibn Tashfin consummated his marriage to Zaynab in the month of *Shaʻban* in the year 463/May, 1071. The newlyweds were pleased with each other, and Zaynab told Yusuf that he would rule the whole of the Maghrib. As she had done for previous husbands, Zaynab threw her political influence in support of Yusuf. She was an ambitious woman, but she could exert power only indirectly. Yusuf might have had his own secret visions of grandeur, but Zaynab undoubtedly urged him on to become an empire builder. She placed all of her immense fortune at his disposal, so, as Abu Bakr had earlier, Ibn Tashfin was able to equip many horsemen and to organize his army.

Yusuf Ibn Tashfin's first year as Abu Bakr's deputy was a busy one. Pious man that he was, Ibn Tashfin set to building the first mosque of Marrakech amidst the half-nomadic, half-sedentary settlement. Chronicles say that he put on some old clothing and worked the mortar with his own hands with the masons out of modesty and humility. His main concern was not to build a lasting monument to himself, but to provide the people with a place to pray. This mosque would later be rebuilt, and nothing of the original mosque can be found today. Yet it is Yusuf who is honored as being the builder of the mosque, indeed, as being the builder of the whole city. In these early days, the Friday worship in the mosque was probably the most urban of the activities in Marrakech.

The military strength of the Almoravids was certainly weakened in the Maghrib when half of it or more returned to the Sahara with Abu Bakr. Since a Lamtuna chief was nothing without an army loyal to himself, Ibn Tashfin created his own personal bodyguard. From Andalusia he brought a number of renegades, former Christians, as mercenaries. He imported some 2,000 black slaves from the western Sudan. He gave them all mounts, paid for with Zaynab's money, so that finally his personal bodyguard numbered 1,250 cavaliers.

When Ibn Tashfin had his army pass in review in that year, chronicles say that it numbered 40,000 strong. He chose among them four generals: Syr Ibn Abu Bakr of the Bani Lamtuna, Muhammad Ibn Tamim of the Bani Gudala, Umar Ibn Sulayman of the Bani Massufa, and Mudrik of the Bani Tilkani. These were men who swore their personal loyalty to him. Ibn Tashfin gave each one of them command over 5,000 men from his tribe and retained the rest of this troop as his own avant-garde that was supposed to war against the Maghrawa, the Bani Yifran, and the rest of the Berber tribes in the Maghrib.

Ibn Tashfin then set out to recruit reinforcements. He wrote to some of his kinsmen in the Sahara, urging them to join with him, and promising them huge benefits. A great number of them came. He had not consulted Abu Bakr, of course, nor did he inform his *Amir* of this. Ibn Tashfin created new legions from the tribes of Aghzaz and Ramat. He recruited heavily among the Bani Gazula, the Bani Masmuda, and the Bani Zanata. With these new units added to the Bani Lamtuna, his army numbered in that year, again according to the chronicles, 100,000 warriors. Whatever the real number, he would need them all. Maintaining control over territory, even once conquered, required constant attention with the continued presence of military force, so Ibn Tashfin needed a constant supply of loyal troops. Though he preferred his own Lamtuna warriors from the desert, there were simply not enough of those.

This army under Ibn Tashfin's command conducted two campaigns in that year of 463/1071, one in the valley of the Moulouya River to the east of Fez and one in the region of Sijilmasa, both of them to subdue tribes that had withdrawn their loyalty to the new regime, and both campaigns were successful. When Abu Bakr learned how God had given these victories to Ibn Tashfin, he began to become concerned about his lieutenant's mounting personal power in the Maghrib. Abu Bakr even began to wonder if his cousin were conspiring against him, and so he decided to return from the Sahara.

Quite apart from what Abu Bakr could see of Ibn Tashfin's power, he knew the woman he had married; he knew only too well of Zaynab's ambition and of her ability. When Abu Bakr arrived in the southern Maghrib, he decided to establish his camp at Aghmat, rather than to move on directly to Marrakech. Many of his troops, on the other hand, did move on to Marrakech to greet its commander, so great had become the reputation of Ibn Tashfin's power and his generosity to those who supported him. The troops were showered with gifts, as Ibn Tashfin planned his strategy to confront his cousin.

Once again, Yusuf turned to his wife, Zaynab, for advice. She said, "Your cousin is too pious to cause blood to flow over this. When you go to meet him, ignore all marks of difference between you and do not be humble toward him as he would expect of you. Rather, assume an air of supremacy, as if you wanted to be his rival. But in addition to that, offer him rich gifts, tunics of honor and other precious gifts from the Maghrib. Offer him all of that in abundance because he lives in the desert and he considers everything from here as rare and curious."

The encounter between the two rivals took place at a distance of nine miles from Marrakech, just about halfway between the camp of each man. It was in the late fall of the year 465/late November, 1072. It was cold and damp, and the wind blowing across the plains was cutting as a saber. Ibn Tashfin waited as Abu Bakr rode toward him. There was tension in the air as the two paused and faced each other at eye level, missing the youthful friendship that was now survived only by mutual respect. Normally, Ibn Tashfin would have dismounted from his horse and bowed before his *Amir* in recognition of his authority, but this time he did not. Rather, the two dismounted together and then sat on a cloak, a burnoose (that spot was known from that time on as the Plain of the Burnoose).

Somewhat overwhelmed by the strength of Ibn Tashfin's army, Abu Bakr said, "Yusuf, what are you doing with these troops?" Yusuf answered, "I need them to oppose anyone who opposes me." At that point, Abu Bakr realized that Yusuf was no longer his lieutenant.

Seeing a thousand heavily laden camels approach, Abu Bakr asked, "What are those camels approaching with such heavy burdens?" Ibn Tashfin answered, "My prince, I have brought everything that I have in terms of riches, furnishings, copper utensils, and the like to make your life in the Sahara easier." Following his wife's advice, he had brought a storehouse of treasures comparable to any king's ransom, provisions that would be luxuries in the Sahara. It was his payoff to send his cousin back to the desert. The list of goods provided in contemporary accounts includes 25,000 gold *dinar*s; 70 horses, of which 25 were equipped with trappings of gold; 70 swords, of which 20 were engraved; 20 pairs of gilded spurs; and 150 choice mules, male and female. There were clothes of all kinds: 100 turbans of fine calico; 400 shawls, *shashiya*s; 100 cloaks; 200 burnooses, of white, black, and red; 100 lengths of linen; 100 lengths of *ashkari* cloth; 700 mantles, both white and colored; 200 shams of different kinds and colors; 200 *jubba*s, of which 52 were of magnificent scarlet; 70 capes; and 7 great banners. For fragrance, he offered aloes wood, musk, ambergris, and incense. He gave his cousin 150 slaves, plus 20 virgin slave girls for his pleasure. The price of the payoff was not merely a token. Ibn Tashfin said, "All this is so little compared to your deserts."

Abu Bakr accepted his fate. He told Ibn Tashfin, "You are my cousin, and you stand in the place of my brother. I have no choice but to help our brothers in the desert and can see none besides you who can take charge of the Maghrib, nor one more fitted than you. So I depose myself in your favor and put you to rule over it. Continue to exercise your rule, for you are deserving of it and fit for it." But he added, "Cousin, let me make these recommendations to you." With both of them still sitting on the burnoose, Abu Bakr said, "It is I who invested you with this power and it is I who am responsible. Fear God in your conduct toward our fellow Muslims. Do not compromise any interest of your subjects. May God help you, may he grant you his providence and permit you to behave with beneficence and equity toward your people. It is he who will be my lieutenant among you and them." Abu Bakr then bid farewell and returned to his encampment on the outskirts of Aghmat. He prepared to go home with a treasure trove that would greatly enhance his life in the desert.

The parting between Ibn Tashfin and Abu Bakr on the plains south of Marrakech was an agreement between the two commanders to divide the Almoravid holdings. The Saharan homeland and the newly conquered Maghrib would be ruled as two domains, but domains whose tribal connection and interdependence would ensure the prosperity of both. The security of each required the continued presence each of its own *Amir*.

Although not entirely by his own choice, Abu Bakr returned to the Sahara, the land of his origin. He would once again live the life of a desert chief. In the Sahara, he would continue to wage war against the infidels, that is, those tribes in the desert who either periodically or continuously resisted Lamtuna domination. The teachings of the *Dar' al-Murabitin* would continue to be the law of the land, and the Bani Lamtuna would maintain control of the caravan routes between Sijilmasa and the Sudan. Abu Bakr's was dedicated to both objectives. He would extend his control over the Sahara all the way to Jabal Dhahab, the mountain of gold in the Land of the Blacks.

Both *Amir*s had been brought up to know the ways of the desert. Abu Bakr had the comfort of returning to his roots and living and commanding his troops the way he knew best. Ibn Tashfin might have remained a nomad in temperament, but his new office in the Maghrib now made it difficult to live like one.

Yusuf Ibn Tashfin, for his part, devoted himself to organizing a new state in the Maghrib. He felt, for the moment, secure within the fortifications of Marrakech with power based on the forces drawn from occupied territories and on the mercenaries and slaves of his own personal guard. Still, he stationed garrisons along his southern border between the Sahara and the Maghrib.

The city of Marrakech continued to develop. When it became clear that the Almoravids were going to stay, settlers converted their temporary dwellings to permanent ones. Tents became fewer and fewer as they were replaced with bourgeois houses. Merchants from Aghmat began to do more and more business in Marrakech.

Ibn Tashfin resumed operation of the mint in Sijilmasa, where he produced coins in the name of the *Amir*, Abu Bakr Ibn Umar. In fact, he struck *dinar*s only in the name of Abu Bakr for as long as that *Amir* was alive, and only in the city of Sijilmasa. He was to continue to send tribute to his *Amir* in the desert and to write to him about his progress.

On the plains of Marrakech, Abu Bakr had managed to save face. Ibn Tashfin still recognized the authority of his *Amir*, at least in name. His parting words to him were, "I will not decree anything without your authority, nor will I, God willing, hold back anything from you." Abu Bakr realized the limits of that authority, and Ibn Tashfin was aware of it too.

CHAPTER 6
War in the Makhzan

The land north of Marrakech and to the northwest of the three Atlas ranges became known as *Bilad al Makhzan*, "land of the storehouse," because it was under the control of Ibn Tashfin's government in Marrakech, even though it was a constant struggle to maintain that control. It stood in contrast to the mountains of the Rif and Atlas ranges, which were constantly just beyond his control.

So far, tribal government had worked reasonably well for the Almoravids. Abu Bakr, and Ibn Umar before him, and Sanhaja chiefs as far back as could be remembered had exercised authority directly or through personal delegates from the inner circle of family or tribe. Abu Bakr had appointed family members as governors of the principal cities that came under Almoravid jurisdiction. But the Almoravid Empire was now growing too large, and it encompassed far too many diverse elements to control in the way that tribal custom had dictated. Ibn Tashfin was faced with the problem of administering a state comprising land quite different from the desert lands, inhabited by peoples even more diverse in lifestyles, customs, and tribal affiliation. If his empire was to survive, he would have to adapt his system of government to ensure the loyalty, or at least the submission, of these diverse elements.

Ibn Tashfin called together the princes of the Maghrib and the *shaykh*s of the Bani Zanata, as well as the Bani Gumara, Bani Masmuda, and other Berber tribes. They came and swore allegiance to him. He offered to them precious gifts and the honorary tunics fitting of a vassal and then made a tour of the country, checking on the condition of those under his jurisdiction.

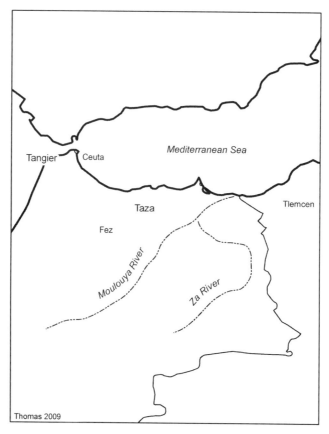

Campaign in the Northern Maghrib. (© Thomas Nolan. Used by permission.)

To maintain law and order in each of the more or less naturally defined divisions of the empire, Ibn Tashfin established garrisons in what amounted to provincial capitals. He still depended upon the tribal elite of his Sanhaja confederation to command these garrisons. The province of Marrakech included Aghmat, the Sus, the High Atlas Mountains, Tadla, and Tamasna, which he considered this to be the very heart of the Maghrib. It was the largest and the richest province. He appointed his own son Tamim as governor here. This was a nominal appointment because Tamim was still a child, so Ibn Tashin would control Marrakech with his own hand.

The province of Sijilmasa, which included the valley of the Draa, was the southern border with the great desert and also a seedbed for rebellion within the ranks of the Lamtuna. The governor in Sijilmasa was Abu Bakr's son, Ibrahim. The *Amir*'s son probably overstepped his authority when the mint at Sijilmasa issued coins in his own name. In deference to the promise that Ibn Tashfin had made to Abu Bakr on the Plain of the Burnoose, all coins were struck in Sijilmasa in the name of Abu Bakr. Ibn Tashfin was so busy trying to submit the Zanata in the central Maghrib that Ibrahim managed to assume this air of independence for five years, from 465/1071 to 469/1076–1077.

In any case, Ibrahim had never accepted his father's forced abdication in favor of Ibn Tashfin. In 469/1076–1077, Ibrahim came to Aghmat to demand that the reins of government be turned over to him. He brought with him a huge number of Lamtuna supporters, so many that Ibn Tashfin knew he had to deal with Ibrahim discreetly. It was a tense moment in Ibn Tashfin's move to establish his own authority, unquestioned throughout most the Maghrib. If he had to confront Ibrahim with force, he would end up at best having to cope with a major rift in the Lamtuna tribe, whose support he desperately needed to control the Maghrib, or at worse having to forfeit his position to him. Either way, he would lose.

Ibn Tashfin sent one of his most loyal and trusted supporters to negotiate with Ibrahim, Mazdali Ibn Tilankan. His grandfather and Ibn Tashfin's grandfather were brothers. Ibn Tilankan was a distinguished and highly respected military commander among the Lamtuna and an insightful diplomat as well. Ibn Tilankan went to Ibrahim and said to the rebel, quoting from the Koran, "Kingship is in the hands of God who gives it to whomever he chooses." Ibn Tilankan cautioned, "God has chosen Yusuf rather than us. If you are wise, you would ask him to endow you with wealth and horses to take back with you to your land. Otherwise, I fear that he may place a shackle on your foot, imprison and enslave you. I tell you this out of my compassion for you."

Ibrahim realized that the odds were against him. He could not challenge both Ibn Tashfin and Ibn Tilankan. And what is more, the latter had strengthened his case by invoking divine will. As his father had done earlier, Ibrahim agreed to withdraw to the Sahara. In a scene that was reminiscent of that on the Plain of the Burnoose, Ibn Tashfin sent Ibrahim off laden with abundant gifts, his honor intact.

Meknes, located in the center of the fertile, hilly plains west of Fez, was another regional capital. The region under its jurisdiction consisted of the land between the Bouregreg River that flowed into the Atlantic Ocean near Sale and the Sebou River to the east. It included the valley of the Fazaz, which was in an almost constant state of rebellion against the Almoravids, and the territory north of the

Sebou up to the frontier. The governor appointed to this province, Syr Ibn Abu Bakr, a Lamtuna tribesman who was both Ibn Tashfin's nephew and his sister's husband, was one of the very best military tacticians that Ibn Tashfin had. He was stationed here so that he could be quickly called into action if need be, either in the Fazaz or against Suqut al-Barghwati, lord of Ceuta and Tangier, whose territory lay to the north just beyond the province of Meknes and extending to the sea.

For generations, the Bani Hammud had ruled Tangier and Ceuta as vassals of the Umayyads of Cordoba. When the latter dynasty collapsed, the Bani Hammud became independent. Suqut al-Barghwati had been a slave, first in the household of *Shaykh* Haddad, a *shaykh* of the Bani Hammud who had purchased him from among the captives taken in the wars against the Barghwata; hence his name "al-Barghwati." Suqut al-Barghwati was then sold to Ali Ibn Hammud. Because of al-Barghwati's loyalty and demonstrated talent, Ibn Hammud appointed him, still his slave, to govern Tangier and Ceuta. The slave-ruler was charismatic. He succeeded, to a degree that few rulers do, in winning the respect and love of his subjects. Even the tribes of the Bani Gumara recognized his authority, that is, until the Almoravids challenged him for that recognition.

In fact, if the truth is ever learned, it may reveal that it was al-Barghwati who incited rebellion against the Almoravids among all of the tribes in this province. Ibn Tashfin would have to deal with those tribes one at a time. In 465/1072–1073 Ibn Tashfin's army attacked the city al-Dimna, southeast of Tangier, one day's march from Ceuta. From there, he proceeded to the mountain of Aludan. By mid-year, C.E. 1073, the Almoravids were finally in control of the Qal'at al-Mahdi in the Fazaz, the very fortress that had constantly alluded his grasp since well before the conquest of Fez. Finally, in the year 470/1077, Yusuf Ibn Tashfin sent one of his ablest generals, Salih Ibn Imran, against al-Barghwati at the head of an army of 12,000 Lamtuna cavalrymen and 20,000 tribesmen from among his vassals in the Maghrib. This was one of the largest armies that the Almoravids had mobilized to date.

Al-Barghwati, now 90 years old, rose to the challenge. He left Tangier at the head of his own troops to confront the Almoravids, resolute, maybe to the point of being foolhardy. As he saw the cloud of dust stirred up by the approaching riders still some distance away, he exclaimed, "As long as I live, by God, the people of Tangier will never hear the drums of the Almoravids." The use of drums to mark the cadence of the army on the march was one of the military innovations that Ibn Tashfin had introduced. Whether it was deliberate on the part of the Almoravids or not, the booming sound of their drums struck terror in the hearts of every enemy who heard it—the thundering drums of the Almoravids had won an ominous reputation.

The two armies met on the banks of the Mina River in the vicinity of Tangier. They clashed, and the number of casualties was high on both sides. Among the warriors to fall on that day was the crusty, old soldier al-Barghwati. When the battle was over, the Almoravids had won the day and had taken the city of Tangier. The city's residents came forth to greet the conquerors as their liberators. General Salih Ibn Imran wrote to Yusuf Ibn Tashfin, telling him of the victory, but the victory was not complete. Al-Barghwati's son, Diya al-Dawla Yahya, had escaped to Ceuta, Tangier's sister city, which had not yet fallen to the Almoravids. Sooner or later, Ibn Tashfin would have to confront him too.

In the meantime, Ibn Tashfin's control over the eastern Maghrib was still fragile. He appointed as governor of Fez the Massufa chief Umar Ibn Sulayman; although Ibn Sulayman was not from the Bani Lamtuna, he was still within the Sanhaja confederation and was also one of the four generals originally chosen in Marrakech. The governor of Fez would be responsible for protecting the Taza Gap, a narrow valley that separates the Rif Mountains and the Middle Atlas and divides the fertile lands of the west from the eastern nomadic steppes. The first Arabs and the founder of Fez, Moulay Idris, had come through the Taza gap, as would every future invader from the east. Beyond that point were the last holdouts of the hostile Maghrawa, many of them refugees from earlier campaigns in the central Maghrib.

The Almoravids had already taken steps to control the Taza Gap. In 467/1074–1075, they had taken the mountains of Ghayyata, the domain of the tribes of the Bani Makkud and the Bani Rahina. These tribes offered bitter resistance, and the campaign cost many lives, but in the end the Almoravids prevailed.

East of Taza, the center of Zanata resistance against the Almoravids was the town of Tlemcen, the stronghold of the Bani Ya'la. The part of the city known as Agadir was walled and had five gates. Its history went back centuries, remnants of a Christian community and Christian churches that were rumored to harbor unknown treasures. Situated on the main road between the Maghrib and the Orient, it was a major market town where merchants gathered from many different places.

In the year 472/1079, from his base camp in Marrakech, Ibn Tashfin dispatched an Almoravid army, some 20,000 troops, under the command of Mazdali. The Almoravids marched up the valley of the Moulouya, where they encountered the enemy, an armed contingent from the Bani Ya'la, somewhere between the Moulouya and the Za Rivers. The Almoravids managed to clear this area of Zanata resistance and captured and executed Mali Ibn Ya'la, the son of the *amir* of Tlemcen. Mazdali chose not to push on to Tlemcen, though, because the Bani Iznasan who occupied the town of Oujda, which stood between him and Tlemcen, were too strong. Ibn Tilankan instead returned to Marrakech to report his victory.

In 473/1081, Yusuf Ibn Tashfin set to direct the campaign against Tlemcen himself. En route, he conquered the towns of Guercif and Melilla, as well as the eastern part of the Rif Mountains that had escaped his grasp on earlier campaigns. He took the city of Nakur, a town one day's march west of Melilla along the coast. Little is said or heard about Nakur anymore. The destruction there was so great at the hands of the Almoravids that the town was never repopulated.

In 474/1081–1082 Ibn Tashfin marched against the Bani Iznasan and took the city of Oujda and the territories around it. Finally, he marched on to Tlemcen, massacring the Maghrawa as well as the *amir* of the city, al-Abbas Ibn Bakhti al-Maghrawi.

His momentum carried him farther eastward the following year, all the way to Algiers, but he considered Tlemcen to be the eastern guard post of his empire. Ibn Tashfin set up his camp in a nearby place that he named Takrart, a Berber word which means station or outpost. Yusuf fortified the post with a large Almoravid garrison, and he installed in Tlemcen his own governor, Muhammad Ibn Tinaghmar, from the Massufa tribe of the Sanhaja confederation.

Ceuta was the only major city in the Maghrib that was still outside of his grasp. News of the Almoravids' victories over the rest of the Maghrib had spread to the courts of the petty Muslim kings in Andalusia, who increasingly felt the pressure of the Christian *reconquista*. As early as the year 467/1074, Mu'tamid bin Abbad, king of Seville, had appealed to Ibn Tashfin to come to Andalusia to jihad war against the Christians. Ibn Tashfin consistently responded, "I cannot consider a war in Andalusia until I have taken Ceuta." The message was quite clear: If Mu'tamid wanted his help against the Christians in Andalusia, he would have to support Ibn Tashfin's campaign against Ceuta now. Mu'tamid bin Abbad offered Ibn Tashfin naval support.

Ibn Tashfin dispatched his son Tamim to lay siege to Ceuta by land. Meanwhile, Mu'tamid bin Abbad dispatched a fleet to blockade the seaward side. Diya al-Dawla Yahya, the son of Suqut al-Barghwati, who had escaped to Ceuta from Tangier, was in command of this last center of Zanata resistance. In the month of *Rabi al-thani* 477/August, 1084, Ceuta was forced to surrender. The conquest of the Maghrib was complete. The Almoravids controlled all of the major urban centers, although the connective tissue between them was fragile.

The Almoravids captured Diya al-Dawla Yahya, bound him, and took him to Tamim. Ibn Tashfin's son sentenced Suqut al-Barghwati's son, the last of the Barghwata opponents, to death. He then sent a victory message to his father, who was in Fez studying the concept of jihad and preparing to embark for Andalusia. Now that Ceuta had fallen, he was compelled to fulfill his promise to Mu'tamid bin Abbad. Malikite scholars in Fez told Yusuf Ibn Tashfin that jihad was a duty of divine institution, that Muslims should not initiate hostilities unless the enemy takes the offensive, and that they should offer the enemy three choices: conversion to Islam, paying the *jizya* (poll tax paid by Jews and Christians in Muslim territory), or war.

CHAPTER 7
Jihad in Andalusia

Gibraltar, *Jabal Tariq*, as it was called in Arabic, was named after the Berber commander who had landed there some three and three-quarter centuries before the Almoravids. For Yusuf Ibn Tashfin, it posed the same sort of barrier that the High Atlas Mountains had posed for the Almoravids almost 30 years earlier—not impenetrable, but known only from afar. The *imam*, Ibn Yasin, had studied in Andalusia and had a sense that it was becoming too secular. The markets of Fez, Aghmat, and Sijilmasa were full of Andalusian merchants and merchandise—candied fruit and almonds, embroidered textiles, brass and iron instruments, and gilded armor—to whet their appetites. The centers of learning, especially the Qarawiyin Mosque in Fez, had attracted Andalusian scholars in large numbers. The latter were possibly among the theologians who had advised Yusuf Ibn Tashfin on the concept of jihad and convinced him that it was his duty to go to Andalusia.

Though his own lifestyle was frugal, Ibn Tashfin knew that Andalusia was a land of prosperity, as he gazed across the straits from the Maghribi coast. Compared to the harsher, more arid plains of the Maghrib, Andalusia was gentle and lush. In many ways, the two regions were like sisters, but Spain was the sister who had married well. Moreover, Andalusia was in the *Dar al-Islam*. But it was also a land of uneasy peace. The Muslim conquerors of Andalusia failed to resolve the chronic differences among themselves, namely the ethnic differences between Arab and Berber. Throughout the Umayyad Empire, the Arab elite regarded non-Arabs as second class citizens; and in North Africa, they were particularly scornful of the indigenous Berber population.

Moreover, the Berbers who were part of the conquering forces of Andalusia felt discriminated against; they felt that they had received an unequal share of conquered lands.

The Umayyad rulers of Cordoba had relied heavily, if not equally, on both Arab and Berber nobles to govern their state. Ibn Abi Amir, for example, was from an Arab family who came with the conquest in the year C.E. 711. He and his descendants served as regents for the Umayyads and eventually carved out states for themselves in Orihuela, Murcia, and Almeria. Zawi Ibn Ziri was among the numerous Berbers to join the Umayyad guard. His descendants formed the powerful kingdom of Granada.

In the end, the forces of factionalism prevailed on the peninsula. The absence of a strong leader toward the end of the Umayyad

Spain in C.E. Eleventh Century. (© Thomas Nolan. Used by permission.)

caliphate, just a generation before the Almoravids emerged from the desert, created a power vacuum that took several petty kings to fill. Chiefs among the Arab and Berber vassals of the Umayyads carved out kingdoms of their own, about three dozen of them in all. They were called *Muluk al-Tawa'if,* or Taifa (party) kings, because the loyalty that they commanded, such as it was, was based on family or tribe, which included their clients and mercenary troops. Their kingdoms were city-states. There were no fixed boundaries, and many cities often changed hands. They battled against one another and formed alliances, sometimes even with Christian states and sometimes to the point of becoming mere tributaries of Christian kings. Eventually, the more powerful Taifas swallowed up the smaller ones so that by the time the Almoravids were in the Maghrib, there were 9 or 10 powerful states left. The two largest and most powerful of the Arab Taifa kingdoms were those of Mu'tamid bin Abbad of Seville, who had even incorporated the Umayyad capital of Cordoba into his state, and that of the Bani Hud of Zaragoza to the far northeast. The most powerful among the Berber states were the Dhu' al-Nun of Toledo, which bordered Christian territory to the north, the al-Aftas of Badajoz in the west of Andalusia, and the Zirids of Granada to the southeast of Cordoba.

Although the Taifa states lacked the political cohesion of the former Umayyads of Cordoba, they were rich. Rulers sought to shed luster on their courts and on themselves by patronizing learning, literature, and the arts. They competed with each other to attract the most learned scholars in science and hydraulics, and in mathematics and astronomy. They commissioned lavish palaces surrounded by elegant gardens and filled them with works of art. Court poets sang their praises. A poet in Toledo described his king:

> You appeared to us like the *wusta* among kings,
> Hence we did not make a halt at small-sized pearls.

A *wusta* is the big, central pearl in a necklace: The Umayyad Caliphate was being likened to a pearl necklace—beautiful, cultured, and wealthy. Now that the Umayyads had fallen, the string of pearls was broken, and the pearls had scattered, but each bead was still a brilliant, worldly pearl. The religious laxity of the Taifa kings managed to alienate the *faqihs,* the legal scholars and guardians of Malikite law who had been preeminent in the Umayyad court but who now found themselves replaced by the scholars and the poets.

North of Andalusia lay the Christian states of Navarre, Leon, Castile, Asturia, Galicia, Aragon, and Barcelona. These, too, had rivalries among themselves, but they shared a common goal—to reconquer Spain, which they had lost to the Muslims. The first to form a successful coalition of Christian states was Fernando I, king of Castile and Leon. In 449/1057 he forced the kingdom of Badajoz to pay tribute. In 455/1062, he reduced Toledo and Seville to Christian tributaries. His son was Alfonso VI. Yusuf Ibn Tashfin, the Almoravid, was soon to learn this name.

Toledo was the first Taifa state to fall to Alfonso VI. Its last Taifa ruler, al-Qadir, was seen as weak and incompetent by his own subjects. His tribute payments to Alfonso in return for protection had kept him in power. In 478/1085, Alfonso decided to seize direct control of Toledo. Al-Qadir sought refuge in the Taifa state of Valencia, a clear sign that the momentum of the *reconquista* had turned in favor of the Christian states to the north. Some Taifa kings, especially those along the frontier, had become concerned as much as a decade earlier and contacted Yusuf Ibn Tashfin to assess his preparedness, if not his eagerness, to cross the straits in the name of jihad. As Ibn Tashfin received these emissaries in Fez and in Marrakech, he sensed that the competition among the Taifa kings was as much a threat to their own survival as was the expansion of the Christian kingdoms. He kept putting them off, saying that he first had to secure his conquest of Ceuta, but at the same time he warned the governor of Ceuta that he planned to conduct holy war in Andalusia.

In the meantime, in the year 475/1082–1083, Alfonso VI sent an embassy of several knights to call on Mu'tamid, king of Seville, to collect the annual tribute. Mu'tamid's prime minister, Abu Bakr Ibn Zaydun, delivered the payment. Since Mu'tamid had been unable to raise sufficient revenues, even though he had levied a special tax for that purpose, part of the payment was in debased coinage. At the head of Alfonso's delegation was a Jew named Ben Shalib. Jews were among the skilled secretaries who worked for Christian and Muslim courts alike. Ben Shalib immediately recognized the debased coinage and refused to accept it, saying that he would take only pure gold, and if that was not forthcoming, he would take Andalusian towns and fortresses instead. Mu'tamid was incensed at the posture of the Jew and ordered his guard to seize the entire Christian delegation and to nail the Jew to a post with his head facing downwards. Some say that Mu'tamid was so angry that he killed the Jew with his own hands. But after his anger cooled, he sent for his theologians to seek "objective," moral assessments of his treatment of the Jew. One of those *faqih*s told him that he was perfectly justified in what he had done, since the ambassador had outstripped the bounds of his embassy and uttered words which deserved death. The *faqih* then told his comrades, "I have hastened to give the king this advice for fear that he would relent in the praiseworthy duty to oppose the enemy and that he would permit Alfonso VI to inflict such an affront upon the Muslims."

The incident, however exaggerated, provoked Alfonso VI. Or, at least, the whole question of paying tribute, or failure to do so, caused Alfonso VI to mount an offensive against Seville. At the head of a large army, the king of Castile invaded Andalusia, burning and pillaging village after village, slaying or enslaving those Muslim villagers who had not taken refuge in some stronghold. He marched south to Seville and laid siege to Mu'tamid's capital for three days. A long siege did not fit his slash and burn plan for a rapid march to the sea, so he withdrew and continued to advance toward the southern coast. Finally, reaching the shore near Tarifa, the southernmost point of the Iberian Peninsula, he supposedly rode his horse into the surf and said, "Here, finally, is the edge of Andalusia, and I have taken it!" Admittedly, Alfonso had reached the southern shore, but he had not yet subdued the Taifa capital cities.

For the rest of the year, Alfonso VI focused his attention on Toledo. The Berber king of Toledo, al-Qadir, had formed an uneasy alliance with Alfonso only to save his throne against the Arab Bani Hud of Zaragoza. The price for Alfonso's help was more than al-Qadir could pay, and eventually he had to surrender the city to the Christian king. On 27 *Muharram*, 478/25 May, 1085, Alfonso VI entered the ancient capital of the Visigothic kingdom.

The Castilian was as confident as the Muslims were fearful. His Christian renegades terrorized the countryside, murdering and raping daughters before their fathers' eyes or wives before their husbands. Alfonso VI, addressing himself as the "king of two religions" in a letter to Mu'tamid, demanded that the king of Seville surrender his fortresses and keep only the plains and open towns. He wrote, "My stay at this place [the outskirts of Seville] has already been too long. The heat is great and the flies intolerable; make me a present of your palace, that I may solace myself in its shadowy gardens and keep away the flies from my face." Mu'tamid met arrogance with arrogance and wrote on the back of the letter, "We have read your letter, and understood its arrogant and taunting contents; we intend to provide you shortly such a shadowy spot, shaded by the hide of the *lamt*." By *lamt* he meant the tall, broad shields of the Almoravids. Ibn Tashfin had offered such shields as gifts to his allies, and they had become a distinctive mark of the Almoravids' prowess in battle.

On the African side of the straits, Yusuf Ibn Tashfin had already taken Ceuta. The king of Seville had provided maritime support for that campaign and was now ready to cash in on Ibn Tashfin's debt and earlier promise to rescue Andalusia as soon as Ceuta was secure. Mu'tamid called for Ibn Tashfin's help against Alfonso VI. But it was not so easy to convince his neighbors to invite the Almoravids to their shores. News of Mu'tamid's plan traveled quickly from court to court. Delegates of several Taifa states met in Cordoba at the home of the chief *qadi* of that city. They transcended their mutual distrust to find a way to defend themselves against a common threat—they were desperate. One of them suggested that they petition the Arabs of Ifriqiya for help. The *qadi* warned that if the Arabs came, they would take control of Andalusia and leave the Christians alone. The Almoravids, he said, were a better choice. The Andalusians were obviously aware of the extent of Ibn Tashfin's authority, the extent of his empire, and the swiftness of his conquests. They were well aware of the fearlessness of his followers, those wearers of the veil, and their skill in wielding the weapons of war, the sharp-edged sword that could cut a horseman in two, the lance, made from Moroccan oak, that could penetrate both horse and rider, and, of course, the shields made of the skin of the *lamt*.

The king of Seville requested that his neighbors send envoys to meet with him. Mutawakkil of Badajoz and Abd Allah of Granada each sent their chief *qadi*. The wise *qadi* of Cordoba who viewed the Almoravids as the lesser of two evils also came to Seville. The delegation was joined by Abu Bakr Ibn Zaydun, the skillful vizier of Mu'tamid whose advice the king frequently sought and always respected. They all met with the king and his son Rashid and wrestled with this dilemma. The delegation warned the king of the dangers inherent in his final, troubled decision to invite the Almoravids to their shore.

Rashid tried to dissuade his father. "A kingdom without heirs and one long sword," he said, "do not find room in the same scabbard." "That is true, my son," Mu'tamid replied, "but I have no desire to be branded by my descendants as the man who delivered Andalusia to the infidels. I am loath to have my name cursed in every Muslim pulpit. And for my part, I would rather be a camel driver in Africa than a swineherd in Castile." He justified his choice with an exercise in logic, explaining, "My present position is of two sorts, one of doubt, and one of certainty, and I must choose between the two. As to the one of

Mu'tamid Bin Abbad was the poet king of Seville who led the effort among the Taifa kings to invite Yusuf Ibn Tashfin to the shores of Andalusia. He was later captured by the Almoravids and brought to live out his life in house arrest in Aghmat. (Photograph by the author.)

doubt, it is whether to apply to Yusuf Ibn Tashfin or to Alfonso VI, since it is equally possible that either of the two may keep his promise faithfully or not keep it at all. As to the position of certainty, if I lean for support on Yusuf [because of Yusuf's reputation as a pious warrior of the faith], I do an act agreeable to God; whereas if, on the contrary, I lean on Alfonso, I am certain of incurring the wrath of God; and, therefore, the position of doubt being in the present instance clear and evident, why should I leave what is agreeable to God to take that which is offensive to him?" In other words, Mu'tamid thought that siding with a Muslim, in the eyes of God, was always better than siding with a Christian. Although not completely convinced, the delegation was persuaded to go along with Mu'tamid. The king of Seville sent a letter to Ibn Tashfin, assuring him that it was God himself who affirmed him as *Amir*, that it was his duty to wage jihad, to strive for truth and righteousness, and to wage jihad against the infidels. Yusuf Ibn Tashfin was ready to carry his jihad to Andalusia.

Alfonso VI was laying siege to Zaragoza when rumors of the coming of the Almoravids forced him to change his strategy. He fell back to Toledo and called for reinforcements and ordered the ablest of his commanders, Alvar Fanez, to come from Valencia. He called for troops from his Christian neighbors in Aragon and Navarre, as well as from Barcelona and from France. One chronicler says that Alfonso VI, again referring to himself as the lord of two religions, wrote to Ibn Tashfin, arrogantly challenging the Berber chief to come to Andalusia. Alfonso taunted the Almoravid, saying that he would even be willing to come to Africa if only he had the ships to do so. According to the same account, Ibn Tashfin scoffed at the taunt. His secretary wrote on the back of Alfonso's letter, "Send no more messages, only swords and lances; send no more embassies, only armies."

During the heat of the summer of 479/1086, the three rival monarchs—Mu'tamid, Alfonso VI, and Yusuf Ibn Tashfin—were perched on their respective vantage points in Seville, Toledo, and Ceuta, keeping a watchful eye one upon the other.

Diplomats traveled back and forth between Seville and Ceuta, negotiating the conditions under which the Almoravids would come to Andalusia. The Taifa kings sought refuge behind the Almoravid shields, but they did not want to surrender any of their sovereignty to Ibn Tashfin. An Andalusian secretary wrote to Yusuf:

> If we acknowledge you for our master, we do that which is wise and prudent, and our names will not be tainted with a foolish act. If you resist taking over our country, that will be a generous act, and your name will not be maligned by an unjust and dishonorable deed. We have therefore chosen for you and for ourselves that which is generous and wise; we will acknowledge you as our lord and sovereign, and you will remain where you now are and allow these poor dwellers in tents to continue as they are; for upon their preservation depends, in a certain measure, the duration and strength of your empire.

Ibn Tashfin recognized that the Taifa kings were negotiating from a position of weakness. Their divisiveness had made them easy prey for the Christian reconquista. Although the balance had swung in favor of the Christians under Alfonso VI, Ibn Tashfin now held the balance of power in his own hand. He could play on the Taifa kings' mutual fear of the Christians to unite them in a force under his command. He could also have Andalusia if he wanted it.

The rocky cliffs across the straits held some mystery for Ibn Tashfin as he looked over from Ceuta. The one-time desert nomad had been in Morocco long enough to know what Andalusia offered. Yet, he assured the Taifa kings that he had no interest in personal gain, that he was fulfilling his duty as a faithful servant of God in rescuing his Muslim brothers from the infidel. That was the advice of the *faqih*s of Fez who had lectured him on the concept of jihad. That term was taking on new meaning. Until now the Almoravids had waged jihad only against pagans in the deep Sahara or against "unpious" or "heretical" Muslims who resisted them in forming their African empire. For the first time, they were about to fight a Christian enemy in the name of Islam.

Yusuf sought strategic advice as well as religious. One of his advisers, Abd al-Rahman Ibn al-Aftas, himself an Andalusian from Almeria, warned Ibn Tashfin that his movement in Andalusia would be restricted. The terrain was rugged, and the Christians controlled a major portion of it. Ibn al-Aftas convinced Yusuf that he needed to control the port of Algeciras to guarantee that he could come and go as he needed. Ibn Tashfin, therefore, requested that Mu'tamid order the evacuation of the garrison of Algeciras so that the Almoravids might use it as a base of operations on the Andalusian side of the straits.

Mu'tamid was suspicious of the Almoravid's true intentions, but he reluctantly agreed. He asked Ibn Tashfin to wait in Ceuta for 30 days to allow the garrison time to withdraw. The rumor was that Mu'tamid was buying time with those 30 days, and that he was playing off Castilian and Almoravid one against the other. Could he use the threat of the Almoravids' crossing to convince Alfonso VI to curb his aggression against him and the other Taifa kings? If so, could he then count on Alfonso's help to block the crossing of the Berbers from the desert? Ibn Tashfin precluded the answer to these questions. At the very time that Mu'tamid's ambassadors returned to Seville with assurances that Ibn Tashfin would wait 30 days before crossing, the Almoravid advance guard was boarding ships for Algeciras.

Ibn Tashfin assembled his army at Ceuta. Troops came from every corner of the Almoravid Empire, from the Sahara, the Sus, and the Maghrib. They came from every major tribe of the Sanhaja as well as from some tribes of other confederations. It was one of the largest armies that the Almoravids had ever assembled. Ibn Tashfin brought in the most skilled of his commanders, including Da'ud Ibn Aisha, whom he had named governor over Sijilmasa and the Draa, and Syr Ibn Abu Bakr, governor of Meknes, to whom he had given one of his sisters in marriage. These were trusted commanders from Ibn Tashfin's own tribe.

During the night of 15 *Rabi al-thani*, 479/30 July, 1086, several ships crossed the straits carrying Almoravid combatants. Once part of the army landed, Ibn Tashfin embarked with a number of Almoravid commanders and warriors. On board the ship, according to one report, he had lifted his hands toward heaven and prayed, "God, if you know that this crossing will be useful to the Muslims, facilitate our crossing the sea. On the other hand, if the contrary be true, make the passage so difficult that I will have to return." The crossing took place with ease. He disembarked and said his morning prayers. It was important for him to believe that he had the support of God, almighty.

Ibn Tashfin had come to take over Algeciras. Its commandant was Razi, son of Mu'tamid. Apparently, Razi had not gotten the message from his father that the Almoravids were to have Algeciras. He remembered Ibn Tashfin's promise to respect the sovereignty of Andalusian rulers, but he was surprised by the demands of the Almoravid. He did provide the provisions requested, but he was a less than willing host. Meanwhile, he sent a letter to his father by carrier pigeon, asking for instructions. Mu'tamid replied promptly, saying that Algeciras was a small price to pay to save their kingdom from the infidel, and he therefore ordered his son to evacuate Algeciras and retire to Ronda.

The local population of Algeciras seemed relieved that Ibn Tashfin was there and greeted him with open arms and supplied his army with what it needed. Some people even joined his force. He immediately strengthened the fortifications of the town, stocked it with munitions of war and stores of food, and provided it with an adequate garrison.

Then he set out for Seville, marching, as one reporter described, army after army, commander after commander, tribe after tribe. Mu'tamid sent his own son to meet him, and ordered to the governors of the districts through which Ibn Tashfin would pass to furnish all that the Almoravids would need or want. That support in kind also conformed to the Koranic notion of jihad. Ibn Tashfin's army marched through green, fertile valleys rich in olives and vineyards, in orange and lemon groves couched between the rocky hills. In late summer, the Andalusian land, baked by the summer sun, looked even more like the Maghrib they had left behind. Ibn Tashfin and his army must have felt at home.

On the outskirts of Seville, Mu'tamid rode out to meet Ibn Tashfin in a stately fashion, surrounded by the chief dignitaries of the state, and, as custom dictated, bearing lavish gifts. When they met, the king attempted to kiss his hand, but the Almoravid rejected the sign of submission and embraced him affectionately. They congratulated each other upon their decision, their determination to wage jihad against the infidel, and prayed to God almighty to render their act pure and acceptable to him. Ibn Tashfin supposedly divided the wealth of gifts among every soldier in his army. Thus, the Almoravids witnessed enough of the splendor of Andalusian royalty to make them covetous.

From the outskirts of Seville, the Almoravid army began to mobilize toward the city of Badajoz, well over 100 miles to the northwest. The Andalusians, slow at first, marched after them. Abd Allah of Granada and Tamim of Malaga joined the Almoravids, the Granadan with 300 horsemen and the Malagan with 200. Even Mu'tamid was late, but then hurried to catch up and follow in the tracks of the advancing Muslim army. The king of Almeria preferred to wait until he could safely predict a successful outcome. He sent a regiment of cavalry under the command of one of his sons, expressing regret that the threatening position of the Christians of Aledo prevented him from appearing in person.

Ibn Tashfin established his camp near Badajoz. The other Andalusian leaders camped some distance from the Almoravids, so that both armies, Andalusian and African, were quite separate. The king of Badajoz came out to greet them and to supply the provisions for the armies, as was requested of him.

Alfonso's army was on the opposite side of the river. It consisted mainly of heavy cavalry like the army of the Andalusians, men wearing mail armor and armed with sword and lance.

The plains to the north of Badajoz are wide and flat. There is not so much as a small hill for miles around. The armies of the Andalusians, those of the Almoravid, and those of the Castilian were just far enough from one another that they were barely within each others' sight. They remained there for three days, preparing for battle and trying to intimidate the opposition.

Ibn Tashfin was very confident. In spite of some setbacks, he had mounted victory after victory, campaign after campaign, in the Maghrib during the past several years until he was in control of it all. Moreover, the *faqihs* had assured him that he had the blessings of almighty God in this fight against the enemy of Islam. Intelligence reports should have told him, though, that the same factors were at play on the other side. Alfonso VI, too, had established momentum in military victories in Andalusia, and Christian theologians had recently made a case for justifiable war, as popes prepared to preach crusade against the Saracens.

On both sides of the river, those whose profession was religion led those in their ranks who were trained to fight.

Messengers and spies scurried back and forth between the camps. The first message that Ibn Tashfin sent to Alfonso VI gave him three choices: to convert to Islam, to pay tribute, or to stand and fight. These are the same three choices traditionally afforded to Christians and Jews since the first century of Islam. The pact of Umar which established these options was shaping Ibn Tashfin's evolving concept of jihad. Ibn Tashfin's letter, as reproduced in the chronicles, was a long one, elegantly written and contained the following: "We understand, Alfonso, that you once expressed the wish of coming over to us and regretted having no vessels to allow you to do so. Your wishes are now accomplished. Here we are, ready to meet you wherever you please, and we shall see how your prayers have been attended to. It is a thing well known that infidels never pray except in the path of error." Yusuf had come prepared for holy war.

Alfonso VI had no trouble choosing among the three alternatives offered. His kingdom of Castile had collected tribute from the Taifa kings for the past 80 years, and he was not about to consider paying tribute to the Muslims now. He too had come to fight.

Muslim scouts were watching the movement of the Christian troops very carefully. On Wednesday, during the night, they observed that the Christian army was preparing to attack at daybreak. The Muslims set up lines of defense that were sufficiently within Alfonso's sight so that he postponed the attack. It was well within the protocol of Spanish chivalry to agree on a time for battle. Alfonso proposed the coming Saturday, since Friday was a holy day for the Muslims, and Sunday was the same for the Christians. Some reports say that Monday was the day designated for the fight since Saturday was holy to the Jews, and there were many Jews in Alfonso's army. As it turned out, it did not really matter. Mu'tamid did not trust Alfonso. He warned Ibn Tashfin to remain on guard throughout the day on Thursday and on through the night, when few slept in any of the three camps. During the night, scouts from Mu'tamid's camp again observed the Christians preparing for battle. The king of Seville dispatched his secretary to warn Ibn Tashfin. Before the secretary returned, the battle had begun.

The battle was wrought with confusion from the very start. Early Friday morning, when Mu'tamid was still saying his morning prayer, scouts rode hard into the Sevillian camp to announce that the Christians were coming "like a cloud of grasshoppers." Alfonso's vanguard, under the command of Alvar Fanez, cousin of El Cid, had three miles of open field to cover before making contact. Mu'tamid barely had time to rally his forces to counter the attack. The Christian momentum still drove the Andalusians back. The front lines were broken on initial contact. Then, whole regiments of cavalry of Badajoz, Granada, and Almeria fled en masse. Only the Sevillians held fast. They were inspired by their king, who fought with tenacity. When Mu'tamid's horse fell from beneath him, he mounted another. This he did three times over. He was wounded in the face and in the hand, but still stood his ground. The only other regiment that remained in the field to resist the Castilian onslaught was the Almoravid cavalry sent by Ibn Tashfin under the command of Da'ud Ibn Aisha.

Syr Ibn Abu Bakr then arrived with reinforcements. The battle was now going according to plan. Ibn Tashfin had devised a strategy whereby the Andalusians would take the full brunt of the initial attack. The Almoravid forces then would envelop the Christians from the sides and from the rear.

As part of the plan, Ibn Tashfin attacked Alfonso's camp while his army was engaged against the Andalusians. The Almoravids inflicted heavy casualties upon those who were left to guard the camp and then set it aflame. Alfonso saw the smoke and realized what was happening. He called off the attack against the Andalusians to try to save the camp, but he was too late. Yusuf's light cavalry was already attacking from that direction. Alfonso was now surrounded and totally confused.

The Almoravids were like a wall of warriors, lightly clad in their blue robes, faces hidden behind the veils that covered all but the slits of their eyes. They formed tight, compact units, each under its own banner, foot soldiers armed with swords and short spears in the front ranks, and javelin throwers in the rear. These units were more effective than the Andalusian archers against the armor of the Christians. The javelin throwers hurled their weapons with such accuracy so as to cut the horses from beneath the Castilian knights. The front ranks then moved in to stab the riders on the ground. The banners, visible everywhere, coordinated the maneuver. Banner down, the unit holds firm. Banner up, the unit attacks!

Yusuf Ibn Tashfin rode among the ranks of his army, urging them to fight for the glory of God. He shouted, "Muslims, be strong and patient in this jihad against the infidel enemy of god; those of you who die today will go to paradise as martyrs, and those who do not die will be rewarded in booty." His warriors fought on that day as soldiers aspiring to martyrdom and not fearing death.

To add to the confusing sound of battle, to the sound of the horses' hooves pounding on the turf and the cries of men, both fighting and dying, the Almoravid drums resounded in a thunderous, rhythmic debut in Andalusia. The shrill of charging camels was another frightening sound that the Castilians had not heard before.

What turned the flow of battle irrevocably in favor of the Muslims was Ibn Tashfin's black guard, which he had been holding in reserve. Armed with short swords, spears, and shields made of the hide of the *lamt*, they dismounted and fought on foot in the same close rank formation perfected by the Almoravids. They penetrated the very heart of the Castilian force, making way to Alfonso's command post. Alfonso, sword in hand, attacked a black slave from Ibn Tashfin's guard, who had thrown all his javelins. Alfonso aimed at his head, but the black avoided the blow, and, creeping under Alfonso's horse, seized the animal by the bridle. Taking out a dagger (*khanjar*) from his girdle, the black slave stabbed the Christian king in the thigh, the weapon piercing both armor and flesh and pinning Alfonso to his horse's saddle. Alfonso VI rode off, barely escaping with his own life.

The Andalusians were now on the winning side. Mu'tamid and his troops charged in pursuit of the fleeing Christians. Even those who had fled from Alfonso's initial attack returned to the field to join the carnage.

Come nightfall, the Christian army was on the run. Mu'tamid urged Yusuf to hunt down the fleeing Christians and to annihilate them. But Yusuf, who was clearly in charge, knew that he had suffered considerable losses; he preferred to wait until his army had a chance to reassemble before they pursued the enemy. Meanwhile, Alfonso VI and a small band of Castilians managed to escape from the vicinity of Badajoz under the cover of darkness. When he reached Toledo, Alfonso had with him, according to various estimates, somewhere between 100 and 500 men. The Muslims may not have pursued them as vigorously as they might have, and Yusuf was criticized by some for failing to fully capitalize on the victory. The Muslims had won the day, but the victory was not decisive. Casualties were extremely high on both sides. Among the Almoravid notables who became martyrs on that day was Abu Marwan Abd al-Malik, the *qadi* of Marrakech.

The battle of Zallaqa was over, and Ibn Tashfin and Mu'tamid congratulated each other for the victory. It was a victory for Islam! Mu'tamid was relieved that the reputation that had preceded the Almoravids to Andalusia had been realized. Ibn Tashfin was pleased as well, but he wished that the victory had been more decisive.

Andalusian king and Almoravid *Amir* returned to Seville side by side in triumph. The victory march into the city was intended to impress the inhabitants and to soften the cost of the victory. But it was Ibn Tashfin who was impressed! Seville at that time was beginning to surpass Cordoba as the leading city of Andalusia, and it was becoming one of the most splendid and magnificent cities in the world.

As the two leaders approached the city, they passed the lush, green groves of olive trees that supplied the oil exported to the Maghrib and to the East. The great river, called *Wadi al-Kabir* by the Arabs, was bustling with activity. The river was filled with boats that ferried passengers and merchandise from one bank to the other, for at that time there was no bridge. Trading ships from all over the Mediterranean crowded the port. Seville was a city of merchants and craftsmen: blacksmiths, broom makers and basket weavers, mat makers, masons and carpenters, tile makers and brick makers, joiners and cabinetmakers, butchers, vendors of fresh fruit and vegetables, spice merchants, weavers and dyers, tailors and shoemakers, furriers and tanners, potters and glass makers. Ibn Tashfin could not avert his eyes from the dazzling sights, and his mind was absorbed in the contemplation of Seville's many beauties.

On the southeast side of the city were the palaces of Mu'tamid and of his father al-Mutadheh, both palaces extremely beautiful in their proportions and most splendid in their decorations. Ibn Tashfin was lodged in one of these palaces, which was furnished for the occasion with everything a victorious king could want—food, drink, clothes, beds. Mu'tamid appointed servants to gratify all the wishes of his royal guest. Several courtiers were calling Ibn Tashfin's attention to the delights of Andalusia. But he himself was uncomfortable and restless. He rejected the advice of the counselor who encouraged him to partake in the privileges of victory. Ibn Tashfin said, "It strikes me that this man (Mu'tamid) is throwing away the power which has been placed in his hands; for there can be no doubt that the sums of money which he is spending daily to support all this pomp and vanity were formerly in the hands of his subjects, from whom he cannot have obtained them by legal means." Yusuf inquired whether or not Mu'tamid's subjects were pleased with this. The answer was that they were not.

After staying in Seville for three days, Ibn Tashfin received word that his eldest son, whom he had left in Ceuta, had died. He felt compelled to go home. Besides, the cautious business of government in the Maghrib beckoned his call. He placed a division of 3,000 cavalrymen under the command of his cousin Majjun Ibn al-Hajj, and he returned to Africa with the rest of his army.

As Ibn Tashfin sailed back across the straits from the land of Andalusian delights to the land where he felt much more at home, the battle of Zallaqa weighed heavily on his mind. In many ways it defined who the Almoravids were, as well as who he was. The Almoravids' acceptance of the teachings of Abd Allah Ibn Yasin in the homeland of the Lamtuna, their march from the desert, their conquest of the Maghrib, their consolidation of the tribes of the Lamtuna, the Gazula, the Massufa, the addition of many tribes from the Masmuda and Zanata, all under the leadership of the clan of the Bani Turgut, and all in the name of Islam, all of this culminated in this victory against the enemy of their co-religionist, against their enemy. Were they not destined to triumph in the name of Islam?

Still, Ibn Tashfin was ambivalent toward this victory. The Taifa kings themselves gave him cause to harbor a growing mistrust. Would they now be able to maintain the status quo achieved by their recent victory, or would their greed and mistrust of each other again make them easy prey for the enemy?

Ibn Tashfin had personally resisted the spoils of victory. He maintained that the delights of Andalusia held no appeal for him. Rather, he turned the booty over to the Andalusian chiefs, saying, "I came not to this country for the sake of booty; I came to wage jihad against the infidel and to merit the rewards promised to those who fight for the cause of God."

He was sure that he had done his duty, that he had conducted jihad to defend Islam against the encroaching Christian forces of Alfonso VI. His Andalusian allies had convinced themselves that Alfonso had been soundly beaten. But Yusuf knew that he had escaped. He wondered how long it would be before the Christian king would threaten the *Dar al-Islam* again.

The Lamtuna chief was now nearly 80 years old. He was born before his tribe had adopted the teachings of Islam, and he still had the burning enthusiasm of a neophyte. But the rigors of the field camp were now harder on an aging frame than were the comforts of urban life. In Andalusia, Ibn Tashfin had gained a glimpse of an urban life that he had never seen before. Whatever satisfaction he sensed as his ship broke the waves across the straits was tempered by the thought that it was only a matter of time before he would return.

CHAPTER 8
The Statesman

Marrakech was Yusuf Ibn Tashfin's city. Here he was far away from the foothills of the High Atlas, far from any stronghold of the Masmuda Berbers whose loyalty he did not fully trust. In Marrakech, there was no established aristocracy, no traditional ideology that he would have to counter with his own. Ibn Tashfin was secure in Marrakech as he busied himself with the weighty affairs of state.

Marrakech was not the typical imperial capital. It lacked the cosmopolitan urban life of Baghdad, Constantinople, or Cairo, or, for that matter, of Fez, Cordoba, or Seville. A generation after the cornerstone was laid on the *qasr* in Marrakech, it had more permanence than the camp of a nomadic chief, but it still had much the same atmosphere. Many of the Berber tents had been replaced by small houses made of stone and mud brick. They stood curiously intermixed with tents of camels' and goats' hair, the poles of the tents pricking the horizon in silhouettes that were all too familiar in the desert sands of the western Sahara. The most distinct structure to pierce the horizon was the mosque. It, too, was made of mud. It was now the site of what was perhaps the most urban of all of the activities that took place in Marrakech with any regularity at all—the Friday prayer.

Near the mosque was the *qasr*, the treasury-armory that Yusuf Ibn Tashfin and Abu Bakr had built together when they first arrived in Marrakech. This was the only fortification in Marrakech. Ibn Tashfin hesitated to go much further with the development of the capital city that owed its birth as much to Abu Bakr as it did to him. It was as if Ibn Tashfin felt that to build more while Abu Bakr was alive would have been an act of defiance to the old *Amir*, who had retired to the desert in 463/1070–1071.

Yusuf Ibn Tashfin had no further contact with his cousin, Abu Bakr. Nor did Abu Bakr interfere with Yusuf's free hand in Morocco or Spain. The old *Amir* ruled in the Sahara in the same way that tribal chiefs among the Sanhaja had done for generations, through a combination of tribal loyalties, religious appeal, and military strength. He had every intention to continue the religious revival in the vein of strict Malikite Islam. He brought to the desert a teacher from the city of Aghmat, the *Imam* al-Hadrami. The latter had studied Malikite law in both Qayrawan and Andalusia. Abu Bakr made him *qadi*, judge, in Azuggi. From there, *Imam* al-Hadrami went out to preach among the unbelievers. It was reported that even the inhabitants of Ghana became good Muslims under the influence of Abu Bakr. From Tadmakka to Gao, the Ibadi school of Kharijite Islam gave way to the Malikite school of the Almoravids.

It was in Ghana that Abu Bakr met his death. Shrouded in legend, he died a martyr's death waging jihad against the blacks in the Sudan. In the region of Tagant on his way to *Djabal al-Dhahab*, the Mountain of Gold, he was wounded, according to the chronicles, by a poisoned arrow, shot by an old black bowman who could not see unless his eyelids were raised up to uncover his eyeballs. The black bowman asked his daughter to hold open his eyes so that he could aim his arrow. It struck the *Amir* in the knee. Abu Bakr turned his horse around and rode off with his troops following close behind. The *Amir* died upon his arrival in Tagant in the month of *Shaban*, 480/November, 1087.

For a decade after the death of Abu Bakr, *Imam* al-Hadrami continued to teach the law of the Almoravids. Yusuf Ibn Tashfin had to rely on diplomacy and the cooperation of foreign rulers, including the kings of Ghana and Zafun, to maintain safe passage across the Sahara. He advised his son and heir not to disturb the tribes inhabiting the gorges of the Atlas or the deserts to the south. Through ties with family and through the tribal confederation that included the Bani Massufa, who had established a camp settlement at the place called Timbuctu, the Almoravids continued to exert some influence among the tribes in the desert. For the rest, Ibn Tashfin had to turn his attention to governing in the Maghrib.

In Sijilmasa, the *dar al-sikka*, the mint, had continued to issue the official coinage of the state in the name of Abu Bakr until the old *Amir*'s death. Now, Ibn Tashfin began to issue coins in his own name as *Amir*, still in the mint at Sijilmasa rather than in Marrakech. The coins were beautifully crafted by Jewish smiths who lived in the Jewish quarter in the eastern part of town, craftsmen known for their precision work in metals and in glass weights. They cast the die with the inscription in mirror image in clear, simple, authoritative script and placed the shiny, blank, gold discs between the two faces of the die and struck the upper die with the heavy mallet, saying, "There is no God but God and Muhammad is his Prophet—the *Amir* Yusuf Ibn Tashfin!" On the opposite side, they inscribed, "In the name of God this *dinar* was struck in Sijilmasa in___(date)—*al-Imam* Abd Allah, *Amir al-Mu'minin*." That last name was of the Abbasid Caliph in Baghdad. It was politic for Ibn Tashfin to honor on his official coinage the titular head of the *Dar al-Islam*, which Ibn Tashfin was sworn to defend.

The first *dinar* to be struck in the capital city of Marrakech was in the year 485/1092. It seemed like a symbolic gesture announcing that Marrakech was, indeed, the capital. Most of the coins continued, at least for a while, to be struck in Sijilmasa. The next year, in 486, a new mint opened in Aghmat, just 18 miles south of Marrakech, still the dominant commercial center in the region.

Even with the opening of new mints, the official coinage remained standardized. The coins were weighed against precisely crafted glass weights that bore the stamp of the ruler. The *sikka*, the official monetary

This *dinar* of Yusuf Ibn Tashfin was struck in Sijilmasa in 484/1091 in his own name after the death of Abu Bakr. (Photograph by the author.)

issue of the Almoravids, guaranteed the same fineness of gold that was established in Sijilmasa a quarter of a century earlier. Ironically, refining techniques in Sijilmasa were not as sophisticated as they were in Egypt, but Almoravids struck coins with gold from Ghana, gold that was renowned for being the purest of all the gold in the world. The name of the Almoravid *Amir* assured their value.

*Dinar*s bearing Yusuf Ibn Tashfin's name commanded respect all over the Mediterranean world. *Murabit*s, as they were called, were quickly on their way to becoming the international standard of currency, so much so that an old Jewish merchant in Alexandria instructed his agents to acquire them in large quantities. "Buy me *dinar*s," he wrote, "*Aghmati*s, or quarters, but not one shred of textiles." The agent of another Jewish merchant from Cairo informed his client that in Mahdiya in Tunisia, Almoravid *dinar*s of full weight cost more than two and a half *dinar*s each in local currency. Merchants from Morocco, when they did business in foreign markets, insisted on being paid in *Murabit*s. Ibn Tashfin's successor, Ali Ibn Yusuf, whose name began to appear on the coins as successor in 496/1103, would later ask the Malikite jurists for a legal opinion on whether, in financial transactions, it was permissible to insist on payment in Almoravid *dinar*s. The *qadi* Ibn Rushd ruled that it was. Indeed, the reputation of Almoravid *dinar*s was so wide spread that in Christian Europe, monetary value was sometimes measured in *marabotini*, the Latin term for Almoravid *dinar*s.

The official stamp of the Almoravids on the coins that circulated daily in the marketplaces all over the empire made the presence of the government visible in the eyes of the people. But the ruler's real authority was assured by the army. To govern in the provinces, Ibn Tashfin relied on his relatives—sons, cousins, and nephews—to serve as military commanders. This was the custom of his native Saharan ancestors for generations before him. Among the Sanhaja, military commanders had to govern, and governors had to defend their land as commanders of the militia. Yusuf assigned his most trusted commanders to the garrisons which controlled each of the four provincial divisions of his empire, two in the northern part of the Maghrib and two in the south.

Ibn Tashfin's nephew, Syr Ibn Abu Bakr, who had again confirmed his trust in the battle of Zallaqa, remained in command of the northwestern province whose capital was Meknes, the province that now also included Tangier and Ceuta, the staging areas for the Almoravids' Andalusian campaign. Umar Ibn Sulayman of the Massufa tribe commanded the garrison of Fez governing the land east of the Bouregreg River all the way to Algiers. This province was naturally broken into two parts by the Taza Gap, a narrow valley 75 miles east of Fez that separates the Rif from the Middle Atlas Mountains and divides the eastern nomadic steppe from the farmland in the west. Ibn Tashfin had established a second major garrison east of Taza in the city of Tlemcen under the command of Muhammad Ibn Tinaghmar, also of the Massufa tribe.

Ibn Tashfin's son, Da'ud Ibn Aisha, who had also distinguished himself at the battle of Zallaqa, returned from Andalusia as governor of Sijilmasa. Ibn Aisha was responsible for securing the southern flank of the state. The garrison of Sijilmasa lay at the southern tip of the axis that runs from the desert, up the valley of the Ziz River through the Middle Atlas, to Fez and up the valley of the Moulouya. In the first decade of Ibn Tashfin's military career in the Maghrib, Sijilmasa was the springboard from which the Almoravids moved from the desert to control the Maghrib. It was the keystone of a string of strongholds that extended along the southern rim of the Atlas into the western Sus, from Sijilmasa to Zagora, to Nul Lamta. It served as the *ribat*, a fortified religious stronghold, at the southern frontier of Ibn Tashfin's empire.

Two of Ibn Tashfin's sons by his first wife Zaynab, al-Mu'izz (the oldest) and Tamim, served their father as ministers of state, as viziers in the capital of Marrakech. Tamim commanded the garrison in the imperial capital.

Outside of this Sanhaja entourage, Ibn Tashfin surrounded himself with religious scholars, Malikite *faqihs* from Andalusia from whom he sought legal advice. These scholars, once powerful, had lost much of their influence under the Taifa kings. As advisors to the Almoravids, they would become more powerful than they had ever been. Malikism, as it was practiced by these *faqih*s, was not characterized so much by its content as it was by its process of formulating law. The *Risala*, written by Ibn Abi Zayd al-Qayrawani, the most complete and authoritative compendium of Malikite law that was available to the *faqih*s of the Almoravids, states very clearly that God revealed to the prophet Muhammad a book full of wisdom, and that Muhammad was the last of the prophets. There was no room for interpretation. The study of law was limited to servile imitation (*taqlid*), as opposed to personal interpretation (*ijtihad*). What Almoravid legal advisers imitated were the legal manuals, like the *Risala*, already worked out by Malikite scholars. It was considered heresy even to question the meaning of one of the prophet Muhammad's words, and the study of the Koran and books of *hadith* was abandoned. This closed club of legal scholars offered a ready-made system of law to the Almoravids, who had already accepted to a rudimentary, even arbitrary understanding of Islam.

The *Risala* says that the faithful must obey their Muslim rulers, those who govern as well as those who make legal judgments. And the faithful must pay their taxes! Right from the beginning, the Almoravids conquered on a platform of "no illegal taxes!" The *Risala* says that the faithful must pay *zakat*, an income tax assessed on one's money, gold and silver, on one's livestock, on one's agricultural produce, and on one's movable property—that is, buildings, furniture, clothing, and slaves. The tax on produce was due at the time of harvest. Tax on the rest was payable once a year. There were standard deductions on certain commodities; for example, the first five baskets of olives and the first five camels were tax exempt. Non-Muslim subjects had to pay the *kharaj*, a land tax. The status of lands subject to this tax was somewhat arbitrarily and inconsistently defined. According to the Malikite legists in North Africa, land, as it came under the control of an Islamic regime, fell into two categories: If the owners were Muslim, they maintained possession of the land and paid *zakat* on what the land produced. If the land was owned by non-Muslims and was conquered by force, the land was forfeited to the state. The former owners, even if they converted to Islam, paid the *kharaj*, which amounted to rent. In practice, the state rarely exercised its rights of ownership and regarded the occupiers as owners. Over time, most *kharaj* payers had converted to Islam; so the tax that they paid legally substituted for *zakat*, even though it still might be called *kharaj*. In some cases, individuals were assessed for both taxes and thus developed a double tax liability.

The Almoravids continued to collect the tax under both names. In fact, they instructed the *qadi*s, whose responsibilities included supervision of the treasury, to promote agriculture in their districts, because that was the basis upon which much of the tax was levied. Under the *qadi*'s supervision, agents called *hurra*s assessed the tax liability of a district. The Almoravids relied on tax farmers to collect the tax in a district as a whole. They were most effective when they had the support and cooperation of the village chiefs.

The Koran permitted customs dues to be levied only on non-Muslims, but it was the well-established practice in the Maghrib and Andalusia to collect this tax equally from all merchants, Muslims as well as non-Muslims, and it provided a major source of state revenue. The same was true for taxes on commodities sold in the marketplace.

The Statesman

These are precisely the taxes that the *faqih*s consistently condemned and that the Almoravids had promised to abolish.

When Ibn Tashfin tried to levy a war tax, a *ma'una* or aid, in Almeria, the people refused to pay. The chief *qadi* there said to Ibn Tashfin:

> You tell me that its legality—in the opinion of the *qadi*s and *faqih*s of the Maghrib and Andalusia—rests upon the example of Umar, companion of the Prophet, who was buried beside him, and whose justice has never been impugned. I reply that you are not a companion of the Prophet, that you will not be buried by his side, that I am not aware that your justice has never been impugned, and that if the *qadi*s and *faqih*s rank you with Umar, they will have to answer before God for their audacity. Umar, moreover, did not demand the contribution in question until he had sworn in the mosque that not a *dirham* remained in the treasury. If you can do the like, you will have the right to call for an aid. If not, you have no right. Greeting!

To make up the deficit caused by the abolition of illegal taxes, Ibn Tashfin heavily taxed the non-Muslim population, who, in addition to the land tax, had to pay a poll tax, the *jizya*. It was well known that the Jews of Lucena, a town in Andalusia that was almost exclusively Jewish, were the richest Jews in the whole of Almoravid territory. A *faqih* from Cordoba alleged that he came across a tradition that the Jews had solemnly sworn to the prophet Muhammad to convert to Islam if their messiah had not come at the end of five centuries. That time was now. Ibn Tashfin threatened to force them to comply. As it turned out, he was less interested in their conversion than in the tax revenues he could extract from them. At the suggestion of the *qadi* of Cordoba, he accepted the sum of 10,000 *dinar*s in lieu of conversion.

It was a tax structure as sophisticated as anywhere in the Islamic world. Ibn Tashfin relied on Andalusian *faqih*s to explain the law and on the Almoravid militia to enforce it. For the most part, his subjects were content that he fulfilled his promise of "no illegal taxes." There were complaints, as there always were, about abuses of the tax assessors and collectors, but not of the tax structure itself. The populace obviously welcomed the tax break afforded by the abolition of commodities taxes, and they experienced an economic boom because of it.

The wealth of the empire, though, was not yet manifest in Marrakech, which was still an armed camp—not a citadel and still less a city. It was a picturesque melee of soldiers, courtesans, tribesmen from the

Sahara, and local countrymen. Yet, it was the administrative heart of the empire from which Ibn Tashfin directed an increasingly complex political program for both the Maghrib and for the Iberian Peninsula, where his level of engagement was quickly increasing. For her part, his wife Zaynab chose to remain in Aghmat. She visited Marrakech from time to time to visit her husband, the Almoravid *Amir*, but she preferred to live in the comfort of the palace where she had lived when she was married to Laqut, whom the Almoravids killed when they conquered Aghmat. She might have ventured out on Friday afternoons to the Grand Mosque, only a few yards to the immediate southeast of the palace, to pray, to be sure, in the rear of the prayer hall with the other women. She might also have walked across the bridge over the Grand Canal Sultaniyya (*al-saqiya al-uzma al-sultaniya*) to the *hammam*, the public bath. Aghmat was well known for its *hammam*. There were none larger nor more monumental in all of the Almoravid Empire.

The *Hammam* of Aghmat was built in the late tenth century and was used through the Almoravid, Almohad, and Merinid periods. It has recently been excavated by the Moroccan-American Project at Aghmat under the direction of the author. (Photograph by the author.)

CHAPTER 9
A War of Sieges with the Taifa Kings

Two years after Yusuf Ibn Tashfin had achieved victory at the battle of Zallaqa, his thoughts began to drift back to Andalusia. It was the spring of 481/March 1088. He had buried a son, his heir, and had set about the business of governing his empire. It is rumored that the Lamtuna tribesman even admitted to a close companion, "Before going to that country I believed that my empire had great worth, but now I have learned that it is nothing. How can I remain master of that country?" He realized what a prize Andalusia would be.

For the past two years, Andalusians, especially the *faqih*s, praised his piety, his valor, and his skill as a warrior, and they called him *Amir al-Mu'minin*, commander of the faithful, a term traditionally reserved for the caliph in Baghdad. They gave alms to the poor, freed slaves, and offered thanksgiving to God. There was a sense of unity among Muslims in Andalusia that had been lost during the last few generations.

Yusuf Ibn Tashfin had appointed one of his cousins, Maju Ibn Hajj, commander of the 3,000 Almoravid troops stationed in Seville and Badajoz. Although the Taifa kings grimaced at the thought of being policed by this Almoravid guard, they felt secure enough inside of their fortresses, secure enough that they no longer paid tribute to the king of Castile.

Ibn Tashfin had been in Andalusia long enough to know that the greed and mutual mistrust among the Taifa kings would prevent them from mounting a united front against the Christian kingdoms to the north. The Muslim states in eastern Andalusia, far removed from the protection of Almoravid forces in Seville, were just as likely to suffer attack at the hands of Christians seeking tribute as by their Muslim neighbors. Their allegiances vacillated back and forth between Muslim and Christian, between the Almoravids and the Christians to the north. Even al-Qadir, the ex-king of Toledo who was installed on the throne in Valencia under the lances of Alfonso, wrote to Ibn Tashfin to declare himself an ally. He, too, ceased paying tribute to the king of Castile. No longer protected by the forces of Alvar Fanez, al-Qadir was besieged by another Taifa rival, Ibn Rashik, king of Murcia, Tortosa, and Denia, whose lands were like a vice around Valencia. Al-Qadir immediately sought protection at the same time from Alfonso in Castile and from his Muslim co-religionist, Musta'in in Zaragoza. He was willing to pay for protection from Christian or Muslim, whoever responded first.

Eastern Andalusia. (© Thomas Nolan. Used by permission.)

The Castilians already had an established stronghold along the southeastern Mediterranean coast, the fortress of Aledo, between Lorca and Murcia. The fortress was perched high upon a precipitous rock, surrounded by bare scrub land. Within the citadel, the Castilians had a reserve of food and munitions to last for months and a garrison of 12,000 to 13,000 troops. Alfonso's lieutenant, Garcia Jimenez, commanded the garrison; he was under orders to terrorize the region on the eastern confines of the kingdom of Seville. From this vantage point, the Castilians launched attacks against Lorca, Murcia, Almeria, and even against Baza some 60 away. The Castilian knights made daily raids in the region of Lorca as a punitive action against Mu'tamid for his role in bringing the wrath of the Almoravids to Andalusia. They ravaged the fields and either captured or put to the sword all with whom they came into contact so that peace and security had vanished from the land under the fatal shadow of the castle of Aledo.

Andalusian poets tell the story of their colleague Abd al-Khalil, a poet from Murcia, who fell victim to such an attack. He was traveling with a friend from Lorca to Murcia. To ease their fear as they approached the dreaded castle of Aledo, the two bards set to improvising verses. Soon after passing a group of tombstones, they were ambushed by a group of Castilian horseman. The knights killed Abd al-Khalil, and they stole everything his companion had and left him for dead.

These violent episodes were especially disturbing to Mu'tamid, still relatively secure in his capital in Seville, since Lorca and Murcia, the two towns most exposed to attack, were supposedly under his protection. The monarch of Lorca had recognized Mu'tamid as his sovereign precisely because of the Christian threat. Murcia was a vassal state to Mu'tamid, but its monarch abetted the Castilian's efforts in hope of winning immunity for himself.

Mu'tamid had no choice but to send his army under the command of his son Mu'tadd. In the vicinity of Lorca, the army of 3,000 was attacked by a small Castilian force of only 300 knights from Aledo. The Castilians won. The Muslim defeat was disgraceful! It is not surprising that Muslim chronicles are silent about this encounter and that Christian chronicles exaggerate the odds. Mu'tamid and the other Taifa kings realized that they were not able to defend themselves against the Castilians without the help of Yusuf Ibn Tashfin.

*Faqih*s and notables from the beleaguered towns came to Marrakech to implore Ibn Tashfin to come and bring his Almoravid forces to their shore a second time. There were representatives from Murcia, Lorca, and Baza. Even the Valencians sent a representative, because their town was being harassed by Rodrigo Diaz de Vivar, better know as El Cid. Reconciled now was that Castilian knight, who had fallen into disfavor with his king and was exiled from Castile. He had come to the east of Andalusia to serve in the army of the Taifa king of Zaragoza and to seek his fortune. In the wake of Alfonso's defeat at Zallaqa, the Castilian king needed all of the allies he could get, including Rodrigo de Vivar. Alfonso restored Rodrigo's lands, granted him new territories, and conferred upon him "sealed privilege," whereby all lands and castles he might conquer from the Muslims in Andalusia would become his own property and that of his heirs.

Because of the strong Almoravid presence in the West, El Cid sought to make his fortune in the East. He was in Zaragoza raising an army at the time that al-Qadir's plea for help came to Musta'in, the Taifa King of Zaragoza. El Cid and Musta'in both saw opportunity in Valencia's need for help. They jointly led an army to Valencia and forced the Murcians to withdraw. El Cid and his forces clearly played the decisive role here. The question is whether he represented the interests of his Muslim ally in Zaragoza or those of his king, Alfonso of Castile. He chose the latter. He accepted tribute from al-Qadir in Alfonso's name, and Musta'in returned to Zaragoza. El Cid also received tribute from the Muslim Taifa kings of Albarracin and Alpuente. He was as much of a threat to Muslim solidarity in eastern Andalusia as was the fortress of Aledo.

Andalusia desperately needed the personal presence of the Almoravid *Amir*. At first, Yusuf appeared indifferent to the pleas of the Andalusian ambassadors. Still, he did promise to cross the straits at a favorable season. He was vague in his commitment, and he made no serious preparations until the king of Seville crossed the straits and met Ibn Tashfin on the bank of the Sebou River, not far from Salé. The reception was warm and worthy of a royal visit: "Why did you make the long trip in person?" Yusuf asked. "Why did you not simply write to tell of your need?" Mu'tamid replied that he had come for the sake of Islam. "Those damned Christians are holding up in the fortress of Aledo which is in the midst of Muslim territory. They are terrorizing the countryside all around. We have come to you because no jihad is more worthy than yours in the eyes of God!"

Ibn Tashfin now had the invitation to do what he wanted to do. The Almoravid *Amir* instructed Mu'tamid to return to Seville and to prepare for war. He ordered Mu'tamid to enroll the support of the whole population, to start making arrows, lances, and catapults. Yusuf then wrote to the other Taifa kings to recruit them for this jihad.

In June 1088, Ibn Tashfin landed in Algeciras for the second time. Mu'tamid greeted him, bringing the requested stores of food and weapons. The kings of Malaga, Granada, Murcia, and some other minor potentates also responded to his summons. When they were all assembled, they marched on to Aledo to begin the longest siege the Almoravids ever imposed on an urban fortress.

Christians from the surrounding area crowded into the fortress, some 13,000 counting women and children, if the numbers are not exaggerated. The siege had begun! It would drag on for several weeks as day after day, the Muslim armies attacked the castle. Carpenters, masons, and blacksmiths from Murcia were called in to build siege machines. They used an extraordinary wooden "elephant" to hurl fire balls upon the fortress. But these machines had little effect. To break the morale of the Christians, the Muslims ravaged the surrounding countryside. From the hilltop fortress, the besieged could see the burning villages, trees, and crops.

Siege tactics were new to these warriors of the desert. Ibn Tashfin had hoped to starve out the defenders of Aledo. To do that, he would have had to surround the city completely. That would have required a large, disciplined army, huge stores of supplies, and more patience than Ibn Tashfin had. Very quickly, the stalled armies of the besiegers became seedbeds of intrigue.

The Andalusian kings who hosted the Almoravids began to grow tired and fearful of their guests. As if the cost of the siege was not expensive enough, King Abd Allah of Granada complained of having to give frequent "gifts," payoffs, to the Almoravids. One Almoravid commander, Garrur, even requested his payoff in Almoravid currency—and was so paid. Abd Allah confessed that he feared that Garrur would speak badly of him to Ibn Tashfin and would put him in disfavor with the Almoravid *Amir*.

Abd Allah had cause to worry. He also suspected his *qadi*, Ibn al-Khulay'i, of discrediting him before Ibn Tashfin. He knew that the *qadi* had encouraged his subjects back in Granada to refuse to pay their taxes, saying that the taxes were not sanctioned by the Koran. That was true, but the Taifa kings collected these taxes anyway. They needed the revenues to support their rather lavish lifestyles, to finance this campaign against the Christians, and to support the ever increasing expense of hosting the Almoravids. Ibn al-Khula'i's advocacy to withhold taxes found a sympathetic ear with Ibn Tashfin. Since it was well known that the Almoravid *Amir* had abolished all non-Koranic taxes in his Moroccan empire, Andalusian subjects hoped that he would do the same here.

The *qadi*'s tent was right next to the tent of his king, who was well aware that his *qadi* held secret talks with the Almoravid *Amir*. He was not sure what was being said, but he suspected the worst. He knew that al-Khulay'i had won the confidence of Ibn Tashfin, since the *qadi* had been one of the four delegates who called on him some four years earlier, inviting him to his first crossing into Andalusia. Abd Allah suspected him of taking advantage of this confidence to advance his own position at the expense of the Taifa kings.

Ibn al-Khulay'i's attitude toward the Taifa kings and his relationship with Ibn Tashfin became evident in another episode during this extended siege of Aledo, the trial of Ibn Rashik, king of Murcia Ibn Rashik and Mu'tamid had quarreled for some time. The king of Murcia was a vassal to the king of Seville but had recently been relaxing on his feudal obligations. The king of Seville actually hoped to depose his vassal so that his own son, Radi, could become the lord of Murcia. Fate played nicely into his hands.

Ibn Rashik, like so many other of the Taifa kings, was playing up to the Almoravids. Back in Murcia, he had ordered his subjects to say their Friday prayer in the name of the Almoravid *Amir* rather than in the name of his overlord Mu'tamid. Here at Aledo, he gave lavish "gifts" to the influential Almoravid commander Syr Ibn Abu Bakr, hoping to win his favor, and it worked. Ibn Rashik was granted *aman*, a special status of protection, much to the envy of the other Taifa kings.

But Ibn Rashik was playing both sides in the conflict between Christian and Muslim. He was here at Aledo along with the kings of Seville, Granada, and Almeria. He did supply materials for the siege as he was told to do, but it is suspected that he also maintained contact with and supplied the besieged Christians inside the city. He had a good reason to do this, for as long as the fortress of Aledo posed a threat in the midst of the Muslim east and continued to preoccupy the armies of Ibn Tashfin and the other Taifa kings, he believed that his throne in Murcia was safe.

Mu'tamid called Ibn Rashik to justice. He submitted the case to the *faqih*s for them to pass judgment against him. Ibn Khulay'i was among the jurists in the case. His general contempt for the Taifa kings came through when he was heard saying, "Ibn Rashik will see what will become of him. I was among the jurists on the case, and if we are called to judge other princes, we will hand them a similar fate!"

Ibn Rashik appealed to Ibn Tashfin. The Almoravid tried to avoid taking sides in these disputes among the Taifa kings, unless it affected his own interests. He knew that in the midst of this siege, he needed the support of the king of Seville more than he needed the king of Murcia. He was not taken in by Ibn Rashik's overtures. He knew full well that Ibn Rashik had no great affection for the Almoravids, and he even suspected that the Murcian was aiding the enemy. But the charge against him was rebellion against his lord. Ibn Tashfin said to him, "If it were a crime against me, I could pardon you, but since it is a matter of the law of the *Sunna*, the law of Islam, I am obliged to comply." Ibn Tashfin spared Rashik's life but turned him over in chains to the king of Seville.

For the moment, Mu'tamid had gotten his way. He appointed his son Radi to be the new ruler of Murcia. But the Murcians were incensed at the treatment of their king, Ibn Rashik. They refused to accept the appointment of Radi and withdrew their support from the siege of Aledo.

Disputes among the Taifa kings even broke out among brothers. Tamim, the king of Malaga, approached Ibn Tashfin to lodge complaints against his brother Abd Allah, the king of Granada, complaints that had to do with rights of sovereignty. Ibn Tashfin chose not to resolve the conflict. If he procrastinated long enough, the problem might resolve itself without his intervention. He did send his commander Garrur to assure Abd Allah of his neutrality. Garrur told Abd Allah that Granada was much more important to the Almoravids than was Malaga. They had to cross his territory to conduct this campaign, and they depended on the Granadans for provisioning the army. Garrur added, "Now, put yourself to the task, and do everything that is in your power to offer the *Amir* a hospitality worthy of him. Before he returns to the Maghrib, he will call on you in Granada."

In the meantime, another dispute was brewing between two other Taifa kings, between Mu'tamid of Seville and Mu'tasim, the king of Almeria. Like everybody else, Mu'tasim bestowed great "gifts" upon Ibn Tashfin, so much so that he had become a court favorite. With this power base, he set out to destroy his fellow Andalusian monarch. Mu'tamid, who suspected nothing of this intrigue, talked freely with Mu'tasim when alone with him. One day the king of Almeria expressed his uneasiness at Ibn Tashfin's prolonged stay in Andalusia. Mu'tamid replied, with a certain degree of Andalusian boastfulness,

> You are right! This man is making a long stay in our country; but when I am tired of him, I shall have but to lift a finger, and he and his soldiers will have to go within a day. You seem to fear that he will do us harm. But of what account is this poor wretch or his soldiers? In their own country they barely had enough to eat.

Wishing to do them a good turn we invited them here that they might eat their fill; when they are satisfied we will send them back to the Maghrib from where they came!

This growing contempt for the Berbers of the Sahara was not uncommon among the Andalusian nobility. But Mu'tasim saw a chance to use Mu'tamid's boasting to discredit him; he reported it to Ibn Tashfin. Little did he know that he would, in the words of an Arab historian, "fall into the well that he had dug for whom he hated and perish by the sword that he had drawn from its scabbard." Ibn Tashfin's wrath began to turn against all of the Taifa kings.

The siege of Aledo was now in its fourth month! Winter had begun to set in. The Murcians had withdrawn their support. And now Ibn Tashfin received word that the king of Castile was marching to the aid of the fortress with 18,000 men. Yusuf's first thought was to meet Alfonso once again on the battlefield, but then he changed his mind. Perhaps it was the wisdom that comes with old age, or perhaps it was old age itself. Either way, the Almoravid *Amir* lacked the confidence that he could win against Alfonso a second time under these circumstances. This was siege warfare, new to the Almoravids, not the open warfare where their military tactics were so effective. He remembered the battle of Zallaqa, where the euphoria of victory was short lived. The flow of that battle had swayed back and forth, sometimes in favor of the Christians, sometimes in favor of the Muslims. Yusuf's victory in that battle had been in no way certain until the end, and when it finally came, it was at a high price. He remembered, too, how the Andalusians fled the field when the battle's momentum had turned against them and returned only when it had shifted back in their favor once again. No, Yusuf was not ready to face Alfonso. He called off the siege of Aledo and withdrew his forces.

If only he had held on a little longer. In retrospect, Yusuf's retreat is one of his few tactical errors. The Christians at Aledo had suffered great losses from thirst and starvation. Their resources had just about given out. When Alfonso arrived to relieve the besieged, he found the garrison on its last leg. He evacuated those who remained and returned to Toledo.

The Almoravid *Amir* was disillusioned with the Taifa kings. "If you were truly united," he told them, "you would be able to repel the enemy." As he began to withdraw his troops, the Taifa kings felt abandoned by the Almoravids and begged Ibn Tashfin to leave an army in their defense. He did not. Rather, he left the Taifa kings to fend for themselves.

Abd Allah, king of Granada, sought an alliance with Alfonso, king of Castile. Alfonso himself had just concluded an alliance with the Muslim king of Zaragoza and was stronger than ever in eastern Andalusia. Abd Allah paid tribute to the Castilian king, who agreed not to attack his state.

Back in Granada, Abd Allah had imprisoned Ibn Khulay'i, the same *qadi* who had had private conversations with Ibn Tashfin during the siege. Abd Allah suspected that in these "secret" sessions, Ibn Khulay'i had convinced Ibn Tashfin that the Andalusian *faqih*s could absolve him from his oath not to conquer territory in Andalusia, that it would be easy to obtain from the *faqih*s a *fatwa*, a legal opinion, listing the misdeeds of the Taifa kings, misdeeds whereby they forfeited their right to the thrones they occupied. Abd Allah was forced to dismiss the *qadi* because of popular pressure, and he was soon to regret it.

The *faqih*s charged Abd Allah with treason! He had resumed paying tribute to Alfonso, and he even formed an alliance with the Christian king. A poet described the treasonous act saying, "Like a silk worm, he built for himself a house without shame, but he knows not what will become of that house when the power of the Almighty is no longer favorable toward him." Led by Ibn Khulay'i, the *faqih*s came to Ibn Tashfin to condemn the king of Granada. They came armed with a *fatwa* that condemned all of the Andalusian kings as impious profligates. By their bad example, these kings had corrupted the people and made them indifferent toward sacred things. They were slack in attendance at divine service, and they had levied illegal taxes and had maintained these taxes in spite of Ibn Tashfin's prohibition. Finally, they had allied themselves with Alfonso. For these reasons, they were no longer capable of ruling over Muslims. The *fatwa* said Ibn Tashfin was no longer bound by any pledges he had made to them, and it was not only his right but his duty to dethrone them without delay. In conclusion, the *faqih*s said, "We take it upon ourselves to answer before God for this decision. If we err, we consent to pay the penalty in another world, and we declare that you, *Amir* of the Muslims, are not responsible therefore; but we firmly believe that the Andalusian princes, if you leave them in peace, will deliver our land to the infidels, and in that case you must account to God for your inaction."

Ibn Tashfin endowed the *fatwa* with still greater authority by procuring its approval by his own *faqih*s in the Maghrib. Just in case that were not enough, he sent it to the most imminent theologians in the East, including al-Ghazzali and al-Turtushi, so they might confirm the opinions of the western *faqih*s. The eastern scholars were flattered, and they approved the *fatwa*. Al-Ghazzali confirmed Ibn Tashfin's primacy as *Amir* of the Almoravids and defender of the faith to carry jihad and to defend the borders of Islam. Al-Turtushi added that jihad was an obligation of *all* Muslims. The eastern scholars addressed letters of counsel to Ibn Tashfin, urging him to govern justly and not to stray from righteousness.

Abd Allah was the first of the Taifa kings to feel the cutting edge of the *fatwa* placed into Yusuf's hands. Yusuf set out toward Granada with a division of his army, ordering three other divisions to follow. Abd Allah prepared to defend his city. He assembled shields and arrows and projectile machines and provisioned each of his castles with stores for a year. In the meantime, he sought the advice of his council, particularly of the aged Mu'ammil, who had already served Abd Allah's grandfather so well. Mu'ammil advised the king that it would be useless to resist the Almoravids. All the older councilors of the court agreed with Mu'ammil, but Abd Allah accused the old man of collusion with the Almoravids and continued to prepare for war. He sent an appeal to the Christian King Alfonso to come to his defense; Alfonso refused.

On Sunday, 15 *Ramadan*, 483/10 November, 1090, when Ibn Tashfin had arrived within eight miles of Granada, Abd Allah had to decide what to do. Several of his citizens had already gone over to the side of the Almoravids. There were rumors that his mother had conceived the idea that Ibn Tashfin would marry her. She said, "My son, you have but one choice. Go out to greet the Almoravid. He is your cousin, and he will treat you honorably."

Abd Allah set out, accompanied by his mother and a splendid retinue. The Slavic guards marched first, followed by an escort of Christian horsemen surrounding the king. All the soldiers wore turbans of the finest cotton and were mounted upon splendid chargers covered in rich brocade. When they arrived in Ibn Tashfin's presence, Abd Allah dismounted and asked for the Almoravid's forgiveness. Ibn Tashfin graciously assured him that any grievances he might have had against Abd Allah were forgotten, and invited him to enter a tent in which he should be treated with all the respect due to his rank. But as soon as Abd Allah entered the tent, he was bound in chains.

Soon after Abd Allah was taken prisoner, many of the leading citizens of Granada came to Ibn Tashfin's camp. He welcomed them cordially. When they had taken the oath of allegiance, he issued an edict abolishing all the taxes not prescribed by the Koran. The Almoravid then entered the city, and paraded through streets crowded with cheering Granadans all the way to the palace of Abd Allah, where he had come to inspect and to claim the spoils of his victory. Chroniclers report that the halls were adorned with hangings and carpets of immense value: everywhere were emeralds, rubies, diamonds, pearls, vases of crystal, gold, and silver! A single chaplet consisted of 400 pearls, each of which was valued at a hundred ducats. The Almoravid was astounded by such treasures. As he had done in the past, he divided the wealth among his officers without keeping anything for himself. It was rumored that Abd Allah's mother had buried many precious objects. Ibn Tashfin ordered Mu'ammil, whom he had made steward of the palace, to excavate the foundations and even the sewers of the palace.

As soon as they heard of Ibn Tashfin's victory, Mu'tamid and Mutawakkil, the kings of Seville and Badajoz, came to Granada to congratulate him. Straight away, he saw through their hypocrisy and refused to greet them. Mu'tamid said to Mutawakkil, "We have made a serious error in inviting this man to Andalusia. He will have us drink from the cup that Abd Allah has just emptied." The two Andalusian kings returned to their own abodes and prepared to defend themselves against the Almoravids.

In the month of *Ramadan*, 483/1090, Ibn Tashfin decided to return to Marrakech, leaving one of his best generals, Syr Ibn Abu Bakr, to continue the war in Andalusia. En route to Algeciras where he would board a ship for home, Ibn Tashfin stopped in Malaga. He handily reduced that city into submission and captured its king, Tamim. Now, the two brothers who had appealed to the Almoravid *Amir* to umpire the quarrel between the two of them were carried off together in bondage. Ibn Tashfin took them back with him to the city of Aghmat, where they were to spend the rest of their days in exile with their harems and their children.

After allowing some days' rest to his men, Syr Ibn Abu Bakr conducted a number of forays into Christian territory, plundering and laying waste the land, slaying and making captives of the inhabitants, reducing the best fortified towns and the strongest and most inaccessible fortresses, and collecting rich spoils. He sent word of his success to Ibn Tashfin, telling him that he received no help from the Andalusian kings. While his own troops faced danger, hardship, and privation along the frontier as they waged jihad, the remaining Taifa kings were still steeped in pleasure and sloth. They enjoyed the luxury of their palaces, the company of their boon companions, the entertainment of their buffoons, jesters, and musicians, and the prestige of their lofty titles, but not the responsibility of a Muslim ruler.

Ibn Tashfin's instructions were clear and sharp. "Press them into service against the enemy," he wrote. "If they obey, well and good; if they refuse, lay siege to their cities, attack them one after the other, and destroy them without mercy. Begin with those whose dominions border on the enemy's frontier. Do not attack Seville until you have reduced the rest of Muslim Spain to obedience. To every city or town which may thus fall into your hands, appoint a governor from among the officers of your army."

Syr first marched against Ibn Hud of Zaragoza, who was then residing at Rhoda, a well-fortified castle with enough food and fresh spring water to withstand a lengthy siege. When Syr realized that standard siege tactics would not work in this case, he resorted to the ruse of the Trojan Horse. One day he raised the siege, broke camp, and went away some distance from the castle. Having then selected a division of his army, he dressed them as Christians and directed them to approach the castle as if they were friends, merchants coming to sell them provisions. In the meantime, he and the remainder of his forces lay in hiding, but well within striking distance. What happened next was exactly as Syr had planned. When the garrison saw the disguised Almoravids, seeing them in small number and not suspecting any treason, they came out of the castle. The Almoravids sprung from their hiding place and descended upon them. They seized Ibn Hud and forced him to surrender his castle.

Next, the Almoravids assaulted Mu'tamid's kingdom, toppling fortress after fortress. Abu Abd Allah Ibn al-Hajj was in command of the forces sent against Cordoba. He arrived there after taking the cities of Baeza and Ubeda, and the castle of al-Balata on his way. On Wednesday, the third day of Safar, 484/1091, the Almoravids stormed the city of Cordoba, the former capital of the Umayyad Caliphate. Mu'tamid was depending on Cordoba to provide the line of defense for his kingdom. Cordoba's own citizens delivered the city over to the Almoravids. The governor was al-Ma'mun, one of Mu'tamid's sons. Mu'tamid had told his son that death was easier to take than humiliating defeat. The son had taken his father's advice to heart and fought to the bitter end. Al-Ma'mun tried to cut his way through the traitors, but he was overwhelmed by them. The victors cut off his head and carried it through the streets on a spear.

Seville was the only Taifa state left for the Almoravids to take. Mu'tamid was desperate. All of the fortresses that formed a protective barrier around Seville had fallen to the Almoravids. His only hope was to appeal to the Christian, Alfonso, for reinforcements. Alfonso agreed and sent an army under the command of his very able commander Alvar Fanez. But Syr Ibn Abu Bakr was just as quick to respond. The two armies met near the fortress of Almodovar, about 13 miles from Cordoba. A violent and bloody battle ensued, in which the Almoravids suffered heavy losses. Yet they won the day and dispersed the Christian army.

The news of the defeat of the Christian relief force was a bad omen to Mu'tamid. It came when Seville was already under siege and as two more Almoravid armies arrived at the city's walls. Mu'tamid displayed the same courage that he had shown at Zallaqa. He marshalled a defense that was worthy of a king and, at the same time, faced traitors in his own ranks. Some of his men planned to turn the city over to the Almoravids. But Mu'tamid intercepted their plans and averted the treason. He could have had the traitors executed, but he simply expelled them from Seville. Still, some of the traitors managed to make a breach in the walls through which some Almoravid warriors entered the city. When he heard that the enemy had penetrated the city walls, Mu'tamid, dressed in a simple tunic, without armor or shield, grabbed his sword and went out to confront them. Near the *Bab al-Faraj*, one of the gates of the city, he came face to face with one of the assailants. The Almoravid threw his spear with sufficient accuracy to rip through Mu'tamid's tunic beneath his armpit, but the spear did not pierce his body. Mu'tamid swung his sword and hit the black warrior in the back of the neck with such force that the black's hewn head rolled to the ground. At the sight of this horror, several of the Almoravids who were standing on the top of the city walls threw themselves down and abandoned the gate which they had taken.

The people of Seville were charged by such a display of courage, and they were elated when they saw the Almoravids begin to retreat. But that did not last very long. In the afternoon of the same day, the Almoravid army, commanded by Abu Hamama, entered Seville on the river side. Another Almoravid army, commanded by Hudayr Ibn Wasnu, was again storming the gate. No sooner did they enter than they began to slay the inhabitants and plunder their houses and set them aflame. The Sevillians' will to resist began to wane. Still, the struggle to control the city lasted a few more days. Finally, Syr Ibn Abu Bakr arrived with a large contingent of Almoravid reinforcements, causing the inhabitants of Seville to flee, some overland from the city gates and others jumping the walls. Some jumped into the river and tried to swim across. Still others climbed into the sewers.

Mu'tamid fought valiantly to the end. It seemed as if he feared defeat more than death itself. Mounted and armed, he led one final charge against the Almoravids. His own son, Malik, fell during the charge and was trampled under horses' hooves. In the end, the Almoravids won the day. When night came, Mu'tamid sent his oldest son, Rashid, to the tent of Syr Ibn Abu Bakr to plea for mercy. The Almoravid offered none. Rashid was informed that his father had to surrender unconditionally. On Sunday, the twenty-first day of *Rajab*, Mu'tamid did just that. Syr agreed to spare the lives of Mu'tamid and his family if he could convince his two sons, Razi and Mu'tadd, who were commanders of Ronda and Mertola, respectively, to surrender as well. Mu'tamid reluctantly complied. Syr then told him that he and his family would live the rest of their lives in exile in Morocco in the city of Aghmat.

Razi threatened the security of his family. He felt that Ronda was impregnable and he could hold out indefinitely. He managed to hold off the Almoravids under the command of Garrur al-Hashimi. He was not about to surrender. In the end, both sons complied in order to save the lives of the rest of their family. They negotiated a treaty of surrender. Mu'tadd escaped, losing only his possessions. But in the case of Razi, Garrur went back on his word; he had Razi put to death and his head brought to the camp of Syr, who had it paraded on a spear before the walls of Seville.

The king of Almeria, Mu'tasim Ibn Samadah, soon suffered the same fate as the king of Seville. He shut himself up in his citadel when the Almoravids laid siege. But when he heard that the Almoravids were in the city, he realized that his time was very short. He was in poor health, and he was so afraid of suffering a humiliating defeat that he suffered a stroke before the citadel itself fell to the Almoravids. His son surrendered the city and joined the community of exiled Andalusian monarchs in Aghmat.

In Aghmat, Mu'tamid bin Abbad lived with his wife Rumaykhiya and his daughters, who, the chronicles say, managed to earn a pittance spinning thread. The women worked for, among others, an officer of the guard of their father's prison and so were able to slightly better their condition. Mu'tamid spent most of his time reflecting on his fate and writing verses. On one *aid al-fitr*, marking the end of Ramadan, he wrote:

> In days gone by this was such a joyous feast!
> But sad is the feast that finds me captive,
> like a slave in Aghmat.

> Yesterday, when I spoke men obeyed.
> Today it is I who submits to the will of men.
> Kings who glory in their greatness
> Are the dupes of a vain dream!

Of the chains that shackled his feet he wrote:

> It be said of the snake that is coiled about my leg
> That he leaves the mark of his fangs.
> Yet it is I whose generosity lifted men to heaven
> And I whose sword sent them to hell!

Mu'tamid received many visitors, among them his closest friend the poet Ibn al-Labbana. He told his destitute king that the minds of thinking men back home were agitated by the rule of the new regime and that there was rebellious sentiment to restore the Andalusian monarch to the throne. If that were true, the Almoravid security would soon become aware of it. In any case, these thoughts held out hope for the Sevillian in Aghmat. Ibn al-Labbana offered his king the following verse:

> Patience! You will soon fill me with joy
> For soon you will resume your throne...
> Prepare to shed your rays again
> The eclipse of the moon is passing.

Yusuf Ibn Tashfin came often to Aghmat to visit his wife Zaynab. On some occasions, he also called on Mu'tamid. When Mu'tamid once asked Ibn Tashfin whether he understood the poems recited to him by the Sevillian poets, he replied, "All I understood was that their composers were in need of bread." On still another occasion, the king sent a letter to Ibn Tashfin in which he included these verses from a love poem written by a famous Sevillian poet:

> While you are far from me, the desire of seeing you consumes my heart and I weep floods of tears. Now my days are black, yet not long ago you made my nights white.

Ibn Tashfin replied, "Does the king wish me to send him black damsels as well as white ones?" His secretary explained that "black" signified gloomy in poetic phraseology and that "white" meant clear and serene. "How beautiful," exclaimed Ibn Tashfin. "Tell the king that I have a headache whenever he is out of my sight!"

Ibn Tashfin was a barbarian in Mu'tamid's eyes. Andalusians viewed all of the desert Berbers in the same way, sorely out of place in the cultured environment of Andalusia. Thirty years earlier Ibn Tashfin was a desert warrior, but his time in Andalusia, as well as in the Maghrib, had seasoned his awareness of the subtleties of ruling. Ibn Tashin's simplicity was deceptive. The political program that he envisioned for Andalusia was as sophisticated and far more effective than that of any of the Taifa kings, although it depended on the presence of the veiled men of the Sahara.

The *faqih*s urged Yusuf to legitimize his authority by having it recognized by the caliph of Baghdad, al-Mustansir Billah, the supreme sovereign over the whole of the Muslim world. For this mission Ibn Tashfin sent two envoys from Seville to call upon the caliph on his behalf. At the head of the delegation was the chief *qadi* of Seville, Abd Allah Ibn Muhammad Ibn al-Arabi. Armed with a host of splendid gifts and a letter asking for his official investiture, the ambassadors left Seville shortly after that city came under the jurisdiction of the Almoravids. The two men made the pilgrimage to Mecca before going on to Baghdad to present the caliph with the all important petition on behalf of the Almoravid *Amir*.

The diplomats described Ibn Tashfin as a true defender of the faith who had championed the cause of the Abbasid Caliph for the past 40 years, successfully waging war against all who opposed that cause. They said that the caliph's name was invoked in the pulpits of some 2,500 mosques within Almoravid territory, which stretched from the Christian frontier north of Andalusia to the borders of Ghana, the land of gold, a distance of five months' march from one end to the other. They emphasized his efforts of waging jihad against the infidel and recapturing territory that was rightfully within the Muslim realm, the *dar al-Islam*. They told the caliph that Yusuf placed in the service of Islam an army of 60,000 horsemen.

The two ambassadors from Seville extolled Ibn Tashfin's virtues as a just ruler who imposed none but Koranic taxes. They assured the caliph that routes were safe throughout the Almoravid state and that the currency was sound and bore the stamp of the Abbasid caliph. Surely the caliph would want to reward such a powerful and loyal servant with official recognition.

The caliph acknowledged Ibn Tashfin's virtues, underlining that they conformed to the edicts in the Holy Koran. His secretary issued a letter which the ambassadors carried back to Ibn Tashfin, investing him with the titles Commander of the Muslims, Defender of the Faith, Champion of the Cause of the Commander of the Faithful, the latter being a title reserved for the caliph himself. The caliph thus recognized Ibn Tashfin's sovereignty over the Maghrib and Andalusia, lands which he had conquered in the name of Islam.

CHAPTER 10

The Almoravids Confront El Cid

Rodrigo Diaz de Vivar, El Cid, earned his living by collecting tribute from the Taifa states in the East of Andalusia. Al-Qadir, the former king of Toledo who now ruled in Valencia, depended on the military arm of El Cid, for which he paid the weekly tribute of 1,000 *dinar*s. In 483/1090 after the death of al-Hajib, king of Tortosa and Denia, El Cid offered his protection to the king's young son as well—for a comparable price. Both Denia and Tortosa paid El Cid tribute of 50,000 *dinar*s a year. The small kingdoms of Albarracin and Alpuente each paid 10,000 *dinar*s a year; Murviedro, 8,000; and Segorbe, 6,000; Xerica and Almenara, 3,000 each; and Lira, 2,000, in all a total of 192,000 *dinar*s a year from these Taifa states that had survived in the East. It was a sum worth fighting for, and El Cid was constantly engaged in preserving his tributary income. His Muslim allies, vassals, and tributaries called him *al-Sayyid*, "the lord." Only later did the Christian world call him El Cid. Muslim historians respected his prowess and referred to him as *al-Kanbitur*, after the Spanish *al-Campeador*—the warrior.

During the first several months of 485/1092, El Cid was in the Taifa state of Zaragoza in support of its king, Musta'in, who was facing growing opposition. The more the Muslims living in Zaragoza heard of the Almoravid successes against the Taifa kings in the West, the more they were encouraged to oppose their own king. Any cause for malcontent against their own rulers pushed them to become Almoravid partisans.

A similar scenario was beginning to form in Valencia. Al-Qadir was king, but everyone knew that he was the puppet for Rodrigo Diaz de Vivar. Al-Qadir's vizier, Ibn al-Faraj, took more and more initiative as his king was old and ailing, and he collected the tribute to be paid

Drawing of the Statue of El Cid in Burgos, Spain. (© Willierossin/Dreamstime.com. Used by permission.)

to El Cid. The Muslim regime was supported by small contingents of Castilian and Aragonese knights under the command of El Cid. The Christian population was growing under the care of Alfonso's bishop, who lived in the northern suburb of Alcudia.

Meanwhile, during the last three months of 484/November, 1091–January, 1092, Yusuf Ibn Tashfin's son, Da'ud Ibn Aisha, had marched against the Taifa state of Murcia and the Christian fortress of Aledo and brought them both under Almoravid control. The news of these Almoravid victories brought much excitement to Valencia, especially to those Muslims who grew tired of paying tribute to El Cid and taxes to his ailing vassal al-Qadir. They "longed for the Almoravid, Da'ud Ibn Aisha," said one Valencian, "as the sick man longs for health."

The rising tide of opposition against al-Qadir rallied around the *qadi* Ja'far Ibn Jahhaf, a man from a leading aristocratic family in Valencia, whose mansions lined one of the most central thoroughfares of the city, the "Street of Ibn Jahhaf." Conspirators took advantage of El Cid's prolonged absence from the city. They met regularly in Ibn

Jahhaf's home, where they complained freely about their king being the puppet of a Christian. They accused the vizier Ibn al-Faraj of overstepping his bounds since al-Qadir's illness. Finally, Ibn Jahhaf wrote to Da'ud Ibn Aisha in Murcia, offering to surrender Valencia to him. At the same time, he persuaded the *qadi* of the neighboring city Alcira to do the same.

In the fall of 485/1092, Da'ud Ibn Aisha took Ibn Jahhaf up on his offer and set out for Valencia. Muslim preachers had prepared the way for him so well that as he approached town after town along the way, the people opened their gates to the Almoravids and greeted them with open arms. Denia and Jativa had already expelled their king's vizier. The king himself fled the scene long before the Almoravids ever arrived. Alcira also surrendered, as they had promised. When the news traveled the short distance from Alcira to Valencia, it struck fear in the hearts of the Christians. El Cid's knights, together with the Aragonese and King Alfonso's bishop, "fled like a leaderless rabble, taking with them what possessions they could."

In Valencia, the Taifa king al-Qadir and his vizier retreated to the Alcazar, the garrison, and posted a guard of foot soldiers and crossbowmen. There, they waited for 20 days for El Cid to come to rescue them. But he did not come. Finally, early one morning in October, stationed near the Boatella gate, the guards heard the thunder of the Almoravid drums. The report was that 500 Almoravid warriors were on the horizon. Ibn Jahhaf was called to the Alcazar to take command. When he arrived, the *qadi* seized the vizier and put him in prison. Al-Qadir fled to hide in the city, taking with him women of his harem and such of his vast wealth as he could carry. Beneath the women's garments that he wore to disguise himself, al-Qadir hid the precious girdle of diamonds, pearls, sapphires, rubies, and emeralds, which three centuries earlier had been, supposedly, the possession of queen Zubayda, the wife of Harun al-Rashid.

The *qadi* wanted the treasure for himself. His paid accomplices tracked al-Qadir down and cut his throat. They kept part of the booty for themselves, but they turned the bulk of it over to Ibn Jahhaf along with the king's head. Ibn Jahhaf buried the treasure, but he threw the head into a pond near his mansion.

Meanwhile, Almoravid sympathizers drove al-Qadir's soldiers from the towers and burned the gates that they had been unable to open, allowing the Almoravids to enter. But there were not 500 of them as had been reported. Da'ud Ibn Aisha, staying safely back in Denia, had sent the Almoravid governor of Alcira, Abu Nasr, with only 20

Almoravid warriors. They took with them 20 knights of Alcira, who were armed and dressed in the tunic of the desert warriors, faces veiled, so that the number of Almoravids appeared to be double what it actually was. The reputation of the veiled Almoravid warriors was enough to win the city with the pounding of their drums.

El Cid was seeking revenge when he finally reached the outskirts of Valencia within a month of the loss of his city. This was the beginning of a long siege that lasted through the winter and the spring and into the following summer. This time, the Almoravids and their allies and sympathizers were the besieged. El Cid burned the neighboring villages and reaped the crops that lay in the fields. He built a fortified city of his own at the foot of the castle of Juballa with the timber obtained from the houses and towers he had destroyed in the environs of Valencia. In late summer, El Cid attacked the two northern suburbs of Villanueva and Alcudia. In the attack against the garrison there, El Cid fell from his horse but quickly remounted and fought so fiercely, said an eyewitness, that the Muslims, both Almoravid and Valencian, were terrified.

Inside the besieged city, enthusiasm and support for the Almoravids, which was so strong at first, began to fade. Both Ibn Jahhaf and the Almoravid commander wanted to bring the siege to an end, especially after El Cid had taken the two Christian suburbs to the north, completing the noose around the city. All factions in the besieged city agreed to bid for peace on El Cid's terms.

Those terms were straightforward: The *qadi* Ibn Jahhaf would remain at the head of the government and he would pay the 1,000 *dinar*s a week with full arrears. El Cid returned to Juballa, placing the northern Christian suburbs in the hands of his own tax collectors. The Almoravids left under El Cid's escort as far as Denia. Valencia was again a tributary of El Cid as it had been before the death of al-Qadir.

News of the Almoravid retreat from Valencia provoked the Almoravid *Amir* in Marrakesh. According to a Christian chronicler, the aging Yusuf Ibn Tashfin wrote to El Cid, demanding that he leave the state of Valencia immediately. El Cid sent a scornful reply, taunting that the Almoravid was afraid to cross the straits again. Due more to old age than to fear, Ibn Tashfin chose not to cross. He would leave future wars to younger men. He sent his son-in-law, Abu Bakr, to march against Valencia.

Ibn Jahhaf was still walking the thin line between submission to El Cid and hope that the Almoravids would rescue him. The news of Abu Bakr's approach caused him a dilemma. Should he pay his tribute or not? El Cid, for his part, made it quite clear that resistance would be costly. He closed the noose around the city so tightly that its inhabitants grew hungry. From the tops of the city walls, they could see the prosperous crops and markets in the suburbs that had recognized El Cid as their master. But the Almoravids were on their way; they were in nearby Alcira. On a cold autumn night in 485/1092, the guards mounted the watchtowers and stood in the pouring rain, chilled and soaked to the bone, to scan the horizon, expecting to see the fires of the Almoravid bivouacs just a few miles away. When day broke, no sign of the rescue mission was to be seen. By mid-day a messenger reported that the mere thought of facing El Cid had sent them scurrying under the darkness of night.

El Cid's siege lasted for 20 months. By the end of the month of *Rabi al-Akhir*, 487/April, 1094, the famine in Valencia had become unbearable. Wheat was sold at 70 times its normal price at the beginning of the siege. Meat was more expensive still. The rich ate cow hides or broth made from them, while the poor were driven to eat the flesh of human corpses. The death rate was high. Hunger drove men, women, and children out of the gates into the hands of the besiegers, who either sold them as slaves or burned them alive in full view of the besieged. Ibn Jahhaf was forced to surrender. The forces of El Cid entered the city on 28 *Jumada al-Ula*, 487/15 June, 1094. This time, El Cid took direct control of Valencia as king.

While the Almoravids failed to take Valencia that summer, they did succeed in their campaign to conquer Badajoz. King Mutawakkil had been a loyal ally of Yusuf Ibn Tashfin. In fact, he had even provided assistance in the siege of Seville. But now, he too had given in to Alfonso's pressure and bought protection from the king of Castile. Syr Ibn Abu Bakr, who had been appointed governor of Seville after his successful campaign in that area, had to call Mutawakkil to terms. Badajoz offered very little resistance. The people had turned against their king for his collusion with the Christians. Almoravid soldiers stormed the palace in Badajoz, and Mutawakkil himself was made prisoner. Syr Ibn Abu Bakr compelled him by torture to reveal his hidden treasures and then announced that Mutawakkil was to be taken to Seville with his two sons, Fadl and Abbas. After traveling some distance, the Almoravid commander ordered Mutawakkil and his sons to prepare for death. Mutawakkil begged only that his sons should die first because he believed that his own sins would be redeemed by suffering. His request was granted, and when he had seen the heads of his two children fall, he knelt down in a last prayer; he was killed before the prayer was finished.

The victory over Badajoz restored Yusuf Ibn Tashfin's confidence. Still seething at the surrender of Valencia to El Cid, he appointed his nephew Muhammad to lead a huge army, recruited both in the Maghrib and in Andalusia, to lay siege to the city of Valencia. Yusuf Ibn Tashfin ordered his nephew to capture El Cid alive and to bring him to Marrakech. As the Almoravids approached, El Cid, now besieged in his recently conquered city, sent messengers asking for help, but a small relief force sent by Alfonso VI would arrive too late. El Cid felt sufficiently threatened to order that all weapons and iron tools in the hands of the Muslim inhabitants of Valencia be surrendered under penalty of death. The Muslims were led to believe that if the Almoravids attacked, they would be immediately put to the sword by their Christian captors.

In the month of *Ramadan*, 487/October, 1094, the Almoravid army gathered outside the walls on the west side of the city on the plain called the Cuarte. As soon as *Ramadan* was over, the Almoravids attacked—daily, for 10 successive days. Then El Cid demonstrated his military genius. He divided his forces in two parts: One force launched a sortie with such strength that the Almoravids were led to believe that El Cid himself led the attack. Meanwhile, El Cid personally led the other body of troops out of a different gate and fell upon the defenseless camp of the enemy. The carefully planned and executed tactic of feint and attack from a different direction won the day for El Cid. The poet of the *Song of My Cid* said that it was El Cid's ghost who led his army against the Almoravids. The fame of this victory spread to the neighboring kingdoms, and throughout the following year Christian notaries dated their documents by this event. A document in Aragon records, "This charter was made in the year that the Almoravids came to Valencia, when Rodrigo Diaz drove them out and captured all their *mahalla*." This first major defeat of an Almoravid army in Andalusia taught the Almoravids that El Cid was indeed *al-Kanbitur*, the warrior! Valencia was a mote in Yusuf's eye that robbed him of all ease; its loss to El Cid was constantly in his thoughts and on his tongue; his one aim was to recover it, and he sent troops and money to accomplish this objective. Meanwhile, El Cid had built a chain of fortresses to the south of Valencia along the Rio Jucar. The strongest of these was the Peña Cadiella, just to the south of Jativa. It was of prime strategic importance because it guarded the southern approach to Valencia by the inland route. Late in the year 489/1096, Da'ud Ibn Aisha marched against the fortress at the head of a powerful army of some 30,000 men. El Cid was so frightened that he called for reinforcements from Aragon. As the reinforcements approached, the Almoravids lifted the siege. El Cid led his army back to Valencia, taking the route along the Mediterranean coast. Da'ud Ibn Aisha must have predicted the move, for he laid in ambush in the narrow pass between Mount Mondubar and the sea. The pass was so narrow that the Christian army had to march almost in single file. Almoravid horsemen fell upon them from the mountain slopes while archers showered them with arrows from barges in the sea, which the Almoravids had brought up the coast from Almeria. Victory seemed sure for the Almoravids, but El Cid somehow managed to rally his force. "Choose your man and hold your ranks!" he shouted. "Do not let the number of these dogs frighten you!" Once again, El Cid's presence turned what should have been a sound beating of his own army into another defeat for the Almoravids.

For a while, the Almoravids would do no more than harass El Cid in his Valencian stronghold. In the summer of 491/1097, the Almoravid governor of Jativa led a force across Valencian countryside and established himself at Murviedro on the coast to the north of El Cid's city. El Cid immediately forced the Almoravids to evacuate and chased them all the way to Almenara. The forces of El Cid laid siege to Almenara, which fell to *al-Kanbitur* three months later.

In the same summer of 491/1097, Yusuf Ibn Tashfin crossed the straits of Gibraltar for the fourth time, this time not against El Cid but against King Alfonso VI, who was in Toledo. Ibn Tashfin gathered his army together in Cordoba under the field command of Muhammad Ibn al-Hajj. The rival armies met at Consuegra, between Tage and Guadiana. Again, the same Almoravid tactics and close rank formations, the same tactics that won in the battle of Zallaqa, routed the enemy. The Almoravids were victorious, perhaps because El Cid was not there. El Cid's own son Diego was fighting in the army of his king and was killed in battle.

A few weeks later, another great Castilian military hero, Alvar Fanez, fell victim to an Almoravid army commanded by Da'ud Ibn Aisha in the neighborhood of Cuenca. The Almoravid commander, trying to capitalize on his momentum, marched into the territory of El Cid, who sent an army to meet him at Alcira. El Cid was not with the army, and the Almoravids annihilated it. Only a few managed to escape and return to Valencia.

For the next two years, the Almoravids avoided any direct confrontation with El Cid. For his part, El Cid continued to exact tribute from the dominions that had fallen under his control. He built churches, primarily for the Christian garrison in towns like Almenara and

Murviedro, and gave an endowment to establish the bishopric in Valencia. He converted the principal mosque of the city into a church and dedicated it to the Virgin Mary. Though he did all that he could to consolidate his hold on Valencia and its hinterland, he failed to attract large numbers of Christians from Castile and Aragon, undoubtedly because the threat of the Almoravids was ever present.

Rodrigo Diaz de Vivar, El Cid, died on 18 *Shaban*, 492/10 July, 1099. His widow, Chimene, came to Valencia from Castile to administer his estate and to be regent over her deceased husband's kingdom. For the next three years, she devoted herself to safeguarding the heritage of El Cid.

The commander who dealt Valencia its final blow was the veteran Mazdali, the loyal Lamtuna who fought by Yusuf Ibn Tashfin's side in the early days of conquest in the Maghrib, the same Mazdali who diverted the challenge of Ibrahim Ibn Abu Bakr in Aghmat some 20 years before. He laid siege to the city in the early spring of 495/1102. With El Cid no longer there, neither in life nor in spirit, the veiled Almoravid warriors seemed more threatening than ever. Christian chronicles would later report a legend that in their ranks, a Turkish woman led a band of 300 "Amazons," black female archers, a legend possibly inspired by the ominous veils on the faces of the warriors and the dark skin colored blue by the indigo of their robes.

Chimene appealed to King Alfonso VI to come to her aid. Since she was the king's kinswoman, he could not very well refuse. Still, he had no intention of challenging the Almoravids for control of Valencia. It was simply too far from Toledo. He came merely to provide Chimene and those Christians who chose to evacuate safe escort back to his capital. Mazdali's army entered Valencia in the wake of the exiles' retreat. The last obstacle to Almoravid supremacy in Andalusia had fallen.

It had been a war of long, protracted sieges, a war of patience. Rarely were there pitched battles that would allow the Almoravids the advantage of the tactics that had worked so well for them in the Maghrib and at Zallaqa. And when pitched battles did occur in the East, they sometimes turned out badly. It was a war in which men fought less for ideology and more for opportunity, one of heroes on both sides, a war in which reputations sometimes swayed the course of battle, and in which commanders performed deeds about which poets would write.

El Cid had been a formidable enemy. Not once did the Almoravids defeat him on the battlefield. Whatever victories the Almoravids enjoyed in Andalusia, El Cid was not there. The Almoravids succeeded in taking his kingdom only after his death.

Yusuf Ibn Tashfin knew it was time to provide for a smooth transition of power in what was now a vast empire, spanning the straits and joining two continents. In 496/1102, his son Ali was 19 years old, living in Ceuta where he had been born and raised. Yusuf Ibn Tashfin ensured that Ali was recognized as his heir throughout his Moroccan and his Andalusian dominions. His secretary, Abu Bakr Ibn al-Qasira, drew up the official proclamation that placed his son in command of the Andalusian side, and he gave him the following advice. Ali was to establish his court in Seville rather than in Cordoba, which had been the capital of the once glorious Umayyad dynasty but which was now a fading memory. He was to conclude a peace with Ibn Hud, the king of Zaragoza, in order to allow him to carry on jihad against the infidels. Finally, he was to equip an army of 17,000 troops in Andalusia—stationing 7,000 in Seville, 1.000 in Cordoba, 4,000 in the East, and the rest along the border with Castile.

The following year, Yusuf Ibn Tashfin ordered that Ali's name be added to his own on the official coinage of the state. It was his way of stating clearly to all who used money that the Almoravids were in command, and that his son would carry on following Ibn Tashfin's own death. The formula on the coins varied from mint to mint. In Valencia, for example, the *dinar*s read, "There is no God but God and Muhammad is the Prophet of God—*al-Amir* Ali Ibn (son of) *al-Amir* Yusuf Ibn Tashfin." In Marrakech, the *dinar*s simply read, "... *al-Amir* Yusuf Ibn Tashfin *wa* (and) *al-Amir* Ali." Yusuf Ibn Tashfin died three years later.

CHAPTER 11
Ali Ibn Yusuf Sets His House in Order

Ali Ibn Yusuf was 23 years old when his father Yusuf Ibn Tashfin died of illness and old age. Ali Ibn Yusuf was born in Ceuta in 477/1084–1085. His mother Kamra ("moon") was a Christian captive from Andalusia; she was called Fadl al-Hasan, "more than perfect," because of her great beauty. Ali Ibn Yusuf became the first Almoravid ruler who had not known the desert.

Ibn Yusuf was tall and light-complexioned with an oval face and aquiline nose. Except for his dark eyes and curly hair, he favored his mother in appearance more than his father. In his piety, statesmanship, and military prowess, he was every bit his father's son. Yusuf Ibn Tashfin had groomed his son to be a ruler.

On 3 *Muharram*, 500/4 September, 1106, Ibn Tashfin's family had gathered around his deathbed in the *Qasr* in Marrakech. Just before the old *Amir* died, he offered his mantle to his son and successor, Ali Ibn Yusuf. Tamim, Zaynab's son and Ali's half-brother, placed it on his shoulders. Tamim then took Ali by the hand and presented him to the assembly and said, "Stand and salute the *Amir* of the Muslims!" All who were there, *shaykh*s from the Lamtuna and other Sanhaja tribes, bowed before their new master.

Ali Ibn Yusuf was heir to a sizable empire by any standards. The chronicles state that at the time of his father's death, the treasury housed 13,000 boxes of silver coin and 5,040 boxes of minted gold! It was Ibn Yusuf's intention to rule as his father had, to apply the principles of Malikite Islam, and to maintain the present tax structure of the state based on no non-Koranic taxes. He would continue to rule through members of his extended family and to surround himself with advisers who were religious scholars of Malikite law.

Among the tribes of the Sanhaja, succession from father to son was not automatic. A successor had to be accepted by a consensus of the tribal elite. Ali Ibn Yusuf sent messengers to all parts of the empire, both in the Maghrib and in Andalusia, to announce the death of his father. The returning emissaries expressed their condolences and acknowledged his succession to power, that is, all except for his nephew, Yahya Ibn Abu Bakr, who was at the time the governor of Fez, appointed to that post by his grandfather, Yusuf Ibn Tashfin. Full of pride and supported by a small faction from among the Lamtuna, Yahya Ibn Abu Bakr refused to recognize the new *Amir*. Thus Ali Ibn Yusuf began his career as *Amir* by having to march on Fez.

Camped on the outskirts of Fez, he sent a message to his conspiring nephew, inviting him to reconsider and to offer his obedience. Yahya Ibn Abu Bakr had tried to incite the people of Fez to rebel against Ibn Yusuf. But the presence of the army on the outskirts of the city had a greater impact upon the citizens. When Ibn Abu Bakr saw that he had very little support, he fled, fearing for his own safety. Ali Ibn Yusuf entered the city of Fez on 8 *Rabi al-thani*, 500/6 December, 1106, with his authority unchallenged.

Meanwhile, Yahya Ibn Abu Bakr fled toward Tlemcen, on the eastern frontier of the Almoravid Empire, where he met its governor, the veteran Lamtuna commander Mazdali Ibn Tilankan, who had already proved his loyalty to Yusuf Ibn Tashfin many times. Just as he had negotiated a reconciliation between Yusuf and Ibrahim, the rebellious governor of Sijilmasa, Mazdali Ibn Tilankan sought to do the same with Yahya Ibn Abu Bakr and the new *Amir*. He guaranteed Ibn Abu Bakr's safety and pardon if the latter would return with him to Fez to submit to the authority of the new *Amir*. He reluctantly agreed.

Upon Mazdali's recommendation, Ali Ibn Yusuf extended *aman*, a guarantee of personal safety, to his nephew. He offered him the choice to live in exile on the island of Majorca or to return to the tribal homeland in the Sahara. His nephew chose the Sahara, but asked first to be allowed to make the pilgrimage to Mecca. Upon his return from the holy city, a repentant Yahya Ibn Abu Bakr asked to be allowed to spend the rest of his days serving his *Amir* in the court at Marrakech. Ali Ibn Yusuf showed compassion and agreed.

The new *Amir* worked very hard to make Marrakech a worthy capital. It was rapidly becoming a city. Just to the south of the *qasr* built by his father, Ali Ibn Yusuf ordered the construction of a new palace. It was connected to the *qasr* by a corridor some 10 meters long with a vaulted arch at each end. The east side of the corridor was made partially of dried mud, but the other three sides were made of massive blocks of stone, carried to the site by camel. This grand entranceway led to the royal residence and served as an ante chamber for those waiting for an official audience with the sovereign. As had been the case in the royal courts of Andalusia, Ali Ibn Yusuf dispensed justice weekly from the royal residence to those who "came to the port."

Within the palace itself, Ali Ibn Yusuf enjoyed his *riyad* (garden) designed in Andalusian style. Stone walks crossed the length and width of the patio, dividing the garden into four sections. At the center was a fountain from which water flowed into a catch basin and then drained through underground clay pipes to irrigate the flowers in each of the four sections of the garden.

The water supply of the palace was stored in two large cisterns. Three double arches supported the huge vaulted ceilings, 32 meters long, almost 4 meters wide, and nearly 3 meters high. According to an ancient construction technique, the wall separating the two cisterns was pierced by arched openings that allowed water to flow from one to the other. The cisterns were fed by a conduit connected to the *khettara*, south of the *qasr*.

A *khettara* is an ingenious, gravity-fed, water transportation system. To design the system for the city of Marrakech, Ali Ibn Yusuf commissioned a man named Abd Allah Ibn Yunus al-Muhandis. The surname al-Muhandis means engineer. Ibn Yunus designed a series of wells dug in a line, each one connected to the next by an underground canal that gradually brought the water to the surface at the terminus, due to the slope of the canal, which was more gentle than the slope of the ground surface above. The *khettaras* of Marrakech not only provided an abundant supply of water for the palace, the gardens, and the parks that beautified the Almoravid capital, but they made possible an urban growth that transformed Marrakech from a military encampment to an urban center of international renown. In gratitude, Ibn Yusuf marked Ibn Yunus with distinction and showered him with gifts.

Just north of the center of town, Ibn Yusuf constructed his grand mosque called *Masjid al-Siqaya*, "Mosque of the Fountain." By the time that it was finished, it cost some 60,000 *dinar*s, and it was the largest of all the mosques that the Almoravids built throughout the empire. Its massive minaret dominated the entire quarter.

To ensure that the *qibla* was properly oriented toward Mecca, Ali Ibn Yusuf assembled 40 jurists, including the famous Andalusian scholars Abu al-Walid Ibn Rushd and Malik Ibn Wuhayb. It was custom among the Berbers of the Maghrib to rely upon the judgment of the *ayt arba'ain*, the assembly of 40 notables, but these men were jurists, not scientists. The mosque was oriented several degrees to the south of the true *qibla*, nonetheless, consistent with others built at that time and for centuries to come.

The *minbar*, the chair from which the *imam* preached his Friday sermon, was imported from Cordoba. It was taller than most *minbar*s, and two arches marked the upper and lower limits of the nine-step staircase. Its dark brown surface was inlaid with ivory and a variety of precious woods, a symphony of parts in which each panel was decorated with a separate motif with only subtle variations of the harmonious theme. The *kufic* inscription that bordered the back of the chair underscored the "divine benevolence" of *Amir* Ali Ibn Yusuf.

For the ritual ablutions before prayer, Ibn Yusuf commissioned a monumental fountain, a rectangular structure dressed in stone, divided into three bays by two vaulted arches with a basin in each bay. He proudly imported a spectacular marble basin to grace one of these bays. Three floral patterns were sculpted into the face of the marble, and on one of the faces, winged quadrupeds and heraldic eagles were carved. The *kufic* inscription, square-shaped Arabic letters, identifies the Umayyad *hajib* Abd al-Malik as the one who commissioned the basin more than 100 years earlier and had it installed in Fez. Water fed the basins through a bronze pipe from a small, vaulted cistern behind the fountain. The ground in front of the fountain was paved in stone to avoid the inconvenience of mud.

The coup de grace of Ibn Yusuf's beautification plan for Marrakech was the *Qubba*, a smaller, more elegant kiosk that housed still another ablutions font. The basic plan was simple enough, a rectangular, two-story domed structure pierced by variously shaped doors and windows. The horseshoe, keyhole, and scallop shapes played with the strong Moroccan light to form contrasting light and dark silhouettes. A battlement of merlons framed a dome, which was decorated with a band of interlocking arches and surmounted by a series of diminishing seven pointed stars. The strong, simple forms of the exterior stood in contrast to the delicately carved details of the interior. The *kufic* inscription above the doors identified the builder: "Ali Ibn Yusuf." Above the frieze rested the dome, supported by an octagon of scalloped arches. The space between the arches was carved with fir cones, palmettes, acanthus leaves—and scallop shells, identical to those carved in the great mosque of Cordoba. These motifs appeared here for the first

The Qubba al-Murabitin is the kiosk that housed an ablutions font in Marrakech, part of the large-scale beautification program of Ali Ibn Yusuf. (Photograph by the author.)

time on the African continent. It is clear that the Almoravids had seen Andalusian art, and they liked it! Ali Ibn Yusuf's architects had produced here a prototype that combined the simple strength of the desert home of the Almoravids with the jeweled elegance of Andalusian art.

Before long, Ibn Yusuf's city began to entice many of the merchants and craftsmen of Aghmat, some 20 miles away, to come settle in Marrakech. The center of politics and law attracted industry and commerce—and a swelling urban population. The first to come were the tanners. Because their trade depended on a large and steady supply of water, more than what the wells and man-made transportation systems could supply, they settled along the Issil River on the east side of town. There was ample space along the banks of the river to lay out the hides to dry, the henna reds and saffron yellows—both brilliant in the sunlight. They were far enough out so that the odor of the craft was not too offensive to the city's residents. Other trades followed. Because of the need for water, the potters and the brick makers also settled along the river. They could hardly keep up with the demand for bricks and tiles for all of the new construction. Soap makers and dyers, considered like the tanners to be among the "foul" trades, became established on the east side of Marrakech as well. In most Islamic cities, they were concentrated on the outskirts of town. They certainly were in Fez, and they were so by decree in Seville.

The open lanes that separated the clans and tribes that settled in town over the last three generations became permanent streets crossing town and connecting one gate with another. The main axes were from the *Bab* (gate) *al-Khamis*, on the north side of town where a weekly market was held every Thursday, to the *Bab Aghmat* on the southeast side of town, and from the *Bab Dukkala* on the northwest to the *Bab al-Naffis* on the southwest side.

There was no quarter for the Jews. Buckling under the pressure of the *faqih*s, Ali Ibn Yusuf had passed a decree forbidding Jews from living in the capital city, but Jews still came to Marrakech to do business. They were allowed to stay within the city during daylight hours, but come nightfall they were supposed to leave. Some returned to Aghmat, where there was a rather large settlement of Jews, whereas others, leaving through *Bab Aylan*, stayed in a ghetto on the outskirts of town.

On the north side of town, olive presses became a permanent fixture along the road to Fez, on the street named *Bayn al-Ma'asir* (between the presses). Although Marrakech was blessed with fruitful gardens and orchards, vineyards, and fruit trees of all kinds, the cultivation of olives dominated the local food production of the city. Between the oil presses and the Mosque of Ali, as it soon came to be called, the various craftsmen and merchants established the permanent positions that they would maintain for the history of the city. Many of the wealthy merchants, as the courtiers, built splendid houses in the city, while those whose wealth came from the land, such as plantation owners and sugar refiners, built richly decorated villas outside of town. Their fountained courtyards were bordered by colonnades covered in white stucco, carved in stylized floral patterns that the Almoravids had learned to admire in Andalusia.

In Marrakech, as in so many Islamic cities, the *suq*, or market place, radiated out in every direction from the mosque, the physical as well as metaphorical heart of the community. It was here at the mosque that the Malikite *faqih*s constituted the judicial arm of the state and gave political advice to the *Amir*. When Ali Ibn Yusuf referred a case to a Muslim judge or sought a legal opinion from one of them, he recommended that the judge not issue a ruling, however minor the issue, without the presence of four other *faqih*s. During his entire reign, Ali Ibn Yusuf never ruled on a single matter without consulting the legal scholars. He once asked the *faqih*s if the Almoravids would be obliged to remove the *litham*, the veil, from their face when they prayed. Those Almoravid warriors who settled in Marrakech, as in other urban centers in the Maghrib and Andalusia, continued the practice of veiling their face as they did in the desert. The *faqih*s ruled that the Almoravids could retain the veil. It set the Almoravids apart and made people conscious of their presence. The wearing of the veil made such an impact in Andalusia that the legal code in the city of Seville forbade the practice for all but the Almoravid militia. Other "less honest" mercenaries and brigands apparently wore the veil to strike fear in the hearts of the populace for their own profit.

The *faqih*s in the court at Marrakech, as well as those who served in every other major city in the Almoravid Empire, were paid for their service from the public treasury, and were paid very well. An Andalusian poet, Abu Ja'far, protested and wrote: "Hypocrites! You have gained recognition as a wolf that moves in the darkness of the night. The doctrine of Malik has made you masters of the world, and you have used the name of Abd al-Qasim (one of the principal compilers of Malikite law) to gather all your riches."

In a later poem, Abu Ja'far specifically attacked a particular *faqih*, the *qadi* of Cordoba, Abu Abd Allah Ibn Hamdin. He wrote: "Ibn Hamdin would have us seek justice from him, he who is further from generosity than he is from the sun! When he is asked to apply the customary law, he scratches his behind in affirmation of his pretentiousness."

This same Ibn Hamdin condemned the books of the famous Islamic theologian Abu Hamid al-Ghazzali, who revealed the science of jurisprudence of the Almoravid *faqih*s as a purely temporal pursuit having little or nothing to do with religion. Al-Ghazzali denounced the *faqih*s for abandoning the study of the Koran and the *Sunna* and for claiming to ensure the salvation of the soul by means of an empty legalistic exercise. Still worse, he criticized them for meddling in politics. "Better to be a fly on a heap of excrement," he told them, "than to be a theologian at the door of kings."

The *faqih*s felt threatened by al-Ghazzali's teaching. The *qadi* of Cordoba ruled that any man who read al-Ghazzali's *Ihya Ulum al-Din* (*The Revival of Religious Science*) was an infidel and was ripe for damnation. Possession of a copy was likewise a crime, and the *qadi* issued a *fatwa* to that effect. This presented the Almoravid *Amir* with a serious dilemma. Al-Ghazzali had earlier endorsed the Almoravid regime. Should the Almoravids side with the distinguished but distant theologian or with the local *qadi*? In the end, the local *qadi* won out.

During the first days of 503/August, 1109, in the small square in front of the west portal of the Great Mosque of Cordoba, the *faqih*s gathered in the presence of the *qadi*. They soaked a bound copy of the *Ihya* in oil and, in a scene that foreshadowed others in history, they burned it! Word went out over the empire to burn the works of al-Ghazzali, and these book burnings occurred in other cities, including the capital of Marrakech.

Scholars who defied the order risked severe reprisals. In Almeria, the Sufi Ibn al-Arif was interdicted. Ali Ibn Yusuf summoned him to Marrakech and then ordered his execution. The *Amir* later regretted his acquiescence to the *faqih*s—only too late to save the Sufi master. The scholar Ibn Barrajan was also brought from Cordoba to Marrakech, where he died in prison. Even the famous philosopher Ibn Bajja, who worked in the service of the state as vizier to the Almoravid governor of Zaragoza, was imprisoned for a short time for heresy. Abu Marwan, the *Amir*'s court physician, who had not only studied medicine but had a solid literary and juridical education as well, at one point referred to the *Amir* as "the wretched Ali." It was no surprise that the physician fell in disfavor of the *Amir* and was imprisoned in Marrakech.

Sijilmasa was known to be a sanctuary for religious dissidents, but even here religious tolerance was tested during these trying times. Abu'l-Fadl Ibn al-Nahuwi was a scholar who had immigrated to Sijilmasa from Tozeur. At the Mosque of Ibn Abd Allah, he taught dialectic reasoning and applied it to the study of dogma. He was especially interested in al-Ghazzali's *Ihya Ulum al-Din*, and he refused to comply with the edict to ban the book. In fact, he had more copies of it made. One day, Abd Allah Ibn Bassam came to the mosque to confront Abu'l-Fadl. Ibn Bassam was the *qadi* appointed by the Almoravid regime to uphold the law in Sijilmasa, and his authority was such that he could expel from the mosque, and even from the city itself, anyone who did not conform to the law of Malikite Islam.

Ibn Bassam interrogated the scholar and concluded that "he spreads learning about which we know nothing." Ibn Bassam banished Abu'l-Fadl from the mosque. Indignant, Abu'l-Fadl implored God to bring harm to Ibn Bassam. The next day, the *qadi* was killed by Sanhaja Berbers as he assisted at a marriage in the same mosque. Abu'l- Fadl fled to Fez, but he was also shunned by the *qadi* of that city.

By siding with the Almoravids and offering them a ready-made system of law, the *faqih*s, most of whom came from Andalusia, leap-frogged the power of the old Arabo-Andalusian aristocracy, who found the legists so repressive. But their influence was not unlimited. They could not dissuade the Almoravids from employing Andalusian intellectuals as *katib*s (secretaries), who were Andalusian to a man. These secretaries drafted the official letters for the chancellery, but they also frequently advised the rulers. Yusuf Ibn Tashfin had earlier attracted Ibn Qasira, the vizier of the Taifa king Mu'tamid in Seville, to work for him as secretary. Now, Ali Ibn Yusuf recruited Ibn Abdun, who had been the vizier for the Taifa king, Mutawakkil.

Ibn Abdun knew Seville very well, and that knowledge is the basis for his small manual on marketplace supervision that described the civil administration for the city. Although it describes city government in the city that he knew best, it provided a model for local government in other major cities of the empire and especially in Marrakech, where no urban institutions existed prior to the Almoravids.

In Seville, as in most cities, the Almoravid *Amir* had appointed a Lamtuna military governor supported by a garrison of Saharan warriors. The dark-skinned Berbers seemed conspicuously out of place in the sophisticated city streets, still dressed in their dark, blue robes and the *litham*, the veil that hung over their nose and mouth with only their eyes visible. The *litham* provided anonymity to those who enforced the law as well as to some who took advantage of the mark of distinction of these desert warriors. Andalusians came to fear these strange outsiders and preferred to keep their distance.

The most effective government in the cities of Andalusia and the Maghrib was the administrative structure that was already in place. In Andalusia, the Almoravids relied on the well-established political and judicial elite, *faqih*s, who interpreted the law, and other local officials. The chief *qadi* of each major city, the *qadi al-qudat*, was an official administrator for the Almoravid state, appointed by and exercising authority in the name of the Almoravid *Amir*. He was the most powerful and influential official in the entire administrative hierarchy under the Saharan military governor. Most *qadi*s were Andalusians, nominated by a local governor. But, as is made clear in a *fatwa* of the famous *qadi*, Ibn Rushd, the *Amir* had to ratify the appointment for it to be legitimate. As for the dismissal of a *qadi*, another *fatwa* of Ibn Rushd explains the procedure. The residents of Algeciras once complained about their *qadi* to the *Amir* Ali Ibn Yusuf, who submitted the complaint to the *qadi* of Ceuta for judgment. The latter judged against the *qadi* of Algeciras and recommended that he be dismissed. When the *qadi* demanded to be informed of the identity of his accusers, Ibn Rushd issued a *fatwa*, saying that a *qadi*'s "dismissal did not fall under the jurisdiction . . . of witnesses."

The chief *qadi*'s stated role was to "direct matters of religion and to protect the Muslim citizens." That rather broad mission gave to the *qadi* jurisdiction over much of the urban life of Seville, which was also the case in the other major Andalusian cities Cordoba, Granada, Murcia, and Valencia. The *qadi* was chief of the judiciary, and the chief reviewer of the law; he advised the Almoravid rulers how to govern in compliance with the edicts of the Holy Law of Islam—that is, as always, Malikite Islam. He was the superintendent of education; it was the *qadi* who set the standards to be met by the teachers in each of the neighborhood mosques that taught the Sevillian youth to recite the Koran and to respect the law. He supervised the treasury and was called upon to ensure that the tax assessors and collectors "weighed with a just scale." The qadi, whose power was both political and judicial, was at the head of a hierarchy of officials. To advise him, the *qadi* had a staff of legal counsels, two to serve him at his chambers and two more to serve at the Grand Mosque. The chief *qadi* did not usually rule on individual civil cases in the court. That was the job of secondary judges (*hakim*s), who sat at the Grand Mosque to hear such cases. Judges, *qadi*s and *hakim*s handed decisions over to officers (*awn*s) of the state who saw that their rulings were enforced. Some of the *awn*s were Almoravid officers who presided over those cases that involved people of the veil. The rest of the officers were Andalusians. In the Muslim world, law was personal rather than territorial, meaning that a person was subject to the law of his religious denomination (*madhhab*) rather than the law of the state. The Malikites, though, had gained so much control over western Islam, especially under the Almoravids, that no other *madhhab* was considered.

The Grand Mosque of Seville was much too small for the ever increasing population. Seville was not nearly as populous as Cordoba, but it was getting bigger all the time. The mosque had not undergone a single expansion since its corner stone was inscribed in the year 214/829-830 during the reign of the Umayyad Caliph Abd al-Rahman II. Now, at the time of Friday prayer, the faithful filled the prayer hall, spilled out into the lateral galleries, and even onto the square outside the mosque itself. The square and the streets leading to the mosque were always crowded and noisy. The bazaars that surrounded the mosque, the hawkers who set up temporary stalls on the stone and brick benches attached to the buildings, beggars, the beasts of burden, all made access to the mosque more difficult.

The official who could do something about this was the *muhtasib*, the supervisor of the marketplace. He was the *qadi*'s spokesman in the marketplace. It was his job to license the installation of each commercial enterprise in the city and to regulate the flow of commercial traffic in the town itself. He organized artisans of the same trade together along the same street, making that particular trade easier to regulate. He also decided where the hawkers could set up shop. In the vicinity of the Grand Mosque, the law forbade the sale of commodities that would impede traffic or dirty the streets. On Fridays, the shops could not open during the hour of congregational prayer. No beggars, horses, armed men, or children with dirty shoes were allowed around the mosque. The *muhtasib* and his appointee the *amin* were to ensure the accuracy of the weights and measures of the city's merchants. The *amin*'s job was to calibrate scales, to check the weights and counterweights, and to mark with his seal those that were within the margin of tolerance.

There were city building codes and regulations against throwing garbage in the streets. Each household was responsible for the upkeep of the street outside its door. The *qadi*'s responsibility extended to the cemetery on the outskirts of town. Here too, overcrowding in the city threatened the sacredness of the place. It was a favorite spot for the city's youth to congregate. Tanners and parchment makers were wont to lay out their skins to dry, and other merchants to set out their stalls. All of this activity impeded the women who came, face unveiled, to mourn.

The chief of police, the *sahib al-madina*, was also an Andalusian. His job was to maintain law and order in Seville. He employed a local police force to patrol the public space in and around the city both day and night. The *sahib*'s men conducted criminal investigations, interrogated witnesses, and when decisions of the court required, they incarcerated those condemned or subjected them to the whip. Troops from the Almoravid garrison were never far away. The mere presence of the veiled desert warriors in the streets of Seville, on the rare occasions that they appeared, inspired fear and respect on the part of the populace and lent authority to the Andalusian administrators.

The local officials did not always measure up to the task. In describing how government ought to be run, Ibn Abdun alluded to abuses that needed to be corrected, like the vicious extortions of the customs officials at the gates of the city and the brutal methods of the police and the night watchmen. Still, his manual provided sound advice to the Almoravid *Amir* and a good model for cities throughout the empire of local urban government with minimal centralization. Local officials provided the manpower and the skill to do the daily, nitty-gritty tasks of administration, office work, and bureaucratic work which had little appeal for the Saharan Sanhaja and for which they had little experience. It was an Andalusian model, and the Almoravids needed Andalusians to do it.

Ali Ibn Yusuf was one generation removed from the desert. He was settling in and even becoming quite comfortable in the urban environment of Marrakech, though he had not yet begun to fortify the city with heavy walls. The *faqih*s had provided him with a ready-made system of law, even though it was more strict, moralistic, and intolerant of personal expression than many of the Almoravids' subjects would have preferred. But they were willing to put up with all of that, at least as long as the Almoravid tax structure of no non-Koranic taxes and the commercial network that linked West Africa to the Mediterranean world brought such prosperity like they had never seen before.

Taxation, always a touchy issue with the Almoravids, was not a local matter. From the beginning, the Almoravid *Amir*s controlled the tax structure from the capital. For the first 50 years, they had been adamant in forbidding non-Koranic taxes, a tax break that was enthusiastically welcomed by their newly conquered subjects everywhere. The empire continued to collect the tithe (*zakat*) and the land tax (*kharaj*) and from the Christians and Jews the poll tax (*jizya*). For Ali Ibn Yusuf, this was not enough. He was felt compelled to reinstitute the *maghram*, a general term that meant taxes not proscribed in the Koran. Tax was levied on foodstuffs and on most manufactured goods. So unpopular was this decision that Ali Ibn Yusuf had to employ Christian mercenaries to collect the tax—a challenge to his popularity.

CHAPTER 12
Ali Ibn Yusuf Faces Muslim and Christian Challengers

Ali needed new tax revenues to finance his jihad in Andalusia. The Almoravids had been fighting a war against Christians in Andalusia for a full decade before Pope Urban II issued his call for crusade on the plains of Clermont in southern France. Muslim zeal to wage jihad against the Christians because they were Christian was a relatively new thing. During the last year of his life, Yusuf Ibn Tashfin had dispatched a fleet of 70 ships from the Atlantic port at Salé to Jaffa in Palestine to defend the port of Jerusalem. That was in the year 499/1105–1106, shortly after Muslim teachers and writers in Damascus and Baghdad began to call for jihad, a war to defend against the Christians who had invaded their land. The Christian crusade to the Holy Land of Jerusalem had started very shortly after Yusuf's diplomatic mission had officially recognized the authority of the caliph in Baghdad, and the caliph in return bestowed on Yusuf the titles Commander of the Muslims, Defender of the Faith, and Champion of the Cause of the *Amir* of the Faithful. The Almoravids had justified their presence in Andalusia by coming to the defense of their faith against the Christians and bringing moral reform to the Muslim aristocracy. The indigenous population of Andalusia, Mozarabs, felt the aftershock of this turn of events. At this very time, large numbers of Mozarabs from Malaga and its environs were deported to the Maghrib, the first such forced emigration under Almoravid rule.

Ali Ibn Yusuf, in turn, found himself committed to that defense and moral reform. He was determined not to incur the criticism of his own propagandists. That policy committed Ibn Yusuf to one campaign after another, some of them successful and some of them not, but all of them costly, in revenues, in manpower, and in some of the ablest commanders in his empire.

Within a year after coming to power, Ali Ibn Yusuf dispatched his brother Tamim to Andalusia to wage jihad against the Christians. Until that time, Tamim had been serving as commander of the garrison in Marrakech. He was now commander of the Almoravid forces in Andalusia from his new post in Granada. It was quite common for the *Amir* frequently to rotate the ablest and most trusted military commanders from his own family or tribe to respond to emergencies or simply to shore up his authority all over the empire.

In the year 502/1108, Tamim laid siege to the fortress of Uclés, a Christian stronghold between Cuenca and Toledo. The besieged Christians managed to get a message to Alfonso VI, who immediately dispatched an army to rescue them. Alfonso gave the command of this army to the ill-starred Garcia Ordoñez, entrusting to him the safety of his son and heir, Sancho, who was symbolically sent to fight at the tender age of nine. The chroniclers reported that it was Alfonso's wife who convinced him that he should send his son to confront Tamim, the son of the famous Almoravid.

Tamim doubted that he had the forces sufficient to continue the siege of Ulcés and to defend against the advancing Christian army. But his trusted commanders convinced him that he did. They said that the Christians were advancing with no more than 3,000 cavalrymen and that they were still some distance away. When the attack came, sooner than Tamim had expected, the Christian army numbered several thousand strong. Tamim's army could neither advance nor retreat. He was forced to fight. The Almoravids desperately fought a battle "like no one had seen before, and God gave victory to the Muslims." At the day's end, many prisoners were taken and many Christians had been killed, including Alfonso's son, Sancho. To demonstrate their dominance, the Muslim warriors burned the church of Ulcés to the ground.

Jihad against the Christians in Andalusia was important enough for the Almoravid *Amir* to come in person. On Thursday 15 *Muharram*, 503/14 August, 1109, Ali Ibn Yusuf set sail for Andalusia for the first time. He left Ceuta with an extraordinarily large army and crossed the straits to wage his own first jihad in Andalusia. He proceeded directly to Cordoba, where he stayed for one month before beginning his campaign. He had already dispatched Tamim to become the governor of Tlemcen.

Ali Ibn Yusuf began by taking the city of Talavera by assault, as well as 27 fortresses in the vicinity of Toledo. He also took Madrid and

Guadalajara. For one month, he scorched the earth in the vicinity of Toledo, but failed to take the city that had been the first to fall in the Christian *reconquista* started by Alfonso of Castile. Ibn Yusuf returned to Cordoba, and the first city that had fallen to the Christians in their reconquest of Andalusia remained in Christian hands.

Ibn Yusuf's father Yusuf Ibn Tashfin had always insisted that the key to the defense of Andalusia was the Taifa state of Zaragoza. He had instructed his son that in order to continue the war against the Christians, he had to maintain a peace with the Bani Hud who ruled there. Zaragoza had been a good buffer between Valencia and the Christian states of Barcelona and Aragon. Its independent king, Musta'in, had been a friend of El Cid and intermittent ally of Sancho Ramirez, king of Aragon and Navarre; and he maintained a delicate political balance between the Christians and Almoravids. But Musta'in did not trust diplomacy. He maintained a solid army of Christian mercenaries for those times when the balance tilted to one side or the other. In the month of *Rajab*, 503/January, 1110, Musta'in was killed on the plains of Valtierra in a skirmish against the Aragonese. He was succeeded by his son Imad al-Dawla. The young king was unable to counter the swell of Almoravid propaganda that had already taken root in Zaragoza. Under the threat of popular revolt, Imad al-Dawla Ibn Hud took refuge in Rueda in the region of Huesca, a small castle that the Bani Hud had used as a storehouse and a dungeon. There he maintained a low profile in his own little fief.

The death of Musta'in was a signal to the Almoravid *Amir* to make his move. Ali Ibn Yusuf transferred one of his ablest commanders, Muhammad Ibn al-Hajj, from his post in Fez to take command of the garrison in Valencia. His first and foremost responsibility was the conquest of Zaragoza. He did just that in the year 504/1110, and he established Zaragoza as his base from which he roamed the countryside between Valencia and Zaragoza, attacking one Christian stronghold after another and taking all the booty he could get, sending the booty home to Valencia. He continued on the march for four years.

In 508/1114, Ibn al-Hajj reached the outskirts of Barcelona, the sight of his final battle. His army was ambushed by a band of Christians in a pass so narrow that the Almoravid warriors were forced to march in single file. They were easy prey for the Christians. Ibn al-Hajj was killed along with most of his army.

This was the third time within a year that Ali Ibn Yusuf mourned the death of one of his tribesmen and key military governors in Andalusia. The first major loss had been Syr Ibn Abu Bakr, who had died and was buried in Seville. That commander had been a key to the Almoravid success against the Christians from the very start. In recent years, he had succeeded in taking the cities of Santarem, Badajoz, Oporto, Evora, and Lisbon, and he ranged more or less at will in the whole western part of Andalusia. To announce his victory in Santarem, Syr Ibn Abu Bakr instructed his secretary to address a letter to his *Amir*. The letter read: "The fortress of Santarem—may God permit the empire of the *Amir* of the Muslims to endure—was among the strongest that the polytheists had erected against the Muslims. But, following the strategy that you provided us, under your direction which is all that we needed, we relentlessly sought to remove this thorn." The letter continues to describe Syr Ibn Abu Bakr's success in gory detail, praising the commander in the full eloquence of the pen of Syr Ibn Abu Bakr's secretary.

The second Almoravid commander to fall in battle late in the year 508/spring 1115 was Mazdali, the longtime faithful servant of the family of Tashfin, the able commander and trustworthy diplomat who had twice negotiated a truce within the ruling family. For a year leading up to his death, he had conducted a mostly successful campaign in the north around Toledo and its dependent provinces, confronting among others the famous Christian King Alvar Fanez and sending valuable booty back to Cordoba. He was killed in battle fighting against the Castilians, and his body was taken back to Cordoba to be buried. Mazdali's son Abd Allah became the next governor of Granada.

While the Almoravids mourned the death of Mazdali, they occupied the Balearic Islands. In the month of *Dhu al-Qa'da*, 508/April, 1115, the ruler Mubasir Nasir al-Dawla, who had nominally recognized the authority of the Almoravids, died. An Almoravid squadron attacked Majorca. Its Christian population fled, leaving the city in flames. The Almoravids occupied the city without a fight. Ali Ibn Yusuf appointed the first of a succession of military governors over the Baleares.

To replace Muhammad Ibn al-Hajj as commander in Zaragoza, Ali Ibn Yusuf appointed Abu Bakr Ibn Ibrahim Ibn Tifilwit, a Massufa tribesman from the Sahara. Ibn Tifilwit made that city the Almoravid administrative center of eastern Andalusia. He then set out to avenge the death of Ibn al-Hajj. Ali Ibn Yusuf had no more maverick warrior in his service than Ibn Tifilwit, a legend in his own time. The Almoravid *Amir* had met him eight years earlier, in the year 500/1107–1108. He was a tribal leader among his people, when he left the desert in great haste following a mild indiscretion concerning his cousin's wife. As the story goes, he visited his cousin one day and was so overcome by his cousin's wife's beauty that he subconsciously uttered her name in his cousin's presence. When his cousin chided him, he felt shame and disgrace. The desert warrior mounted his camel and rode day and night until he reached Sijilmasa, the first of the provinces of his cousin, the *Amir* of the Almoravids. He felt somewhat overwhelmed in this bustling city. When he was hungry, he slaughtered one of the goats that he had with him. He invited a blacksmith whom he had just met to share his meal. When they finished eating, Ibn Tifilwit continued his journey with his new companion. When they reached Marrakech, Ibn Tifilwit sought an audience with the *Amir* Ali Ibn Yusuf. The *Amir* presented gifts to the man of the desert, fine thoroughbreds, a suit of clothes, and a thousand *dinar*s of gold. Ibn Tifilwit gave it all to the blacksmith. Ali Ibn Yusuf recognized the nobility of the Saharan. The *Amir* took the noble warrior into his service and offered the hand of his own sister in marriage. He then sent his new brother-in-law to Granada to fight the Christians. After a few years of distinguished service in the jihad against the Christians, he became governor of Murcia. And, finally, he was appointed governor of Zaragoza.

To avenge the death of Ibn al-Hajj, Ibn Tifilwit launched a full-scale, punitive campaign into Barcelona. For 20 days, he ravaged the countryside around the city, burning crops, uprooting trees, and leveling whole villages. The king, Raymond Berenger III, rushed home from a campaign in the Balearic Islands to defend his kingdom. He dispatched his bishop to France to seek the help of King Louis the Fat, warning that in five days the Almoravids could be in Monpellier and Saint-Gilles. The Christians, a combined army of Catalans, Aragonese, and French, marshaled a counterattack and forced the Almoravids to retreat to Zaragoza. For two years, Ibn Tifilwit ruled in Zaragoza in the fashion of a Taifa king. He wore the dress and regalia of kings and became seduced by the pleasures of courtly life, addicted to drinking wine. Always to the north was the pressure of the threat of a Christian attack by Alfonso I of Aragon, nicknamed El Batallador (the Fighter). Still, Ibn Tifilwit managed to provide relatively secure control over Zaragoza and the whole northeastern part of Andalusia for two years. In mid-year 510/1117, El Batallador seized the advantage and renewed the pressure that he had continually pressed against Zaragoza under the Bani Hud. Initially, Abd Allah Ibn Mazdali, who had been in Granada, came to the rescue and forced Alfonso to withdraw from the vicinity of Zaragoza, at least for the time being. But before the battle was over, Ibn Tifilwit had been killed.

Seeing that Almoravid control over Andalusia was slipping more and more from his grasp, Ali Ibn Yusuf ordered all of his commanders in Andalusia to rally under his brother Tamim. El Batallador had turned his attention against Lerida. By the beginning of the year 511/1117, Mazdali's son Ibn Mazdali and Ali's son Abu Yahya Ibn Tashfin arrived with their troops from Granada and Cordoba, respectively, and joined Tamim, who had come from Valencia with his Lamtuna warriors. In a direct confrontation between Muslim and Christian armies, the Christians took such heavy casualties that they had to withdraw.

In the meantime, El Batallador appealed for help to the nobility of southern France, men like Gaston de Bearn, Centule de Bigorre, and Bernard Ato de Carcassonne, who had taken part in the First Crusade. At a council held at Toulouse, Christian church leaders, bishops, and

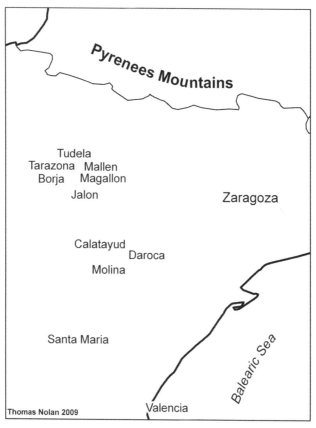

Northeast Andalusia. (© Thomas Nolan. Used by permission.)

archbishops urged French knights to join the crusade against Zaragoza. Pope Gelasius II, who was traveling through southern France at the time, granted crusade indulgences to all who joined their cause. When the Christian army convened, it included Aragonese, Catalans, Castilians, and Frenchmen. This combined force was ready now to turn its attention once again to Zaragoza. The Spanish *reconquista* was now very much identified with the larger Christian movement known as the Crusades.

The Christians laid siege to the city of Zaragoza in the month of *Muharram*, 512/May, 1118. The French, especially Gaston de Bearn, had experience using siege towers and catapults against the walls of Jerusalem, and they now directed the use of these war machines against Zaragoza. The Christian army encircled the city with tall, wooden siege towers and catapults. On the verge of famine, the population of Zaragoza sued for peace, hoping that rescue would come before they suffered total defeat at the hands of the Christians. As it turned out, the Muslim army sent from Adoua arrived too late to save them. Alfonso I had already entered the city in triumph on 3 *Ramadan*, 512/18 December, 1118. Zaragoza was in Christian hands.

The loss of Zaragoza was enough of a setback that Ali Ibn Yusuf came to Andalusia personally to assess the situation. This was his second voyage across the straits. He came with a large number of Almoravid warriors and Arab volunteers, as well as Zanata and Masmuda Berbers. He arrived in Cordoba and met with all of his commanders in Andalusia, asking them to describe the status of one city after another. Much of the news was not good. The Christians stood astride the Ebro River and soon began to move southward. Within a few months after the fall of Zaragoza, the city of Tudela fell to Alfonso's army on 9 *Dhu al-Qa'da*, 512/22 February, 1119. Soon after that, Mallen, Magallon, Borja, and Tarazona fell from Almoravid jurisdiction. The whole region south of the Ebro River and west of Zaragoza was now in Christian hands. And Alfonso was still marching south. In the spring of 514/1120, Alfonso besieged Calatayud and handed a relieving force of Almoravids at Cutanda the worst defeat they had suffered thus far. As a result, Calatayud and Daroca fell to the Aragonese, and the frontier was pushed well south of the Ebro. The northern tip of the Almoravid Empire was lost. Ali Ibn Yusuf set up his defense in the city of Santa Maria to prevent further advances by the Christian army. He resorted to a scorched earth policy, burning fruit trees and destroying houses in the region to slow the Christian advance, which was gaining momentum.

If the situation in Andalusia was not bad enough, back in Marrakech, a challenger of Ali Ibn Yusuf's own faith arrived in the capital city in the winter of 514/1121. His name was Ibn Tumart. Born in the small village of Igiliz some 30 years earlier, high in the Atlas Mountains south of Marrakech, Ibn Tumart, even as a child, was interested in little more than the study of religion. As a teenager, he, like many Maghribis, had an irresistible desire to make the pilgrimage to the Orient and to study there with some of the great masters. He left home in the year 500/1105 and, over the next 15 years, spent time in several centers of learning including Cordoba, Alexandria, Baghdad, and ultimately Mecca itself. In each of these places, he studied with some of the most prominent *ulama*, religious scholars, of Ash'arite theology. It is likely that he even met the famous al-Ghazzali, whose books the Almoravids had burned in 503/1109.

Central to the teaching that Ibn Tumart was now spreading around the countryside was the absolute unity of God, what Muslims call *tawhid*, a notion that was contrary to the much more personal image of God held by the Malikite *faqih*s, who had taught the Almoravids. Ibn Tumart openly criticized the Almoravids, calling them *mujassimun*, anthropomorphists. Likewise, he criticized the Almoravids for their strict reliance upon the books of Malikite law, rather than being open to the use of analogical interpretation of the Koran and traditions of the Prophet. He taught that the *imam* should be a person of impeccable virtue, that it was his duty, nay, everyone's duty, to promote good and combat evil, even if that meant rebelling against the *imam*.

On his way back home from the Orient, Ibn Tumart gained quite a reputation as a strict censor of mores at each place that he stopped. Many viewed him as a troublemaker. In the city of Bijaya on the Atlantic coast east of Algiers, for example, at the time of the *Id al-Fitr* (the feast of the breaking of the fast of *Ramadan*), he took a stick to a group of men and women whom he saw intermingling in the streets. He went so far as to criticize the Hamdanid sovereign al-Aziz Ibn al-Mansur for surrounding himself with the pleasures of life. The people of Bijaya turned on him and chased him out of town.

Closer to home in Fez, Ibn Tumart was received warmly at first. But when he and some of his companions began to smash drums, castanets, flutes, and guitars, the townspeople complained to their *qadi*. When Ibn Tumart introduced Ash'arite doctrine into a discussion attended by the Malikite *faqih*s of Fez, he was forced to leave the city.

When Ibn Tumart arrived in the capital of Marrakech, he proceeded directly to the "mosque with the mud-brick minaret." He went unnoticed in the capital until he began to censure the mores of the people and went around overturning vats of wine and smashing musical instruments. On Friday, he went to the community mosque where he met the *Amir* Ali Ibn Yusuf. Ali Ibn Yusuf was wearing a veil, as his Lamtuna custom dictated. Ibn Tumart refused to acknowledge the presence of the *Amir*, saying, "I only see veiled women here." When the *Amir* removed the veil, Ibn Tumart said, "The caliphate belongs to God, not to you." He reminded the *Amir* that a ruler had to answer to God for the sins of his people, that those sins that the ruler did not condemn would be placed on his account on judgment day. Finally, Ibn Tumart rebuked the *Amir* for sitting in the mosque on a mat that was ritually unclean, because of the dung used in the dye.

When the Friday prayer was over and the faithful had left the mosque, Ibn Tumart reentered to discuss law with the *faqih*s. Having studied with Ash'arite jurists, he tended to read the Koran as allegory. He rebuked the Malikite *faqih*s for limiting themselves to the literal interpretations of the early Muslims, for viewing God in corporal form. For this, Ibn Tumart accused them of being infidels.

Ibn Tumart spent the next few days at the Arafa Mosque. The final affront came when Ibn Tumart met the *Amir*'s sister riding through the streets of Marrakech. She, as was the custom of all Lamtuna women from the Sahara, did not veil her face. The preacher was shocked. He ordered her to cover herself as he slapped the haunch of her mount. The animal was startled and threw its rider to the ground.

Ali Ibn Yusuf, indulgent at first, could no longer let the rantings of the itinerant preacher go unchecked. Upon the advice of Malik Ibn Wuhayb, one of the most prominent *faqih*s in Ali Ibn Yusuf's court, the *Amir* summoned Ibn Tumart to the palace. Ibn Tumart arrived dressed in poor clothes and saying that he was a simple, poor man who was more concerned with the next world than with this one. He then began to debate with the *faqih*s in the *Amir*'s presence.

"Are there any limits to the path of science," Ibn Tumart asked, "yes or no?" One of the *faqih*s answered, "Yes, it is limited by the Koran, the *Sunna*, and its commentaries." This answer was consistent with the rather narrow base of Malikite law. But it was not the answer that Ibn Tumart sought. He came back at the *faqih*s, saying that the sources of good and evil are four: knowledge, which is the right path, and ignorance, doubt, and opinion, which are the source of evil. The *faqih*s fell silent and were embarrassed.

Malik Ibn Wuhayb recognized that the fiery preacher had the ability to stir people, and that if he got to the Masmuda tribes to the south he could well foment a rebellion. "Put him in prison," Ibn Wuhayb advised. But Yintan Ibn Umar appealed to the *Amir*'s piety, saying that it would not be prudent to imprison a man who was so wise in matters of religion. Yintan was one of the *Amir*'s closest confidants; he was of Ali Ibn Yusuf's own Lamtuna tribe, his vizier and commander of the mercenary troops in Marrakech. The *Amir* took Yintan's advice over that of Ibn Wuhayb and decided to banish Ibn Tumart.

Just as Ibn Wuhayb had warned, Ibn Tumart fled immediately to the south. He went first to the city of Aghmat. where he found an ally in the Masmuda *faqih* Abd al-Haqq. He also ran into more opposition when he resumed the role of the reformer. The people of Aghmat sent a message to Marrakech complaining of his presence, and Ibn Tumart had to flee to the mountains, to the territory of the Bani Masmuda, an area just beyond the effective control of the Almoravids. He went to Igiliz, his ancestral home, and built a small *ribat*, a convent, where he gathered around himself a band of followers. In a Friday sermon in the month of *Ramadan*, 515/November, 1121, Ibn Tumart preached in eloquent Berber his reform theology, a body of teaching that included overt anti-Almoravid propaganda. To him, the Almoravids were worse than polytheists; they were Muslims who placed so much emphasis on their books of law that they elevated those books to the status of God—certainly a justifiable reason to wage jihad against them. The next day, flanked by his circle of 10 closest associates with their sabers at their side, he ascended the *minbar* and announced that he was *Imam al-Mahdi*, the "Guided One," the expected restorer of true Islam who would conquer the world for the true faith. He told them that the true word was that of the Koran and the traditions of the Prophet rather than the secondary works of Malikite *faqih*s, or jurists of any other school, for that matter. These Masmuda mountain tribes became Ibn Tumart's main support. He had great appeal among them because he was one of them, and he became the leader of their community, their religious teacher, and their arbitrator of disputes. Their attachment to him and his teaching was profoundly from the heart. Because of Ibn Tumart's insistence on the doctrine of the absolute oneness of God, *tawhid*, his followers became known as *al-muwahidun*. We call them the Almohads.

Once again, Malik Ibn Wuhayb urged his *Amir* to get rid of this potential threat. This time, Ali listened. He sent a band of horsemen to arrest Ibn Tumart, who now enjoyed the protection of Abu Hafs Umar, a prominent chief of the Bani Hintata. Ali's men captured several of Ibn Tumart's followers, including Abu al-Hasan Yugut

Ibn Wajjaj, one of Ibn Tumart's inner circle, but Ibn Tumart himself eluded arrest.

The Almoravid *Amir* intensified his effort to halt Ibn Tumart's mounting threat. He ordered the Lamtuna governor of the Sus, Abu Bakr Ibn Muhammad al-Lamtuni, to lead an Almoravid armed band against the Bani Hargha, the tribe of Ibn Tumart, where the rebellious preacher was then hiding. This time the Bani Hargha had advance warning and had the help of her sister tribes, the Bani Hintata and the Bani Tinmallal. The Almoravids were caught in a surprise ambush outside the village of Igiliz. They fled, leaving their tents and many of the arms, shields, helmets, and lances in the field, all to the benefit of the Masmuda Berbers. Encouraged by this first major victory over the Bani Lamtuna, the *Mahdi* called other tribes in the region to war against Almoravid authority.

Ibn Tumart placed each tribal contingent of his troops under the command of men who were especially devoted to him, men who were strangers to the tribe under their command. Each unit was under a flag of a different color. The *Mahdi* placed a white flag in the hand of Abd al-Mu'min and put him in command of the Bani Gadmiwa. He handed Abu Ibrahim a yellow flag and placed him in command of the Bani Hargha. To Ibn Malwiya he handed a red flag and placed him in command of the Bani Ganfisa. Yalattan became the commander of the Bani Tinmallal. Only the Bani Hintata were commanded by one of their own, Umar Inti.

The Almoravid *Amir* sent one military contingent after another to root Ibn Tumart from these treacherous mountain hideaways. Time and time again, the Almoravids, completely ill at ease in this mountainous terrain, were either evaded or ambushed, and they returned to Marrakech defeated, empty-handed. The *Mahdi* generously distributed the booty taken from the Almoravids among those who promised to support him, hoping to buy their continued loyalty. The Almohads would learn, as the Almoravids had learned more than a half century earlier, that the mountain tribes of the Masmuda were fiercely independent. It would take such distributions of booty and occasional military reprisals to maintain his grasp on the Atlas and the Sus. His success was an ever increasing threat to the Almoravids.

In direct response to this new military threat posed by Ibn Tumart *al-Mahdi*, late in the year 515/1121–1122, Ali ordered the building of massive walls around the city of Marrakech. The perimeter was roped off to include all of the city, a 15-sided polygon almost six miles around, about one mile from north to south, and about the same distance from east to west. They built hurriedly, using sun-dried mud. The Sanhaja had seen this type of construction before. The walls at Sijilmasa had been built this same way. The workers built the wall in courses by means of a wooden shuttering about two and a half feet high. For the first course, they placed the shuttering directly on the ground and placed each successive course on three putlogs, which rested on the wall below. The workers, using heavy wooden rams, in a steady rhythm pounded a mixture of moist loam, chopped straw, and gravel into the forms. As soon as the course was dry enough, the shuttering was detached, leaving round putlog holes in the wall, which were filled with loam or closed off with a flat stone.

When the wall was finished, it was almost 20 feet tall and 4 to 5 feet thick, all the way around Marrakech. There was a tower every 30 yards or so with a parapet of merlons at the top. Like the walls of Sijilmasa, these at Marrakech were broken by 12 gates. Some of the gate complexes required two or three right angle turns to pass from the exterior to the interior of the city walls, designed that way to discourage frontal attack. The walls completed the definition of urban space in Marrakech while they offered protection against external threat, which seemed to be increasingly imminent.

CHAPTER 13
Voices of Dissent

"Since Andalusia rejects me," wrote a poet from Cordoba, "I shall flee to Iraq, and, there, everyone will rise to greet me." His verse continued, "The profession of the intellect has lost all vitality since it is a life embraced only by those of low extraction and vile manners." He was speaking here of the *faqih*s who represented the law of the Almoravids. And "God does not break the shaft of the lance since that is what brings grandeur; but it is decreed that speech must be silenced." The poet resented the presence of the Almoravid militia as much as the stifling of intellectuals.

Voices of dissent were beginning to speak ever more loudly throughout the empire. What began as whispers were now being heard as outcries of criticism. There were rumors that

> Almoravid chiefs raised pretensions of independence in the various parts of the empire where they exercised authority... [that] women themselves, members of the principle families among the Lamtuna and Massufa, ruled and became the patrons of worthless, evil men, brigands, wine merchants and tavern owners... [while the *Amir* himself] was satisfied in exercising nominal authority and collecting taxes; the *Amir* thought of nothing other than his religious and spiritual practices; he prayed throughout the night and fasted throughout the day, all while he neglected the interests of his subjects.

By this time, the Andalusian citizens had grown weary of Almoravid administration with all its promises of moral reform and abolition of

Western Andalusia. (© Thomas Nolan. Used by permission.)

illegal taxes. Moral reform, on the one hand, was seen as a ruse for the Almoravids, made anonymous by the veil that covered their faces, to impose their will arbitrarily and to install a clique of Malikite *faqih*s in power. Moreover, moral reform brought with it the obligation to wage jihad against the Christians to the north. Jihad demanded resources, so Ali Ibn Yusuf had been forced to revert to older practices of taxation. That had a negative impact on the average person's pocketbook.

The citizens of Cordoba were just waiting for an incident to spark their hostility at the beginning of the year 515/1121. It came on a feast day, the first day of the year, March 22 of the Christian calendar. A black slave in the Almoravid guard molested a woman in the open street. The victim cried for help, and a fight broke out between a crowd of passersby and the soldiers. The riot lasted most of the day. Meanwhile, a delegation of Cordoban notables went to the governor and demanded that the man who had caused the scandal be put to death. Ali Ibn Yusuf's governor in Cordoba, Abu Bakr Yahya Ibn Rawwad, did exactly the opposite. He unleashed his soldiers on the city.

The whole population of Cordoba reacted. Legists, notables, and youngsters whose fathers a generation ago had begged the Almoravids to come to their aid took up arms against the militia. The soldiers retreated to the citadel and the Cordobans immediately laid siege. They stormed the *qasba*, they sacked the palace, and they pillaged and burned the houses of the Almoravids. Ibn Rawwad and his soldiers, fearful for their lives, barely escaped the city.

Ali Ibn Yusuf crossed over once again into Andalusia with a contingent of troops and laid siege to Cordoba. Its inhabitants fought with a tenacity of those who fought for their women, for their property and for their very lives. Ali Ibn Yusuf was touched by their spirit and by the justice of their cause. He agreed to negotiate. The *Amir* granted *aman*, immunity from punishment, to the Cordobans on condition that they compensate for the destruction they caused in the city. The Cordobans grudgingly accepted. When the incident was over, the *qadi* of Cordoba, Ibn Rushd, resigned from his post, and the *Amir* accepted his resignation.

Ali Ibn Yusuf spent most of the next year in Andalusia reviving his jihad against the Christians. He focused his efforts in the West in the region of Santarem, even though the main thrust of the Christian *reconquista* led by King Alfonso of Aragon was in the East along the Ebro River. Ali's forces were stronger in the West, strong enough at least to fulfill his ideological obligation to wage jihad. When the *Amir* finally returned to Marrakech, he left his brother Tamim in charge as governor of Andalusia with fewer troops than he would have liked.

Voices of dissent were not confined to far-off Andalusia. Just to the south of Marrakech, the Almohad movement of the dissident preacher Ibn Tumart now presented a military threat, so that Ali Ibn Yusuf was condemned to fight a two-front war. For the rest of his life, the Almoravid *Amir* would have to shift his focus several times back and forth between Andalusia and the Maghrib. He really needed to give constant, total attention to both sides of the straits, but that proved to be impossible.

At the same time that Ali Ibn Yusuf built walls around the city of Marrakech late in the year 515/1121–1122, Ibn Tumart was proclaimed to be the *Mahdi*, the "Guided One" sent to restore Islam to its original vitality. The *Mahdi* preached to the tribes in the Atlas Mountains and in the Sus. He condemned the regime of the Almoravids, whom he

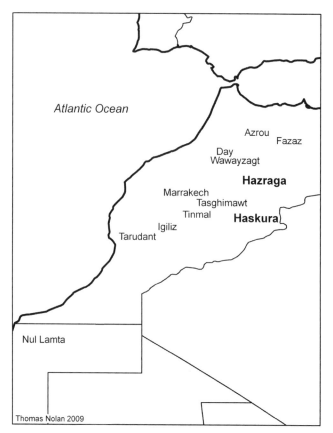

Southwestern Maghrib. (© Thomas Nolan. Used by permission.)

described as unshod, threadbare, and miserable shepherds who were ignorant of God's command before they had come out of the Western Sahara. Now, claimed Ibn Tumart, the Almoravids were shepherds turned kings. They were arrogant and ostentatious in their buildings; they begot offspring by slave women and enjoyed the company of slave girls; and they were deaf and dumb to the truth and were untrustworthy, for they did not carry out the dictates of God. Ibn Tumart promised that he would abolish evil and all illegal taxes. When preaching failed to win over a tribe, Ibn Tumart was not above resorting to skirmishes and surprise attacks. He soon won most of the tribes of the Bani Masmuda confederation to his cause.

In 518/1124, Ibn Tumart decided to withdraw to a stronghold that would be easier to defend. He settled in Tinmal, a village located deep in a canyon between two mountains in the High Atlas, due south from

Marrakech. The name Tinmal means "white," descriptive of a place surrounded by mountains that are covered with snow for much of the year. The valley abounded with trees, cultivated fields, and running water. The village could be approached on horseback only from two directions, the east or the west. Both roads were so narrow that only one horseman could pass abreast, and at times the horseman would have to dismount for fear of falling. In places, gaps between ridges were bridged by wooden planks, which could easily be removed. Ibn Tumart raised ramparts around the village and constructed a fortress-mosque within. Of the 70 or so fortresses in the Atlas, Tinmal became the most impregnable!

The Almohad *Mahdi* did not trust the local inhabitants any more than they trusted him, nor did he tolerate any opposition. To disarm the suspicions of the people, Ibn Tumart would camp outside the town and enter only after the end of the evening prayer. One day, when the people had left their weapons at home, Ibn Tumart ordered the massacre of, allegedly, 15,000 men. He imprisoned their women and distributed their belongings among the loyal Almohads. Those who were now called *Ahl Tinmallal*, people of Tinmal, were not

The Tinmal Mosque was part of the impregnable fortress in the High Atlas Mountains south of Marrakech, which served as the center of Almohad opposition to the Almoravids. (Photograph by the author.)

indigenous inhabitants but rather a heterogeneous group of Almohad supporters. They were also called *muhajirun*, "emigrants," as were the first followers of the prophet Muhammad.

Ibn Tumart pointed out to the people of Tinmal that many of their children had light complexions and blue eyes, whereas their fathers had very dark skin and dark eyes. It was the legacy of the Christians who came every year to collect taxes for the Almoravid *Amir* in Marrakech, he said. He told them to let the tax collectors into their homes the next time they came and then to kill them during the night. He assured the people of Tinmal that they had nothing to fear, because the fortress was strong enough to prevent retaliation. The people complied and killed the Christian tax collectors during the night. Only one Christian escaped, because he had gone out from his host's house to relieve himself.

Ali Ibn Yusuf was angered at the news and ordered an expedition to Tinmal to punish the guilty ones. As the Almoravid soldiers approached, Ibn Tumart told the people of Tinmal to hold back their fire. When the Almoravids were finally in range, a shower of stones fell upon them from above. They battled for a whole day, but then the Almoravid soldiers had to give up and retreat to Marrakech.

During the next six years after his move to Tinmal, Ibn Tumart launched several attacks against Almoravid partisans throughout the High Atlas, but only in the highlands. Wary of the plains that separated him from Marrakech, Ibn Tumart did not stray too far from his mountain stronghold. Once, when he attacked the Almoravid fortress of the Bani Imadidan on the western limit of the Tasghimawt plateau, Ali Ibn Yusuf dispatched a force under the command of Umar Ibn Dayyan to defend the fortress. In the battle that followed, the *Mahdi* fell from his horse, but he was rescued and managed to return to Tinmal. Umar Ibn Dayyan returned to Marrakech, and both sides claimed victory.

In the year 524/1130, Ali Ibn Yusuf again sent a large contingent of Almoravid troops south from Marrakech into the mountains to confront the forces of the *Mahdi*. The troops were under the command of the *Amir*'s brother, Tamim. When they reached the plateau that separates the corridor between the Regaya River and the Nafis River, the baggage train was attacked and the Almoravids lost most of their supplies. Tamim decided to retreat to Aghmat. He was pursued by Almohad forces under the command of Abd al-Mu'min all the way to the very walls of Aghmat. The Almoravid commander Ibrahim Ibn Tabast was killed, as were many of the citizens of Aghmat who tried to flee the city at the onset of the conflict. The Almoravids continued to retreat all the way back to Marrakech, and the momentum carried the Almohads behind them in close pursuit.

The Almohad army that prepared to lay siege to the Almoravid capital city was under the command of Abd al-Mu'min, who had been the *Mahdi*'s closest disciple since the two first met in Algeria more than a decade earlier. They approached from the southwest. The dust rising from the hoof beats of the enemy's mounts was visible for some distance, and, perhaps for no reason other than to see what was going on, many of the city's inhabitants came out of the city through the *Bab al-Shari'a*. When the Almohads charged, the people of Marrakech fell back toward the gate. There was confusion and terrible disorder among the citizens who tried desperately to reenter the city before the gates were closed. A large number were crushed or killed by the charging Almohads. Abd al-Mu'min's army then retreated to the heights on the east side of the city, overlooking the *Bab al-Debbagh*, and laid siege to the city for the next 40 days.

Abd al-Mu'min had sent a message to the besieged population of Marrakech urging them to surrender their allegiance to Ali Ibn Yusuf, to renounce their heresy, and to recognize the *Mahdi*, warning that if they did not, he was under orders to destroy the city. Ali Ibn Yusuf, in turn, reminded the attackers of the law forbidding the shedding of blood within the Muslim community. Somehow, he doubted that would assuage the determination of the besieging army for, at the same time, the *Amir* had called in reinforcements from every region of the empire, from Andalusia, the Balearic Islands, and Sijilmasa.

There were several battles during the next 40 days. If a certain chronicler is to be believed, the battles were so fierce that the Almohads refrained from saying the regular prayers of *Zuhr* and *Asr*, but rather said a prayer of fright. When Ali Ibn Yusuf heard that reinforcements from Sijilmasa were approaching, he took courage and ordered an attack against the besiegers. The battle on the plain of al-Buhayra took place on Saturday, 2 *Jumada al-Ula*, 524/14 April, 1130. The Almoravid commander, Ibn Humushk, led a sortie of 300 cavalrymen out through the Bab Aylan. He ordered his men to shorten their lances to make them easier to maneuver. They attacked the Almohads and returned with three heads atop the lances.

Ali Ibn Yusuf led the next charge himself. The battle took a heavy toll on the Almohad army. The noteworthy commander Al-Bashir al-Wansarisi was killed on that day, and Abu Hafs Umar Ibn Yahya, another principal commander, was wounded. Half of the Almohad Council of Ten were dead, as were 12,000 men of the Hargha tribe.

Abd al-Mu'min himself "was struck by so many arrows, that his shield resembled a porcupine." After burying the dead and tending the wounded, the Almohads took advantage of the alluvial rains to retreat back to Tinmal. The forces of the *Mahdi*, skilled at guerrilla warfare in mountainous terrain, were no match for the Almoravids, who had fought and won so many times on flat and open ground like the plains that surrounded Marrakech. In addition to the favorable terrain on this day, the Almoravids also enjoyed superiority in numbers. They had the reinforcements from Sijilmasa plus the full support of the people of Marrakech.

Four months after the siege of Marrakech, during the month of *Ramadan*, 524/August, 1130, the *Mahdi*, Ibn Tumart, died. Abd al-Mu'min succeeded to Ibn Tumart's position of authority. Twelve years earlier, Ibn Tumart had attached Abd al-Mu'min to his own tribe by adoption and had given him a place in the Council of Ten. Abd al-Mu'min had taken part in all the expeditions and had a say in the deliberations of the general staff. Now, he took charge of the Almohad war against the Almoravids. Drawing a lesson from the crushing defeat on the plains of al-Buhayra, Abd al-Mu'min decided to avoid the plains where the Almoravid cavalry and closed rank infantry formations had a decided advantage. He would concentrate on securing the mountain passes that would give him undisputed control over the crucial trade routes to the south, the lifeline of the Almoravids in Marrakech and the link to their original homeland in the desert.

Meanwhile, Ali Ibn Yusuf recruited an Andalusian by the name of al-Fallaki to organize the defense of the plains. Al-Fallaki was an audacious highway bandit whom Ali Ibn Yusuf had pardoned in order to be assured of his good service. Al-Fallaki's plan was to build a string of fortresses along the north slope of the High Atlas Mountains between the Issil River and the Wurika River. The belt extended as far as the Wurika so the Almoravids could also defend the city of Aghmat, still a vital economic center at the foot of the mountains. The fortresses were built hurriedly out of rock rubble laid in alternating thick and thin courses. Ali did not want to risk losing his best warriors in a mountain campaign, so he manned these forts with local partisans; he convinced those rulers in the mountains who were still loyal to him to wage guerrilla warfare against the Almohads.

Abd al-Mu'min decided to attack the belt of fortresses along the northern rim of the Atlas in the year 526/1131. The fortress of Tasghimawt was his first target. This stronghold was located about

20 miles southeast of Marrakech and 6 miles from Aghmat. Because of the element of surprise attack, the Almoravid garrison of 200 cavalry and 500 infantry offered little resistance. The fort was taken in one night. The victors destroyed the fort and transported the heavy doors to Tinmal, where they were used to close the gate of the potters.

Abd al-Mu'min's march continued eastward to force back into submission the Hazraga and the Haskura tribes who had renounced Almohad doctrine. The loyalty of the mountain tribes of the Masmuda had been far from certain. If they were loyal to an outsider, that loyalty was superficial and temporary. But after nearly a decade of warfare, most of the tribes in the High Atlas and in the Sus found it easier to support a leader from among themselves rather than the Almoravids.

Between the war against the Almohads in the Atlas and the jihad against the Christians in Andalusia, Ali Ibn Yusuf needed cash. He also needed to inspire confidence in the central government; he had to convince his subjects that the empire was prosperous and secure. Gold coins, *dinar*s bearing the name of "Ali Ibn Yusuf, Commander of the Faithful," were the most visible sign of Ali's authority—at least among those who handled money. New *dinar*s were struck in huge quantities in the official mints all over the empire. In the year 524/1130, production of *dinar*s in North African mints surpassed that of Andalusian mints for the first time in 28 years. The mint in Marrakech continued to produce coins, of course, but Ali's authority was secure there, especially after he successfully defended the city against Almohad invasion. His authority was secure in Aghmat and Sijilmasa as well. To benefit from the use of money as propaganda, it was more important to issue coins from cities where loyalty was in question, such as in Nul Lamta, located southwest of Marrakech in the Sus, an area whose governor was still loyal to the Almoravid regime but under heavy pressure from the Almohads. The most productive mint of all on the African side of the empire was Fez. Local opposition there was at its peak, led by the intelligentsia, many of whom had come to Fez from Andalusia. The mints in Almeria and other Andalusian cities along the Mediterranean seaboard continued to produce *dinar*s in large quantities.

The gold for all of this production continued to come from south of the Sahara, but it came along an eastern route, north from Timbuctu, through Taghaza, Warjala, Tlemcen, the Mediterranean port of Oran, and across to eastern Andalusia—a route controlled by the Bani Massufa who, like the tribe of the Almoravids, were part of the Sanhaja tribal confederation. With the Almohads placing a stranglehold on the routes going directly south from Marrakech, the Almoravids depended more and more on their co-confederationists within the Sanhaja to secure a more eastern route. In the year 520/1126, Ali Ibn Yusuf appointed two Massufa noblemen to important posts in eastern Andalusia. He appointed Muhammad Ibn Ali Ibn Ghaniya governor of the Balearic Islands and Yahya Ibn Ali Ibn Ghaniya governor of Cordoba. They were sons of Ali Ibn Yusuf al-Massufi, one of the bravest and most influential chiefs of the Bani Massufa, who had occupied a high position in the court of Yusuf Ibn Tashfin. Now, Yusuf Ibn Tashfin's son Ali was paying off a family debt by making these appointments. He was extending the links between the Bani Massufa and the Almoravids and solidifying the network that ranged from Timbuctu to eastern Andalusia, facilitating the flow of wealth all along the way.

The appointments of the Massufa nobles were also made to offset the steady loss of Lamtuna commanders in the ongoing jihad against the Christians in Andalusia. Even as Ali Ibn Yusuf was embarking for his return voyage to Africa in 516/1122, Alfonso I of Aragon, El Batallador, led an army made up of his own Aragonese troops and some French crusaders against an Almoravid army led by Ali's brother, Ibrahim Ibn Yusuf. Ibrahim's army consisted of army regulars and a large number of volunteers, pious Muslims from Africa who felt that it was their duty to come to Andalusia to wage jihad.

Indigenous Christians, the Mozarabs, had been living among the Muslim population for some time in cities like Seville, Cordoba, Toledo, and Saragossa. In some places, such as Valencia, they lived in Mozarab quarters or in suburbs outside of the city. There were incidents when a certain *faqih* might issue a *fatwa* against the Mozarabs, as was the case in 492/1099 when Yusuf Ibn Tashfin ordered the destruction of their church in Granada, and the Muslim population set out to enforce it with gusto. For the most part, they went about their daily lives like anyone else, as long as they paid the *jizya*, the tax owed by non-Muslims. As the war between the Almoravids and the Christian kings to the north heated up, life became more difficult for them. Whatever security they had earlier under Almoravid rule became jeopardized with the arrival of Christians from the north.

In Granada, Ibn al-Kalas, leader of the Mozarab community, convinced the king of Aragon that certain Almoravid strongholds of Andalusia were poorly guarded, and that having sent most of their ablest troops back to Africa, they would not be able to offer much resistance. He also assured the Christian king that the Arab Christians would welcome him with open arms and would, in large numbers, join the ranks of his army.

In the summer of 519/1125, Alfonso assembled an army of 400 cavalrymen followed by their-men-at arms. Again, there were Frenchmen among the ranks of the Aragonese under the command of Gaston de Bearn. Keeping secret the exact route and military objectives from the troops, El Batallador led his army south from Zaragoza. He followed a mountain route where his soldiers were in their own element and the Almoravids were ill at ease. He arrived quite by surprise in the plains on the outskirts of Valencia where, in fact, a large number of Mozarabs did indeed join his ranks. They were most useful in serving as guides and providing crucial intelligence reports. He did not have the siege machines necessary to take the walled city, so he passed it by and moved on to Alcira, another city with a significant Mozarab population that lived in a suburb called *al-Kanisa*, "the church." Again, he passed the city by, picking up still more Mozarab recruits. On the night of the feast of *al-fitr*, the ending of the fast of Ramadan, he attacked Denia and ravaged its surroundings. By now it was late autumn and the granaries were full, the olives gathered, the wine pressed, and the flocks were in from the mountains. The season was perfect for taking booty, and the Christians pillaged everything in their path. Then, Alfonso marched on to Murcia. It seems that he chose his route of march because of the location of large Mozarab populations, from which he planned to tap the resource of recruits promised to him.

It was the dead of winter by the time the Christian army reached Granada. Ali Ibn Yusuf's brother Tamim was in Granada preparing his defenses. The population prayed a *salat al-hawf*, a prayer of fear, and kept their weapons at close hand. But, even though Alfonso's army grew with Mozarabs coming over to his side, he still lacked the resources to take a well-fortified, walled city. It is rumored that he reproached Ibn al-Kalas for having overstated the ease of victory. Ibn al-Kalas reportedly answered that the Christian army, seduced by the prospects of booty, had advanced far too slowly, giving the Muslims time to establish their defenses.

El Batallador withdrew and marched toward Cordoba. He pillaged the countryside around Ecija, Luques, Baena, Cabra, and Aguilar. Tamim followed the campaign step for step but did not dare attack. Finally, on 11 *Safar*, 520/9 March, 1126, Tamim knew he had to take the offensive. At Arnisol, not far from Lucena, the two armies clashed. Tamim launched a surprise attack at first light and managed to assail but a few Christian tents. The Christian army, divided into four columns, counterattacked. Tamim was forced to abandon his position to seek higher ground, causing his troops to fall into complete disarray. The Almoravids were overtaken by panic and began to retreat. By nightfall, Tamim had abandoned his camp, which was taken by the Aragonese. In this first open battle of the entire campaign, a combat situation in which the Almoravids normally excelled, the Almoravid troops were not able to seize the advantage over the Christians, who drove the Almoravids from the field in defeat.

The *qadi* of Cordoba, Abd al-Wahid Ibn Rushd, went to Marrakech to denounce the Christian traitors who had defected to the Aragonese. Ali Ibn Yusuf responded by taking two decisive steps. First, he endorsed the *fatwa* issued by Andalusian *faqih*s denouncing those Mozarabs who had collaborated with El Batallador. He ordered a mass deportation of Christians from Andalusia to the Maghrib, where many of them settled around Salé and Meknes. Second, he removed Tamim from his command in Andalusia. He appointed Yahya Ibn Ghaniya in his place and sent his own son Tashfin Ibn Ali to take up the banner of the Almoravid jihad against the Christians.

Tashfin Ibn Ali's mother was a Christian slave named Dhu al-Sabbah, which means Dawn. Since his father was also born of a European mother, Ibn Ali was only one-fourth Saharan. Still, the courageous youth bore the name of his Saharan great grandfather. He landed in Andalusia with a handful of Almoravid commanders and 5,000 cavalrymen, a far cry from the enormous army that his grandfather Yusuf Ibn Tashfin led into Andalusia almost exactly 40 years earlier. He closed the marches in order to restore Almoravid control over the frontier between Muslim and Christian lands. He restructured the Almoravid garrisons, giving preference to the professional army, adding to the number of archers and giving them mounts, all while recruiting volunteers to fight for the faith—all of this to be better poised to wage jihad against the Christian enemy. He moved his residence to Cordoba, where he immediately won the respect of the population for his faithfulness to Islam, his determination to follow the straight path, and his dedication to jihad.

Tashfin Ibn Ali led frequent attacks into enemy territory and several times laid siege to Toledo. Although he never took that city, he ravaged its suburbs more than once. He established a bridgehead on the north bank of the Tajo River east of Toledo in spite of vigorous counterattacks by the opposition. Once, when Ibn Ali was marching through the night, his *hasham*, his mixed military corps and bodyguard, were ambushed and dispersed. Ibn Ali fought single-handedly, according to the official court historian, to save the *hasham* from total defeat. In the thick of battle, a lance struck Ibn Ali in the buttocks and left him with a limp for the rest of his life, a trophy for his courage that became legendary.

Beginning in 525/1131, Tashfin Ibn Ali split his residence between Cordoba and Seville, the cities from where he directly controlled the western half of Andalusia. Ali Ibn Yusuf, still wanting to profit from the Massufa connection that brought wealth into the empire, appointed Abu Bakr Ibn Ibrahim al-Massufi as governor of Valencia. In the West, Ibn Ali attacked Coimbra and Santarem, while in the East, Ibn Ghaniya put continuous pressure on the kingdom of Aragon.

In 527/1133, the new king of Castile, Alfonso VII, led a campaign from Toledo to Cadiz. He left little more than a scorched earth in his path: He cut olive and fig trees and uprooted vines, destroyed mosques, massacred *imam*s, and burned their sacred texts. The devastation set the tone for other raids that had less strategic planning. A state of march warfare developed between Christian and Almoravid territory, a state of perpetual conflict in which a class of professional pillagers thrived on both sides. For them, the zest for jihad had become secondary as the land was scourged and Andalusia profaned.

The Muslims of Andalusia blamed Ali Ibn Yusuf, who was safe in Marrakech and could no longer defend them. An earlier Andalusian king had likened the Andalusians to a camel who cried when it was loaded and cried again when the load was taken off. They took as their model Sayf al-Dawla Ibn Hud, the son of Imad al-Dawla, who had been exiled from Zaragoza back in 504/1110. In 525/1131, Sayf al-Dawla, whom the Christians came to call Zafadola, formed an alliance with Alfonso VII. He exchanged his fief in Huesca for territory on the outskirts of Toledo. He also accompanied Alfonso on his raid of 527/1133. Now, Sayf al-Dawla's co-religionists came to him to complain: "The Almoravids devour the marrow of the earth, our goods, our gold. They oppress our women and our children.... Let us chase them from Andalusia.... Ally yourself with the king of the Christians so that we will be delivered from the yoke of the Almoravids. Once freed, we will pay to the king of Castile a tribute larger than what our fathers paid to them, and you and your sons will rule over us." This was the beginning of a swelling wave of local Muslim rulers defying the Almoravids.

It was in eastern Andalusia that the Almoravids won their last major battle against the Christians. El Batallador, with the help of his French allies du Bearn and du Languedoc, laid siege to Fraga in 528/1134. Tashfin Ibn Ali responded and sent 2,000 cavalrymen from Cordoba under the command of Zubayr Ibn Amr al-Lamtuni. Yahya Ibn Ghaniya sent 500 from Valencia, and Abd Allah Ibn Iyad sent 200 from Lerida. Muslim chroniclers say that El Batallador, with 12,000 men, was overconfident. When he came within range, Ibn Iyad charged head on and broke the Christian's lines. Ibn Ghaniya charged in turn, and Ibn Iyad continued to press. During the melee, the occupants of Fraga—men, women, young and old—came from within and fell upon the tents of the enemy. The men killed wantonly while the women carried off all the arms and provisions that they could get their hands on. When Zubayr took to the field of battle with his troops, El Batallador was forced to retreat.

The death toll among the Christians was heavy. A number of Aragonese nobility were killed, as were many French commanders, including Gaston de Bearn. The Almoravids captured the jeweled reliquary of Alfonso that contained a fragment of what they believed to be the true cross, a relic that Alfonso had pillaged from the church in Leon. The clergy who accompanied the relic were taken prisoner. The Bishop of Lescar was carried off to Valencia, where he was circumcised. *El Batallador* himself died shortly after this defeat, possibly of wounds suffered in the course of the battle. In 532/1137–1138, Tashfin Ibn Ali ordered yet another deportation of Mozarabs from Andalusia to the Maghrib, perhaps the largest deportation in number under the Almoravids.

The Almoravids might have been able to follow up on this victory had Ali Ibn Yusuf not been forced to recall some of his desert warriors from Andalusia to defend the empire in the Maghrib. On the African side of the straits, Abd al-Mu'min and his Almohads increasingly threatened the empire. The *Amir*'s son, Tashfin Ibn Ali, returned to Africa to join the fight. He joined Reverter, the Christian who had become an Almoravid and who, at the same time, was one of the most feared names among the Almohads.

Reverter was among the many Christians captured in Spain by the Almoravid admiral Ali Ibn Maymun and sent to Marrakech to serve the Almoravid *Amir*. He was a noble warrior from Barcelona, an honest, simple, God-fearing man who had never lost a battle. Ali Ibn Yusuf placed him in command of a militia made up of Christian captives as well as Berbers. He became one of Ali Ibn Yusuf's most trusted military advisers in this war against the Almohads.

Tashfin Ibn Ali and Reverter faced the Almohads for the first time about 50 miles west of Tinmal. The Almohads had attacked the Bani Haha, and Ali Ibn Yusuf sent troops in relief under the joint command of his two ablest commanders. At first, the Almoravids managed to entrap the Almohads, who had retreated to a defensible mountain peak, and held them under siege. But then the Almohads attacked. The battle lasted a day and a half, and when it was over, the Almohads had prevailed. The Almohads returned to Tinmal, having captured the red flag of the Almoravids. Tashfin Ibn Ali's army, defeated, returned to Marrakech. Reverter, himself wounded, suffered heavy losses among his Christian militia.

Farther west in the vicinity of Tarudant, Al-Fallaki, the architect of Tasghimawt and other Almoravid fortresses, defected with several of his men from the ranks of the Almoravids and surrendered to the Almohads. At the same time, 400 women were also taken prisoner by the Almohads. One of them, the daughter of an Almoravid chief, interceded on behalf of these women captives and gained their freedom. Reverter, on the other side, also set free women that he had taken prisoner from among the Almohads.

By 534/1139, Abd al-Mu'min was finally in total control of the mountains south of Marrakech. He was ready to begin an all-out campaign to conquer the rest of the Maghrib in a contest that came to be known as the Seven Years' War. Still determined to avoid the plains, Abd al-Mu'min led his army northeast along the ridges of the Middle Atlas range in a maneuver designed to isolate the Almoravid heartland. He easily took the towns of Damnat, Wawayzagt, and Day on his way to Azrou. From there he conducted a campaign into the valley of the Ziz and then laid siege to the Qal'at al-Mahdi, the ancient capital of the Fazaz. Abd al-Mu'min then marched north.

Ali Ibn Yusuf again ordered his two best military commanders to pursue. Tashfin Ibn Ali and Reverter led an army from Fez to confront the Almohads. They arrived in the Fazaz too late to save the Qal'at al-Mahdi, but they began a chase that would last for the duration of the seven-year campaign. They marched on a route parallel to that of Abd al-Mu'min but always stayed in the open plains as the Almohads sought the protection of the mountains. The Almohads took Sefrou, passed on to the Bani Makkud, Lukay, and Igan as the Almoravids moved toward Qasr al-Kabir. After Igan, the Almohads won the valley of the Law while Tashfin Ibn Ali and Reverter occupied Tetouan. The Almoravid fleet watched from the sea as the troops of Abd al-Mu'min reached the Mediterranean coast and began to move east toward Tadjra, the town where Abd al-Mu'min was born. The Almohad leader entered his hometown in triumph and began immediately to consolidate his following. At almost every stage, the ranks of the Almohads grew as neutral tribes joined and as Almoravid supporters deserted the flag of Tashfin Ibn Ali.

The complexities of holding the empire together had taken every bit of Ali Ibn Yusuf's statesmanship and military resources. As the two branches of the empire, Saharan and Maghribi, became more independent from each other, Ali Ibn Yusuf could not depend on a steady supply of desert warriors to maintain his jihad in Andalusia. He relied more on Christian mercenaries and upon a tax base that he had previously abolished. That reliance put in question his ideology of moral reform and jihad. His ideology had been threatened further by an itinerant preacher from the High Atlas who, like the Almoravids had done a hundred years earlier, became a warrior against moral weakness. Still, the *Amir* managed to cope with these challenges and held the empire together for more than 35 years. His subjects failed to appreciate his statesmanship. They heard only the voices of dissent.

In 537/1142, Ali Ibn Yusuf's long struggle came to an end. As the sun was beginning to fall below the horizon of the Almoravid Empire, the *Amir* died after a reign of 36 years and 7 months. He died as he had lived most of his life, quietly at home in Marrakech, while his empire was being torn apart all around him. As he had requested, he was buried in a common grave in a public cemetery. His death was not publicly announced for three months, when word of the *Amir*'s death finally reached Tashfin Ibn Ali. He had been chasing the Almohad ruler for more than three years, and he was with his army surrounded by the forces of Abd al-Mu'min when he received word of his father's death. The position of the *Amir* and the struggle on two fronts were now his.

CHAPTER 14
The Center Cannot Hold

Tashfin Ibn Ali, the new *Amir*, was determined to take his stand in Tlemcen. That city had become a vital link in the Almoravids' commercial network, which stretched from Almeria to Timbuctu. Through its markets came gold from south of the Sahara. In the opposite direction went Andalusian finery, artwork that found its way to the distant banks of the Niger River. The Almoravids benefited from this network largely because of their co-confederationists, the Bani Massufa, and it made eastern Andalusia the richest part of the empire. The mint in Almeria struck more gold *dinar*s during the reign of Ali Ibn Yusuf than any other Almoravid mint, including Sijilmasa, and along with a few other mints along the Mediterranean coast of Spain it struck almost two-thirds of all of the *dinar*s produced under Almoravid rule.

The Massufa connection was now coming unraveled! Worse, it was symptomatic of a downward spiral in the Almoravids' hold on the empire from one end to the other, an erosion of loyalty from within and an escalation of attacks from without. Within months after the *Amir* Ali Ibn Yusuf died, a dispute broke out among the Bani Massufa and the Bani Lamtuna. Several *shaykh*s of the Bani Massufa, among them Berraz Ibn Muhammad, Yahya Ibn Takaght, and Yahya Ibn Ishaq, who had been governor of Tlemcen, withdrew their support from the Almoravids and went over to Abd al-Mu'min with all of their warriors. They sided with the charismatic leader into whose grasp the momentum had clearly swung.

Tlemcen was a major hub for the Massufa network. When Yusuf Ibn Tashfin first decided to pitch camp there just to the west of the nearby fortified town of Agadir, Tlemcen was no more than an outpost in the eastern part of the empire, a garrison to guard the eastern frontier. The new section called Takrart, which stood adjacent to Agadir, was inhabited mostly by Almoravids. Now, in little more than a half century, Tlemcen had become a major city, sprawling out from the Great Mosque that the Almoravids had built at its heart.

Tashfin Ibn Ali appointed a new governor to Tlemcen, Abu Bakr Ibn Mazdali, and began to set up his defenses as Abd al-Mu'min camped on the top of the mountain called Two Rocks that overlooked the city on the south side. In the Almohad army were contingents from Tinmal as well as members of Abd al-Mu'min's own tribe from Tajdra and Nedroma and members of the Bani Wamannu, a Zanata tribe. Joining the Almoravid garrison of Tlemcen were not only the troops from Marrakech who had come with Tashfin and Reverter but also reinforcements sent by the governor of Sijilmasa and by Yahya Ibn al-Aziz, a prince among the Bani Hammad. The Bani Hammad were also Sanhaja Berbers who lived immediately to the east of the Almoravid empire. They were co-confederationists and felt compelled to help. The day that the Hammadid contingent arrived, its commander, Tahir Ibn Kabbab, assessed the position of the opposition, boasted his own courage, and lashed out his contempt for the Bani Lamtuna because they were reluctant to engage in battle. "I have come," he shouted, "to deliver to you Abd al-Mu'min who is at the moment your master. As soon as I have finished, I will return home." Tashfin was irritated by Tahir's arrogance, but gave him leave to attack. The Almohads met the Hammadid attack head on and cut part of the corps to pieces. The rest took flight back to Bijaya.

The Almoravids launched a second attack on the plain of Mindas when the Almohads came down from the Two Rocks into Zanata territory to "punish Zanata rebels," the Bani Ilumi and the Bani Abd al-Wad. The Almohads moved into square formations in the open plain. In the first rank were the infantry, armed with long lances and protected by armor. Behind them were soldiers carrying shields and short lances and men carrying leather bags filled with rocks and slings. In the middle of the square were the Almohad cavalry. The Almoravid cavalry attacked. They suddenly found themselves surrounded by Almohads. Every direction they turned, they ran into first the long lances and then the short lances as they were showered by heavy stones and sharp arrows. Then, the Almohad cavalry made a sortie and crushed the Almoravid cavalry. Those who were not killed fled. Somehow, Tlemcen managed to survive the Almohad attack in mid-year 539/early 1145, but hope was fading fast for the city.

A ghost had returned to haunt the Almoravids—the burning of the books of the famous theologian al-Ghazzali, an event that had stunned Ali Ibn Yusuf's subjects more than three decades earlier. Tashfin Ibn Ali had repeated the order during the first year of his reign. He issued a decree in the month of *Jumada al-Ula*, 538/November, 1143 which said: "When you come across heretical books or the perpetrator of some heresy, guard yourself against them, especially the works of Abu Hamid al-Ghazzali ... so that his memory will be totally obliterated by means of a relentless *autodafe*!" The ban was one of the most unpopular stands that the Almoravids had taken, especially among the Muslim mystics on both sides of the straits. By now, opposition to Almoravid doctrinal censorship was so strong, even in the southern border town of Sijilmasa, that two *sufi shaykh*s were expelled from the mosque and were forced to take refuge in the city of Fez. There were even rumors that al-Ghazzali had damned the Almoravids with the curse, "Oh God, tear this kingdom apart just as they have torn my book in pieces. Take away this kingdom as they have burned my book!" Whether al-Ghazzali actually said that or not, the malediction seemed to be taking effect.

Opposition to the Almoravids over this issue focused in the west of Andalusia where a certain *sufi* preacher, Abu'l-Qasim Ahmad Ibn Qasi, preached with fervor about the works of al-Ghazzali. He was a disciple of Abu'l-Abbas Ahmad Ibn al-Arif, a *sufi* teacher in Almeria. Ibn Qasi won many converts in the area between Silves, Niebla, and Mertola. He built a *ribat*, a religious stronghold, just outside of Silves, and he called his confraternity installed there *al-Maridin*, the insurgents. At first, the Almoravid militia managed to keep the *Maridin* under cover, but now that the regime was quickly losing ground everywhere, Ibn Qasi became bold and encouraged his confraternity to take up arms.

In 539/1144, the *Maridin* stormed the walls of Mertola, the stronghold that secured the western region of Andalusia. On 12 *Safar*, 539/14 August, 1144, Ibn Qasi arrived and declared himself *imam al-mahdi* in the city. It was a spark that ignited the west of Andalusia in revolt against the Almoravids. When the *Maridin* tried to take Seville, the Almoravid governor, Yahya Ibn Ghaniya, led whatever forces he could gather to push the *Maridin* back. He forced them back to Niebla but was unable to follow through on his momentum to take Mertola and Silves because trouble was again breaking out in Cordoba.

Now that Andalusia was collapsing all around the Almoravids, the Christian King Alfonso of Castile began to pressure Ibn Ghaniya, the governor of Cordoba. Alfonso took the fortresses of Baeza and Ubeda while Ibn Ghaniya was forced to take refuge within the walls of his city. Alfonso was in a position to demand more and more tribute from Ibn Ghaniya, who became so desparate that he finally had to appeal to the Almohads for help. The Almohad commander, Berraz Ibn Muhammad, granted Ibn Ghaniya an audience and offered him Jaen as a fief in exchange for Cordoba and Carmona. Ibn Ghaniya accepted. As soon as Abd al-Mu'min ratified the treaty, Ibn Ghaniya took possession of Jaen, and the Almohads took control of Cordoba. Ibn Ghaniya then persuaded Maimun Ibn Yaddar al-Lamtuni, who was in Granada with a contingent of Almoravid troops, to do what he had done and submit to the Almohads as well.

Alfonso of Castile laid siege to Cordoba one more time. This time it was defended by a contingent of Almohads under the command of Yahya Ibn Yaghmur. The Christians were forced to withdraw because the strength of the Almohads was now manifest all over Andalusia. The remainder of the local rulers who had shed the authority of the Almoravids now came to Yahya Ibn Yaghmur and asked him to intercede on their behalf in the court of Abd al-Mu'min.

Meanwhile on the African front, Reverter, the Christian who continued to be Tashfin Ibn Ali's ablest commander, was busy trying to control the tide of defections of Zanata tribes over to the side of the enemy. He led a campaign in the region of Uyda, upstream along the Za River. After taking much booty from the Bani Sanus and other Zanata tribes in the region, he, in turn, was attacked by a large Almohad force. Reverter's army was completely destroyed. Barring the chronicler's exaggeration, there were only six survivors, three Christian militiamen and three Muslims. Reverter himself was killed. His body was later found on the field of battle laid out in the form of a cross. His Almohad opponents respected his military prowess but were relieved at the death of this "villain (*al-shaqiy*) al-Abritayr." Tashfin Ibn Ali, for his part, cried at the news.

Defections, defeats, and now the death of his ablest commander—Tashfin's defenses crumbled all around him. Tashfin Ibn Ali was forced to pull back to the citadel of Oran, Tlemcen's Mediterranean port, which was normally a two-day journey to the northeast. First, he sent his son and designated heir to Marrakech under an armed escort of Lamtuna warriors, along with his chief minister, Ahmad Ibn Aita. He then sent word to Muhammad Ibn Maimun, the admiral of the Almoravid fleet, to send 10 ships to facilitate his passage to the Andalusian port of Almeria on the opposite shore. Ibn Ali took shelter in a small fort by the edge of the sea, not far from Oran, and waited for help to arrive. He waited for more than a month.

Abd al-Mu'min sent an army in pursuit, 80 units containing as many Zanata as Almohads. Tashfin Ibn Ali was completely surrounded by his enemy, who set fires all around the fortress. During the night of 27 *Ramadan*, 539/23 March, 1145, Ibn Ali fled the fortress on horseback. Under the shelter of darkness, the *Amir* rode through enemy lines. As he approached the sea, he was blinded by the same darkness that guarded his escape. His horse fell, and Tashfin Ibn Ali fell to the ground—dead! The following morning, Almohad soldiers found Ibn Ali's body at the bottom of the ravine. They cut off his head and sent it to Tinmal, where it was hung from a tree.

When news of Tashfin Ibn Ali's death reached Marrakech, Tashfin's young son, Ibrahim Ibn Tashfin, was proclaimed *Amir* everywhere that Almoravid authority was still recognized. Tashfin Ibn Ali had every intention of his son succeeding him to power. As was the custom, he had his son's name as his heir stamped along with his own name on the official coinage. But Tashfin Ibn Ali had died too soon. His son was only 10 years old. The tribal elite again searched for a formula that would balance legitimacy and effectiveness. Tribal succession might have been easier in their Saharan homeland. Ibrahim Ibn Tashfin's name did appear on imperial decrees for the next couple of months, but the coins were still stamped in his father's name. Ibrahim was simply too young to be effective. Finally, the family decided to transfer power to Ishaq Ibn Ali, grandson of the first Almoravid *Amir* Yahya Ibn Umar. Ishaq Ibn Ali, too, was very young. He did provide the desired legitimacy for the office, but his effectiveness was still untested. Even in the best of times, the Almoravids needed a stronger leader. The spring of 539–540/1145 was far from the best of times.

Three days after the death of Tashfin Ibn Ali, Oran fell to the Almohad commander Abu Hafs. Many of the city's inhabitants had already died of thirst. Abu Hafs destroyed the city and killed most of its defenders, except for a few who managed to escape to Tlemcen or to Fez.

When the Lamtuna warriors in Tlemcen learned of the death of their *Amir*, they withdrew from the city, leaving it easy prey for Abd al-Mu'min. The city sent a delegation of 60 prominent men to plead with the Almohad, who promptly had all 60 of them killed. He showed mercy to the inhabitants of Agadir but unleashed the Almohad army on the Almoravid section of Takrart. The fires in Tlemcen were not yet extinguished when Abd al-Mu'min received word of other victories, including the homage of the people of Sijilmasa.

In early 540/1145, Abd al-Mu'min began a siege of Fez that would last for seven months. Second only to Marrakech, Fez was beyond a doubt the most important city in the Almoravid Empire, important as an economic and intellectual treasure chest. The Almoravids had put considerable effort into the city's development from the very beginning when Yusuf Ibn Tashfin tore down the wall that divided the city's two parts and formed a united city within new ramparts. Since then, the city's commercial establishments multiplied and its population grew. The city became a haven for Andalusian intellectuals who sought new careers. Yusuf Ibn Tashfin's son Ali made the Qarawiyin Mosque one of the most beautiful in the empire. To enlarge the mosque, houses were bought and torn down, many of which belonged to Jews whose quarter was pushed just to the north of the sanctuary. Ali Ibn Yusuf's mosque renovation extended the prayer hall in the direction of the prayer niche, added an axial nave perpendicular to the old and new transverses, and built a chapel for the dead. Even with the help of *habus* (religious endowments), the *qadi*s could not have financed such decorative quality and heavy reliance on Andalusian art without the support of the Almoravid *Amir*. Next to Marrakech, Fez was Ali's favorite city.

Fez was also a potential seedbed of dissent. Some of the intellectuals who moved to the city of the Qarawiyin Mosque and university came as political exiles. Such was the case of Abu Muhammad Ibn Qasim al-Fihri, the last representative of a famous family from Medina who had settled in Andalusia. Having fallen in disgrace after Yusuf Ibn Tashfin's conquest of Andalusia, he took up residence first in Salé and then in Fez, a prison that was less disagreeable than Aghmat had been for the king of Seville. The *qadi* Abu Umayya visited him there, as did his secretary, the lettered Abu'l-Hasan Baki Ibn Ahmad. Ibn Baki, the Andalusian poet who had threatened to move to Iraq, complained about his own stay in Fez: "I am among you," he wrote, "miserable and destitute; if I had been a free man, a proud soul, I would never have stayed."

In command of the Almoravid garrison in Fez was Yahya Ibn Abu Bakr Ibn Yusuf, surnamed al-Sahrawi, that is, the Saharran. He had fled from Tlemcen with those Lamtuna warriors who had managed to escape after that city was destroyed. He was a grandson of the famous Yusuf Ibn Tashfin.

From the top of the ramparts, the people of Fez could see the campfires of the Almohad army bivouacked on the hilltops all around the city. As they watched the maneuvers of the enemy forces, they became increasingly nervous. Abd al-Mu'min grew impatient, so he built a dike out of earth and trees to divert the waters of the river to form a body of water large enough to navigate. He then ordered the dike to be smashed and the waters plunged into the ramparts, causing a breach in the wall. But the defenders of Fez stood fast, and the Almohads could not penetrate.

In the end, it was an act of treason that opened the city to the enemy. The city's provost (*mushrif*), along with a number of the city's notables, sent a message to Abd al-Mu'min offering him the city in exchange for immunity. When the Almohad caliph agreed, the conspirators opened one of the city gates during the night. Early in the morning, the Almohad army entered Fez. Al-Sahrawi had already escaped to Tangier and crossed over to Andalusia.

It was hard to believe that Fez was taken. After its fall, the *ulama* told the story of how the night before Abd al-Mu'min was to enter the city and perform the Friday prayers at the mosque, the *shaykhs* ordered that the decorations around the *mihrab* be camouflaged to

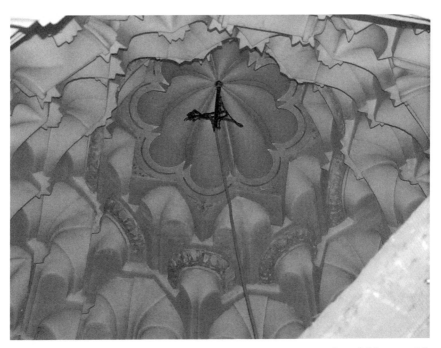

Cupola in the Qarawiyin Mosque in Fez is an example of Almoravid decoration that was covered over by the Almohads after their conquest of Fez and since restored. (Photograph by the author.)

prevent them from being destroyed. In truth, the Almohads plastered over the decorations themselves sometime after the year C.E. 1148 to reflect the more austere aesthetic of the new regime.

Within weeks after the fall of Fez, several other cities in the Maghrib fell. Meknes opened its gates to the Almohads. Ceuta sent a delegation to Abd al-Mu'min seeking protection. Salé surrendered without resistance. Abd al-Mu'min next turned his march toward the Almoravid capital, Marrakech.

The Almohads had become quite adept at taking a city by storm. After a long siege and five inconclusive pitched battles on the plains outside the city walls, a band of Almohad warriors built ladders and succeeded to scale the walls and to open the city's gates to their comrades. The Bani Hintata and the people from Tinmal entered the city through the *Bab Dukkala*, and the Bani Haskura and people of other tribes entered on the side of the *Bab Aylan*.

The Almohad caliph refused to enter Marrakech at this time, some say because he claimed that the mosques were not properly oriented. So the mosques were destroyed, say the chroniclers, and were rebuilt to conform to the proper orientation. Only then would Abd al-Mu'min make his grand entrance in the month of *Shawwal*, 541/the end of March, 1147. The young Almoravid *Amir* Ishaq Ibn Ali Ibn Yusuf, who had succeeded the weak and ineffective Ibrahim Ibn Tashfin, took refuge in the palace. When he was captured, the *Amir* begged for mercy, saying that he was not responsible for what the Almoravid *Amir*s before him had done. His plea was viewed as weakness unbefitting the *Amir* of the Almoravid Empire. Abd al-Mu'min ordered that his head be cut off.

The line of Almoravid *Amir*s, faltering at best since the death of Tashfin Ibn Ali, had now run its course. To be sure, there were Andalusians and Maghribis who were relieved, but there were also serious pockets of resistance to the new occupants of the palace in Marrakech. Even with the Almoravid capital in the hands of the enemy, some loyal supporters refused to submit to the new regime. Among the loyalists, Muhammad Ibn Abd Allah Ibn Hud, a native of Salé, led a series of revolts against the Almohads. His career started in Ribat Massa in the Sus, southwest of Marrakech, where he began to preach against the new regime and to gather a substantial following. He took the title *al-hadi*, "he who guides." Before long, his following included tribesmen from the Bani Dukkala, the Bani Ragrara, the Bani Tamasna, and the Bani Huwara, as well as from the valley of the Draa and from Sijilmasa.

Abd al-Mu'min was quick to respond to the threat. The Almohad labeled Ibn Hud's preaching as heresy and sent an army under the command of Abu Hafs Umar in pursuit of the rebel army, estimated at some 60,000 infantrymen and 7,000 cavalry. Even with such a large force, Ibn Hud could not prevail. He was killed by the Almohads on the field of battle during the month of *Dhu al-Hijja*, 541/May–June, 1147. Within a year, all of Ibn Hud's supporters were forced to submit, including the Almoravid's port on the edge of the Sahara, the city of Sijilmasa.

When the Almohads were firmly in control of Sijilmasa, they enlarged the Mosque of Abd al-Allah. The mosque was far too small to serve as the Friday mosque for an ever-growing population. Again, claiming that the Almoravids had improperly oriented the prayer niche toward Mecca, the Almohads changed the orientation a few degrees more toward the East, as they had done at the Kutubiya Mosque in Marrakech. They also plastered over the carved stucco as they had done at the Qarawiyin Mosque in Fez. These were effective symbols of their victory and of their religious reforms.

The city of Ceuta also made a desperate attempt to hold out against the Almohad conquerors. The new governor, Yusuf Ibn Makhluf of Tinmal, was killed along with all of the Almohads in the garrison. Even

The Sijilmasa Mosque has undergone four distinct phases of occupation, two of which are pertinent to this story, the occupation of the Almoravids and the expansion by the Almohads when the latter replaced Almoravid rule in Sijilmasa. (Photograph by author.)

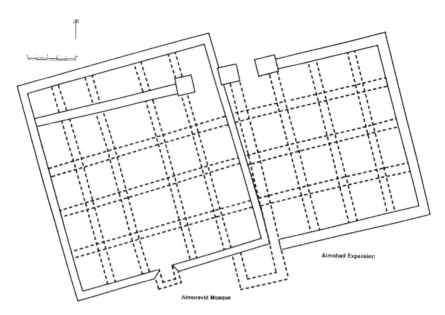

Plan of the Sijilmasa Mosque shows the original floor plan of the Mosque of the Almoravids and the addition and slight change in orientation by the Almohads. (© MAPS [Moroccan-American Project at Sijilmasa, Ronald Messier, project director]. Used by permission.)

in this last hour, the *qadi* of Ceuta, *qadi* Iyad, continued to be a loyal supporter of the Almoravids and led the opposition against the Almohads. He crossed the straits to Algeciras and appealed to the Almoravid governor, Yahya Ibn Ali Ibn Ghaniya. *Qadi* Iyad asked Ibn Ghaniya to reestablish Almoravid rule over his city and to send a new governor. Ibn Ghaniya obliged and sent Yahya Ibn Abu Bakr al-Sahrawi, the same Almoravid commander who had escaped the siege of Fez and made his way to Tangier and then on to Cordoba. Al-Sahrawi managed to rally once again a group of rebels against the Almohads, a group so diverse that it included some of the heretical Barghwata. It took six months for Abd al-Mu'min to crush this opposition. When he finally succeeded, he issued a letter of pardon to al-Sahrawi, and the people of Ceuta submitted. Salé submitted too. Still, its walls were razed, but the people were spared by the conquering Almohads.

Not only were the Almoravids losing the Maghrib, but their loss of Andalusia moved into its final phase. Within months after the news of Tashfin Ibn Ali's death in 540/1145 had reached Andalusia, local rulers of Andalusian cities broke allegiance from the Almoravids one after the other. Andalusians knew of the fall of the city of Fez and the defection of the admiral of the Almoravid fleet. While Tashfin Ibn Ali had been waiting for the admiral to come to his rescue in Oran, the latter went to the Almohad camp beneath the walls of Fez and surrendered. He then returned to Cadiz as an Almohad partisan and prayed there in the mosque in the name of Abd al-Mu'min. It was the first time that the *khutba* prayer was pronounced in the name of the Almohad ruler.

Ibn Qasi, the leader of the *Maridin* revolt, had already expressed his loyalty to the Almohads; he had been in contact with Abd al-Mu'min during the siege of Tlemcen, and he had, after all, led an open revolt against the Almoravids. Now he decided to cross the straits and appeal to the Almohad caliph. When he landed in Ceuta, he was immediately escorted to Marrakech, where he told Abd al- Mu'min how easy it would be to conquer Andalusia. To lead this campaign, Abd al-Mu'min appointed Berraz Ibn Muhammad al-Massufi, one of the Massufa chiefs who had abandoned Tashfin to join the Almohads shortly after the death of Ali Ibn Yusuf. His job was to fight the Almoravids and those rebellious local rulers who thought that they could remain independent. He focused this first campaign on the western part of Andalusia, where opposition against the Almoravids seemed to be the strongest. He quickly took the cities of Xeres, Niebla, Mertola, Beja, Badajoz, and Silves. He granted Silves to Ibn Qasi as a reward for his loyalty, and he received the homage of Abu Ghamr Ibn Azzun of Ronda, Yusuf Ibn Ahmad al-Batrugi of Niebla, and Seddrai Ibn Wazir of Beja and Badajoz. This completed the Almohad conquest of western Andalusia, except for Seville.

In the month of *Sha'ban*, 541/January, 1147, Berraz appeared before the walls of Seville. He formed a blockade and waited for the city to surrender. The Almoravids fled toward Carmona, and the Almohads pursued, killing all the Almoravids that they caught. Meanwhile, the *qadi* of Seville, Abu Bakr Ibn al-Arabi, led a delegation to submit to the authority of Abd al-Mu'min, who received them and granted them fiefs. In the year 545/1150, Abd al-Mu'min sent a message to all the Muslims in Andalusia announcing that he was prepared to accept their homage. He went to Salé to wait for their response. People came from all over Andalusia to swear an oath of fidelity and to surrender their sovereignty. Those who did not, like Ibn Qasi of Silves, would later pay with their lives.

The last refuge for supporters and sympathizers of the Almoravids were the Balearic Islands. Ali Ibn Yusuf's appointee, Muhammad Ibn

Ghaniya, was still governor there. After the fall of Marrakech and the defeat of the last Almoravid *Amir* Ibn Ghania proclaimed his independence on the Islands and held fast in his opposition to the Almohads. His son Ishaq managed to make the little kingdom prosper for several years to come through piracy, aimed mostly against the Almohads. When Ishaq died, his son Muhammad was inclined to submit to the Almohads, but his brothers resisted. They deposed Muhammad in favor of another brother, Ali, and together the Bani Ghaniya waged war against the Almohads in the central Maghrib and Ifriqiya, (what is today Algeria and Tunisia). Their descendants continued the struggle for the better part of a century after the death of the last *Amir*.

The torch of the Almoravids was all but extinguished. What survived was a religious, political, and cultural hegemony in Maghrib and Andalusia that was unprecedented in western Islam, a hegemony that was taken up and carried on by the dynasties that succeeded them. The torch would flare up from time to time to rally the opponents of the Almohads, or to stir the memories among the tribes of their Saharan confederation, memories of the ghosts of a fallen dynasty.

CHAPTER 15

The Almoravids and Ibn Khaldun

More than 250 years passed after the fall of Marrakech before Ibn Khaldun began to chronicle the history of the Almoravids. He based his account on what earlier historians, travelers, and storytellers had said, some of them contemporary to the events, and most of them themselves relying on the memory of others. Ibn Khaldun blames the collapse of the dynasty on their defeat by another, the Almohads. Ibn Abi Zar said the same thing nearly a hundred years earlier:

> The Lamtuna were a people of the desert, religious and honest, who conquered an immense empire in Andalusia and the Maghrib; they imposed good government and waged jihad . . . ; the *khutba* was prayed in their name in more than 2000 pulpits . . . ; their days were happy, prosperous, and peaceful . . . ; for a half ducat we bought four charges of wheat . . . ; there was no tribute, taxes or contribution for the government other than the *zakat* . . . ; their reign was free from lies, fraud and revolt and they were cherished by all until the Mahdi, the Almohad, rose against them in the year 515.

Nostalgia clouds the accuracy of Ibn Abi Zar's recollection, to be sure. After the Almohads became masters of the Maghrib and "massacred the Lamtuna," Ibn Khaldun writes, "Abd al-Mu'min crossed to Andalusia with the Almohads and became masters. From all sides, death overcame the Lamtuna and their *Amir*s fell." Ibn Khaldun concludes his account of the Almoravids by saying that "a small band managed to escape to the eastern islands. . . . Later these refugees would found a new empire in Ifriqiya." He talks here about the Bani Ghaniya, who were the last of the Almoravid resistance against the Almohads. As for the rest of the Almoravids, those who were not killed returned to their ancestral homes, where the Almoravid aristocracies live on in memories and folklore of the northern and western Sahara.

The corruption and fall of a dynasty and its replacement by another nicely fits the paradigm that Ibn Khaldun formulated to explain the rise and fall of regimes. It completes one of the cycles. The medieval Arab writer Al-Marrakushi explains why the Almoravids fell prey so easily to the Almohads. He blames it on an *Amir* who lost himself in religious asceticism and was content with collecting taxes as he surrendered control of his empire to a ruling elite who were seduced and softened by the delights of Andalusia, who

> raised pretensions of independence in the various parts of the empire where they exercised authority.... Women themselves, members of the principle families among the Lamtuna and Massufa, became the patrons of worthless, evil men, brigands, wine merchants and tavern owners ... [while Ali] was satisfied in exercising nominal authority and collecting taxes; he thought of nothing else other than his religious and spiritual practices; he prayed throughout the night and fasted throughout the day, but he neglected the interests of his subjects.

But there is more in the chronicles than a simple virtue to corruption story. There is opportunism. It was a chief of the Sanhaja confederation who invited Ibn Yasin to the Sahara to preach to his people. Could he have envisioned that the preacher would launch a jihad? It was the religious elite of Sijilmasa who invited the Almoravids to free them from their oppressive Maghrawa rulers. It was the disunity and political instability among Arab and Berber tribes that opened the Maghrib to Almoravid conquest. And it was the Muslim Taifa kings of Andalusia who begged the Almoravids to come to Andalusia to defend them against the Christian *reconquista*. There is no evidence to suggest that the Almoravid *Amir*s foresaw at any of these points what the empire would become.

The shields of the Almoravids cast their shadow from the Senegal River in Africa to the Ebro River in Spain. The Almoravids were richer than any previous regime in western Islam. Their wealth resulted from their control over such a wide network of trade routes that stretched across the empire. The Almoravids were ideally situated to totally dominate the gold trade between West Africa and the

Mediterranean world. The dramatic increase in the striking of gold coins in the name of the dynasty shows that the state benefited directly from the gold trade. The Almoravids struck large quantities of *dinar*s from Sudanese gold in several mints at critical points of connection between the Mediterranean basin and the Sahara; five of the sites were the seats of Almoravid governorships. The gold shipments that passed through their territory provided the revenues to support local governorships and their garrisons. Gold revenues were derived as payment for protection. With gold as the principal state revenue, the main political and military concerns of the Almoravids would have been to defend the routes of trade against external threat and to block the emergence of competing local elites.

Gold was not their only resource. Additionally, they were able to call upon the agricultural wealth of the Maghrib, resources that would allow a regime that originated in the desert to grow well beyond the economic limitations of their homeland. When the Almoravids went to Spain, they added to their resources the profits of Andalusia's rich agricultural and industrial production. Because of their policy of no non-Koranic taxes, the prosperity filtered down to many of their subjects. Both Ibn Abi Zar and the *Hulal* highlight the relative peace, prosperity, and contentment of the Almoravids' subjects. They were seen as liberators by those who were ruled by the Maghrawa, who were tyrants by comparison. They were hailed as saviors by the Andalusians, who lived in fear of a Christian onslaught.

The Almoravids brought not only prosperity to their empire but also a greater degree of political unity than western Islam had ever seen before. The Almoravids seized their empire as religious zealots. They began in the western Sahara at the same time that scholars in the East sought to emancipate themselves from caliphal control and were looking back nostalgically at a mythical simplicity in the faraway Arabian desert. It was easy enough for a charismatic religious preacher to play on the similarities between the Arabian desert of the seventh century and the western Sahara desert of the eleventh century. At least at first, the Almoravids stressed egalitarianism among members of the movement, a fundamental belief of the Kharajite Islam that first appealed to the Berbers of North Africa. It was an ideology that was rooted in resisting the political and social domination of the Arab ruling classes.

But the Almoravids did not adopt Kharijism. Rather, they secured an alliance with the Malikite *faqih*s who offered a ready-made system of law and who instructed the faithful to obey their Muslim rulers. The *faqih*s were not Almoravids; they were themselves opportunists who supported the new regime only to perpetuate their own positions of power. They were even more strict than the Almoravids were inclined to be and more so than the Almoravids' subjects would tolerate in the end. Overreliance on the *faqih*s eventually cost the Almoravids the support of local rulers, who felt that they were passed over and had never been successfully integrated into the Almoravid hierarchy. When the Almoravids fell, the *faqih*s went down with them, not out of loyalty to the old regime, but rather because the new regime had *faqih*s of their own.

In keeping with the ideology of the *Dar al-Murabitin*, the Almoravids believed that they were first and foremost "bound together in the cause of God." Under the guidance of Ibn Yasin, they adopted, as a cornerstone of their ideological platform, waging jihad first against pagans in the western Sahara, and then against "bad Muslims" in the Maghrib, and finally against the Christians in Andalusia. That ideology did limit their choice of opportunities to exploit. It did permit them to expand northward into Andalusia but not eastward into the territory of their co-confederationsists, the Sanhaja of Ifriqiya. Jihad against the Christians was the Almoravids' justification for remaining in Andalusia, and Andalusians were willing to put up with them as long as they provided the much-needed defense. This jihad against the Christians did not abate; the Christians, too, were motivated by the ideology of Holy War.

At the same time, another threat arose from the south of Marrakech, the Almohads who were themselves motivated by an ideology of religious reformism. The Almoravids were condemned to fighting a two-front war. To relax on either front would have eroded whatever support they had from their subjects. To continue the two-front war, however, consumed vast resources in revenues that came from across the desert and manpower that came from the desert itself. Moreover, their lines of communication with the desert were obstructed by the Almohads, who had formed a semicircular stranglehold to the south of Marrakech.

The Almoravids could not sustain their jihad against the Christians in Andalusia and their war against the Almohads without raising taxes. Two cornerstones of their ideology, jihad and "no non-Koranic taxes," turned out to be mutually exclusive. Such an ideological dilemma proved deadly. Raising taxes was so distasteful that they even brought in Christian mercenaries to collect them. Reversing their initial tax policy not only caused the regime to loose credibility among their subjects, but prosperity no longer filtered down to the people.

The Almoravids' subjects could accept austere religious reformism as long as it brought prosperity. Eventually, the Almoravids lost the support of the masses because they failed to meet the expectations they had created among their subjects—expectations of a better life, security, low taxes. Former subjects turned, albeit reluctantly, to the new regime, the Almohads, who formed a new paradigm that, at least for the moment, better served their wants.

The new paradigm was based on victory rather than on defeat. In terms of religion, the Almohads offered a belief in the absolute unity of God, an idea that is straightforward and has wide appeal among Muslims, and, more importantly especially for the Bani Masmuda, it was taught by one of their own. In terms of reformist ideology, they offered the same as did the Almoravids: morality, tax reform, peace, and prosperity—new promises, the same hopes. The difference was that the Almohad star was rising while that of the Almoravids was in decline.

Having failed to integrate the local aristocracies or to form a loyal local bureaucracy, in the end the Almoravids could only rely on themselves, on the tribal aristocracy of the Saharan Sanhaja, which at best felt awkward and out of place beyond the confines of the desert. Within three generations after the Almoravids emerged from the Sahara to conquer the cities of northwestern Islam, senility had set in, and their desert virtues of austerity, discipline, and hardiness had given way to defeat. So, in that sense, Ibn Khaldun was right when he saw the move from desert to city as weakening the dynasty. But it is not the city itself that spelled their doom. Ibn Khaldun is himself somewhat ambivalent toward the relative merits of the desert and the city. At the same time that he admires the desert nomad for his simple life, he clearly prefers the city. For him, Almoravid civilization is the Maghrib and Andalusia as defined over and against "the various tribes of veil-wearers ... who stayed in the desert and remained in their primitive state of dissension and divergence." But ultimately it was the desert which had been the very source of strength for the Almoravids that spelled their doom. The Almoravid identity, their ethos, was so tied to the Sahara that they were unable to adjust to any other environment. The *litham*, the dark veil that covered all but their eyes, was a mark of pride and nobility in the desert. It made them foreboding to their subjects in the streets of Fez and Seville. And when the Maghribis and Andalusians rejected them, the Almoravids had only the desert to go back to, a home where their brethren still lived.

The Sahara had never really let the Almoravids go. What is it about the desert that holds captive the identity of its inhabitants? Its vastness, to be sure. The Almoravids, whose homeland is at the very heart of the western Sahara, had to travel very long distances before they were out of the desert. With effort, they could leave physically, but not psychologically, and not for long periods of time. And on a practical level, the source of military manpower on which they continuously and ultimately relied was simply too far away from the Maghrib and Andalusia. History, too, is part of the captivating force of the desert, history which is measured in centuries rather than in years. The Almoravids' experiment with "empire" was but the briefest of episodes, and the home to return to made finite their willingness to put up with the difficulties of maintaining an empire beyond the desert. It is the harshness of the desert that demands extraordinary skills and habits from its residents for mere survival, but not the administrative skills to run an urban empire. William Langewiesche, in his powerful book *Sahara Unveiled*, describes the power of the desert and its impact on the ethos of its inhabitants quite eloquently. He says that the desert teaches by taking away. The desert taught the Almoravids, or at least reminded them, of who they were by taking away their empire. The Sahara reclaimed their spirit.

What survives is not the memory of defeat, but a legacy of achievement. The Almoravids achieved a degree of political unity in western Islam that was unprecedented, a unity that previous regimes, the Idrissids, the Umayyads, and the Fatimids, failed to achieve. The Almoravid Empire did not survive, but the land that would become Morocco would never again be the same; it would never again be as fragmented as it was before. Likewise, the Almoravids forged a cultural fusion between the Sahara, the Maghrib, and Andalusia that expressed itself in art and literature and would forever leave its mark on all three. The desert warriors provided ample subject for Andalusian authors to write about. When they became kings of Andalusia, they were seduced by much of the high culture that Andalusia offered. They brought scholars and poets, sculptors, and architects back home with them to Africa. The writers retold their stories and the artists adapted their refined, intricate designs to the strong, simple forms seen in Saharan architecture. The result was a composite style that their successors would later re-export to Andalusia in the likes of the great square tower of the Giralda.

The geographer Yaqut, writing in the third quarter of the thirteenth century, more than a hundred years after the collapse of the Almoravid dynasty, says of the western Sahara, "Their tribes are Lamtuna, Massufa, and Gudala. Gudala are the most numerous, Massufa the most handsome, and Lamtuna the bravest. Authority resides in the Lamtuna and of them was the *Amir* of the veiled men, Yusuf Ibn Tashfin, who ruled over the whole of the West." Those memories live on today.

Main Characters

The following are the main characters who appear in this narrative of the Almoravids. Minor characters or those who appear only once in the story are identified only in the text. The names appear here in alphabetical order, disregarding the prefix "al-."

Abd Allah Ibn Buluggin Ibn Badis. The last Zirid ruler of Granada (1073–1090). His memoirs which have survived are an important source for the history of the Almoravids in Andalusia.

Abd Allah Ibn Yasin. The preacher who came from the *Dar al-Murabitin* to preach Malikite Islam to the Sanhaja tribes in the western Sahara.

Abd al-Mu'min. One of the early followers and closest associates of the founder of the Almohad movement, Ibn Tumart. He succeeded the latter as leader of the movement from 1130–1163.

Abu Imran al-Fasi. The Malikite scholar in Qayrawan who directed Yahya Ibn Ibrahim to seek a preacher at the *Dar al-Murabitin* of Wajjaj Ibn Zalwi.

Abu Bakr Ibn Umar. Appointed as the second *Amir* of the Almoravids by Ibn Yasin to replace his brother, Yahya Ibn Umar.

Alfonso I. King of Aragon. Nicknamed El Batallador (the fighter).

Alfonso VI. King of Castile, conqueror of Toledo, champion of the Christian *reconquista* against the Taifa Kings and the Almoravids.

Ali Ibn Yusuf. Son of Yusuf Ibn Tashfin, born in Ceuta in 1084/85, Yusuf's successor as *Amir* of the Almoravids.

Alvar Fanez. One of Alfonso VI's greatest commanders.

Chimene. Wife of Rodrigo Diaz de Vivar, the El Cid, ruled Valencia after the death of her husband until it was conquered by the Almoravids.

Da'ud Ibn Aisha. Son of Abu Bakr and Aisha, second cousin to Yusuf Ibn Tashfin, appointed by the latter as governor of Sijilmasa.

al-Ghazzali. One of the greatest theologians of Islam, author of the *Ihya Ulum al-Din*, which was burned under orders of the Almoravid *faqih*s.

al-Hajib. The Taifa King of Murcia, Tortosa, and Denia (king of Valencia?).

Ibn al-Aftas, al-Mutawakkil. The Taifa King of Badajoz.

Ibn al-Hajj, Abu Abd Allah Muhammad. Of the clan of the Bani Turgut, a distinguished commander of Almoravid forces in Andalusia, a distant cousin of Yusuf Ibn Tashfin, appointed by the latter as commander of forces at Cordoba, then stationed in Fez, transferred to Valencia, and then to Zaragoza.

Ibn Rashik. Taifa King of Murcia.

Ibn al-Khulay'i. *Qadi* of Granada during the reign of Abd Allah.

Ibn al-Faraj. Al-Qadir's vizier in Valencia.

Ibn Ghaniya, Muhammad. He was appointed governor of the Balearic Islands by Ali Ibn Yusuf. Muhammad's brother Ali Ibn Ghania and Ali's son Yahya continued the Almoravid struggle against the Almohads long after the death of the last Almoravid *Amir*.

Ibn Hud, Musta'in. The Taifa King of Zaragoza.

Ibn Tifilwit, Abu Bakr Ibn Ibrahim. A tribesman from the Bani Massufa who was appointed by Ali Ibn Yusuf to replace Muhammad Ibn al-Hajj as governor of Zaragoza. He had a reputation for his ability as a warrior, for his generosity, and for being seduced by the luxuries of Andalusia.

Ibn Tumart. Founder of the Almohad movement. Born about 1084 to the Harghah tribe in the region of the Sus.

Ibn Wuhayb, Malik. One of the most prominent *faqih*s in Ali Ibn Yusuf's court.

Ibn Yasin, Abd Allah. The preacher from the Sus who accompanied Yahya Ibn Ibrahim back to the Sahara to preach a reformed Islam to the Sanhaja. He is the founder of the Almoravid movement.

Ibrahim Ibn Abu Bakr. Son of the Almoravid *Amir* Abu Bakr, governor of Sijilmasa for five years (1071–1076).

Ibrahim Ibn Tashfin Ibn Ali. He succeeded his father Tashfin as *Amir* of the Almoravids.

Ishaq Ibn Ali. A distant cousin to Yusuf Ibn Tashfin, he succeeded Ibrahim as *Amir* of the Almoravids.

Ja'far Ibn Jahhaf. *Qadi* in Valencia.

Jawhar Ibn Sakkun. A jurist from the Bani Gudala. He served as interpreter for Yahya Ibn Ibrahim, the chief of the Sanhaja confederation, who went on a pilgrimage in the 1030s C.E. and brought the preacher Abdallah Ibn Yasin back to the Sahara.

Main Characters

Mazdali Ibn Tilankan. A cousin of Yusuf Ibn Tashfin, one of the most trusted commanders of both Yusuf and Ali Ibn Yusuf, serving in several campaigns; governor of Cordoba, Granada, and Almeria.

Mu'ammil. The aged advisor to Abd Allah of Granada and of his father before him.

al- Mu'izz. The oldest son of Yusuf Ibn Tashfin and Zainab, born in 1070/1071. One of his father's ministers, he participated in the campaign against Ceuta.

Mu'tadd. The son of Mu'tamid of Seville.

Mu'tamid. The Taifa King of Seville, he organized the delegation that appealed to the Almoravids, inviting them to invade Andalusia. He died in exile in Aghmat.

Mu'tasim Ibn Samadah. The Taifa King of Almeria.

Mutawakkil. The Taifa King of Badajoz.

al-Qadir. The Taifa King of Toledo who went to become king of Valencia after Toledo was taken by Alfonso VI in 1085.

Radi. The son of Mu'tamid of Seville, appointed ruler of Murcia after the deposition of Ibn Rashik.

Reverter. A Christian warrior from Barcelona, captured by the Almoravid admiral Ali Ibn Maymun, placed in command of an Almoravid militia, one of Ali Ibn Yusuf's most trusted military advisers in the war against the Almohads.

Rodrigo Diaz de Vivar. Better know as **El Cid**.

Syr Ibn Abu Bakr. Nephew of Yusuf Ibn Tashfin, married to Yusuf's sister Hawwa, one of Yusuf's ablest commanders and advisors, appointed governor of Meknes and the region of Fazaz; distinguished himself in the battle of Zallaqa.

Suqut al-Barghwati. A slave among the Bani Hammud; because of his loyalty and talent, he was appointed governor of Tangier and Ceuta; a stalwart opponent of the Almoravids.

Tamim. The Taifa King of Malaga.

Tamim. A son of Yusuf Yusuf Ibn Tashfin and Zaynab, appointed governor of Marrakech; it was he who announced Yusuf's death and proclaimed his half-brother, Ali, to be the new *Amir*; later, he was successively named governor of Granada, governor of Tlemcen, governor of Seville, and finally, governor of Granada and Cordoba; he distinguished himself in several military campaigns.

Tashfin Ibn Ali. A son of Ali Ibn Yusuf, he succeeded Ali as the Almoravid *Amir* at Ali's death in 1143.

Wajjaj Ibn Zalwi. The *sufi* master at the *Dar al-Murabitin*, the teacher and mentor of Abd Allah Ibn Yasin.

Yahya Ibn Ibrahim. Chief of the Bani Gudala, great chief of the Sanhaja confederation, he made a pilgrimage to Mecca cir. 1036 to 1039. He invited the preacher Abd Allah Ibn Yasin to come to the Sahara to preach to his tribesmen.

Yusuf Ibn Tashfin. A cousin of Abu Bakr Ibn Umar, he became the Almoravid *Amir* in the Maghrib when Abu Bakr decided to return to the Sahara in 1072.

Zaynab. The daughter of a merchant in Aghmat, she was the concubine of a tribal chief of the Masmuda, then was married to Laqut, the ruler of Aghmat, who was killed by the Almoravids. She then married Abu Bakr and later Yusuf Ibn Tashfin.

Glossary

Aghmati: A gold coin struck in the mint in the city of Aghmat.

al-Kanbitur: After the Spanish *al-Campeador*—the warrior. One of the terms used by Muslim historians to describe Rodrigo Diaz, better known as El Cid.

Almohads: An Anglicization of Arabic *al-Muwahidin* (pronounced almuwahideen) from the root W-H-D, which means one. It refers here to a Muslim group bound together by a religious ideology of absolute monotheism. The group formed in the High Atlas Mountains south of Marrakech; it became the main threat to the Almoravids and provided the dynasty of rulers who replaced them.

Almoravids: An Anglicization of the Arabic *al-Murabitin* (pronounced almurabiteen), from the root R-B-T, which means to bind, to tie up, make fast. In the context of the Almoravids, it means those who are bound together in the way/service of Islam.

amin: An official appointed by the director of marketplace supervision to ensure the accuracy of weights and measures.

amir: (pronounced ameer) A commander. Military commanders usually had administrative responsibilities, and political rulers had military responsibility. The term *amir* refers to a ruler at some level, the title of princes of a ruling family, a tribal chief. In this story, *Amir* (uppercase) refers to the ruler of the Almoravid empire.

aman: A guarantee of personal safety and protection under the law.

Andalusia: Muslims called the Spain that they ruled "al-Andalus." In this story, Andalusia refers to Muslim Spain. In modern times, Andalusia is the southern most province in Spain.

asabiya: Tribal solidarity.

Ash'arite: In Islam, a school of scholastic theology which attempts to reconcile religious doctrine with Greek thought. It was the theology adopted by the famous theologian al-Ghazzali, and it became the dominant theology in Sunni Islam.

awn: An official of the state whose job it was to see that rulings of the *hakim*s (judges) were carried out.

bab: (pronounced baab) A door or gate.

Bani Lamta: One of the Sanhaja tribes of the Western Sahara.

baraka: A special blessing/gift/power given by God.

Barghwata: A tribe located along the Atlantic coast of the Maghrib whom the Almoravids regarded as heretics.

bilad al-makhzan: Land controlled by the central government.

bilad as-siba: Land beyond the control of the central government, "lawless land."

caliph: Literally the successor to Muhammad. It came to mean the ruler of the Muslim world, ruling during the time of the Almoravids from Baghdad. There were occasionally rival caliphs, like those ruling in Cordoba in the tenth century and in Cairo in the tenth, eleventh, and twelfth centuries.

caliphate: The office of the caliph.

dar: House.

Dar al-Islam: Literally the House of Islam. It applied to the parts of the world under Muslim rule.

dar al-sikka: House where coins are struck, the mint.

Draa: Valley south of the High Atlas Mountains, west of Sijilmasa.

dinar: A gold coin weighing 1 mithqal (about 4.72 grams), a unit of currency.

dirham: A silver coin, a unit of currency. The "official" exchange rate of gold to silver coins in the eleventh century was around 1:18, whereas the actual rate of exchange could reach 1:35 or 1:40, depending on a number of factors such as deterioration of the silver content, hoarding in time of panic or calamity, and so on.

faqih: A scholar of Muslim law, a theologian, an expert of *fiqh*, a legist, one whose legal opinions are accepted as a basis of law.

fatwa: A formal legal opinion in Islamic law.

fiqh: Understanding, Islamic jurisprudence.

funduq: A caravansary, an inn, an enclosure to shelter travelers and their beasts of burden.

funduqiyya: A woman who frequents or who is employed at a *funduq*, usually a woman of ill repute.

gamamin: Agricultural zone; a series of enclosed fields within a larger enclosure.

Gazula: One of the tribes in the confederation of Berber tribes known as Sanhaja.

habus: (pronounced habous) Religious endowments.

*hadith*s: Sayings and traditions attributed to the prophet Muhammad through an unbroken chain of reliable sources.

hajib: (pronounced haajib) A chamberlain.

hakim: A secondary judge who ruled on individual civil and criminal cases in the court.

hasham: Entourage; military corps that serves as a bodyguard.

hisba: Manual for marketplace supervision.

huerta: The belt of irrigated land around the city.

Ifriqiya: What is today Tunisia and the eastern part of Algeria.

ijtihad: Independent judgment in a legal or theological question.

imam: A Muslim prayer leader; a leader of the religious community.

jami': A Friday mosque or congregational mosque; the central mosque where the public prayer is performed on Fridays.

jihad: From the Arabic root J-H-D, it means to struggle. In Islam, it means to struggle in the way of/for the sake of Islam. It evolved to mean holy war.

jizya: A poll tax paid by Christians and Jews who were citizens in a Muslim state. It was viewed as a form of submission.

katib: A secretary or scribe.

kharaj: A land tax, paid usually by non-Muslims.

Kharajite: One of the three main sects of Islam, the other two being Sunni and Shi'ite. Kharajite Islam is the sect that was predominant in North Africa in the early centuries of Islam.

khettara: A gravity-fed, underground aqueduct, constructed by digging vertical shafts in a line and connecting them by digging a horizontal tunnel through which water travels. This system is called *qanatir* in much of the Arab World.

khurras: A tax assessor.

kufic: A style of Arabic script that consists of square-shaped letters.

lamt: An oryx, a large African antelope whose hide was used to make the broad shields of the Almoravids, shields for which they became very famous. The shields were three cubits long (four and a half to five feet) and protected both rider and steed.

Lamtuna: One of the main tribes of the Berber confederation of tribes known as Sanhaja. In another sense, it was (and still is) a caste name applied to a nobility and to a military aristocracy.

litham: A veil worn over the lower half of the face.

madhab: (pronounced math-hab) One of the four accepted schools of law or legal interpretation in Sunni Islam. Sunni is one of the three main sects of Islam, the other two being Shi'ite and Kharajite.

madrasa: A theological university.

maghram: Illegal taxes, those taxes not sanctioned by the Koran.

Maghrawa: A tribe from the Berber confederation known as Zanata. They invaded Sijilmasa and defeated the Almoravids shortly after the latter had taken control of it, necessitating a second conquest by the Almoravids.

Maghrib: Literally "West"/*al-Maghrib* = "the West." It is a common abbreviation for Jazirat (pronounced jazeerat) al-Maghrib, which means island of the west and refers to Muslim land west of the Libyan Desert, north of the Sahara, and bordered by the Atlantic and Mediterranean seas.

mahalla: Encampment.

Mahdi: The divinely guided one, the one who will conquer the world and restore it to true Islam. Belief in the coming of the Mahdi became an essential creed in Shi'ite Islam as well as for the Almohads.

Masmuda: One of the three great confederations of Berber tribes who were located mainly in the Atlas Mountains.

Massufa: One of the tribes in the confederation of Berber tribes known as Sanhaja.

ma'una: A special tax or aid levied in time of war. It is a tax that is not sanctioned in the Koran.

Mecca: Holy city in Saudi Arabia, the birthplace of Muhammad, location of the holy shrine, the Ka'ba. One of the five duties of Muslims is to make a pilgrimage, once in a lifetime, to this city.

minbar: The chair from which the imam preaches his Friday sermon.

muezzin: The man who calls Muslims to prayer.

muhtasib: The director of marketplace supervision.

mujassimun: (pronounced mujassimoon) Anthropomorphists.

murabit: A gold coin struck by the Almoravid state.

maridin: (pronounced marideen) Insurgents.

Muwatta: The book of Malikite law.

qadi: A judge.

qasba: A fortress or citadel.

qasr: A fortified village.

qibla: The direction toward Mecca.

qusur: Plural of *qasr*.

rak'a: In Muslim prayer ritual, a bowing of the body from an upright position, followed by two prostrations, accompanied by the repetition of liturgical formulae. A normal prayer service consists of a varying number of *rak'a*s.

Reconquista: Re-conquest. Refers here to the effort made by Spanish Christians to recapture land that was conquered by Muslims beginning in A.D. 711.

ribat: A fortified post, where horses were sometimes stabled, and the garrison which combined military duties with agriculture and pious and ascetic practices, geographically located on or near the frontier of *Dar al-Islam*. A fortified monastery or convent. At times, however, this word had a metaphorical meaning and indicated a frame of mind, a spiritual resolve, or that which combined deep devotion to Islam, self-sacrifice, and the courage to face alone, or with a like group, those enemies which threatened the faith.

riyad: A garden.

sahib al-madina: The chief of police in a city.

salah: Righteousness or piety or godliness.

Sanhaja: A confederation of Berber tribes, mainly from the Sahara Desert. The Almoravids were from this confederation.

shaykh: An elderly, venerable man; an elder; a chief of a tribe.

sikka: The striking of official coinage; the official insignia/inscription that appears on the coinage.

Shari'a: The law of Islam.

sufi: (pronounced souffy) A Muslim mystic. The term comes from the Arabic *suf*, which means wool and probably refers to the wool clothes worn by communities of mystics.

Sunna: The prophet Muhammad's way of doing things based on traditions going back to the life of the Prophet and his companions. It included the ritual ablutions, prayer, almsgiving, and the other duties taught by the Prophet.

suq: A market place.

sura: A chapter from the Koran.

Sus: A region in the southwestern part of the Maghrib.

Taifa: Party or factionalized kings/states. It refers to the several independent Muslim states that emerged after the collapse of the Umayyad state based in Cordoba, Spain.

taqlid: Blind, unquestioning adoption; the study of law limited to uncritical imitation.

tawhid: Belief in the absolute unity of God.

ulama: Religious scholars in Islam.

ushr: Tithe.

vizier: A minister or administrator in the service of the state.

zakat: Legal alms. One of the five duties of Muslims is to give alms. At the time of the Almoravids, it amounted to a form of tax, one of the few sanctioned by Islam. It was an income tax assessed on one's money, gold, and silver, live-stock, agricultural produce, and movable property—that is, buildings, furniture, clothing, and slaves.

Zanata: One of the three great confederations of Berber tribes who were located mainly in the plains north of the Atlas Mountains.

Commentary on Sources

INTRODUCTION

There are very few modern monographs about the Almoravids. In 1946, J. Beraud-Villars wrote a popular account in French, *Les Touaregs au Pays du Cid*. A decade later, Spanish historian Jacinto Bosch Vila wrote *Los Almoravides*, an excellent summary of the medieval chronicles. There are a number of monographs in Arabic. In 1962 (?), Ibrahim Harakat published *Al-nizam as-siyyasi fi ahd al-Murabitin*, and in 1969, Muhammad Abd al-Hady Shu'ayrah published *Al-murabitun, ta'rikhihim as-siyyasi*. The latter was especially useful in describing the Almoravids' strategy in conquering the Maghrib. More recently, French scholar Vincent Lagardère wrote *Le Vendredi de Zallaqa*, which, although it focuses on the first battle of the Almoravids in Spain, is a comprehensive description of the dynasty. Lagardère's book *Les Almoravides*, published three years later, is a general history of the dynasty but ends at the beginning of the reign of Ali Ibn Yusuf.

There are several good journal articles on the Almoravids which will be described in the notes of individual chapters as they apply. The best, most comprehensive, article in English is by I. Hrbek and J. Devisse, which appears in volume III of *Unesco, General History of Africa*.

The author who is most relevant to the introduction is Ibn Khaldun, born in Tunis in 1332. His family had moved there from Seville when that city fell to the Christians in the thirteenth century. His ancestors were famous for the bravery they showed in the battle of Zallaqa when the forces of the king of Seville fought alongside the Almoravids against their dreaded enemy, King Alfonso VI of Castile. Ibn Khaldun was fond of the Almoravids.

Ibn Khaldun's family had a long and distinguished tradition of public service and scholarship. Growing up in a household frequented by many scholars, Ibn Khaldun studied theology, philosophy, logic, mathematics, astronomy, medicine, and, of course, history. He also learned administrative affairs, that is, how to properly draw up official documents. When Ibn Khaldun was 20 years old, he began his career in politics as a secretary for the sultan. For the next two decades, he held a number of political offices in several royal courts in North Africa, in Fez, in Granada, and in Algeria. He often witnessed and sometimes was a part of political intrigues. His own political fortunes rose and fell with those of the rulers he served. He spent almost two years in prison in Fez for taking the wrong side, and he barely escaped imprisonment a second time; rather, he spent another four years under the protection of an Arab chieftain. He knew the political life of North Africa from the inside, and he spent his later life as a scholar trying to explain it. It was during C.E. 1375–1378 that he wrote most of his *Muqaddimah*, a three-volume *Introduction to History* in which he laid out his paradigm for the rise and fall of dynasties.

The most accessible version of *The Muqaddimah* to the English reading public is the three-volume translation by Franz Rosenthal published in 1958. In 1967, N.J. Dawood edited and abridged the Rosenthal translation. Biographical information on Ibn Khaldun comes from Yves Lacoste's *Ibn Khaldun* (1966 and 1984), whose work also provides interpretive insights; Philip Hitti's *History of the Arab Peoples*, who refers to Ibn Khaldun as one of the greatest historians of all times; and the *New Encyclopedia of Islam*.

Recent sociological analysis of tribes and Berbers comes from Ernest Gellner's *Saints of the Atlas* (1969) and *Arabs and Berbers* (1972). Especially useful from the latter collection of essays is David M. Hart's essay, "The Tribe in Modern Morocco: Two Case Studies." Richard Fletcher (1992) provides a good description of the wealth of medieval Spain and cites Ibn Hawqal and Recemund of Elvira regarding the "green revolution," the introduction of new crops and agricultural technology. The medieval Arabic sources will be identified and discussed as they apply to individual chapters. Editions of these sources are identified in the bibliography.

CHAPTER 1. ISLAMIC REFORMISM COMES TO WEST AFRICA

Dialogue about how and when Islam spread to West Africa is ongoing. The classic work by J. S. Trimingham (1962) says that during the tenth century the Sanhaja chiefs of the western Sahara converted to a nominal Islam and that trading centers, like Awdaghust, with their large foreign population, assumed the characteristics of Muslim towns. In an earlier work (1959), Trimingham describes the process in distinct stages: first, a preparatory stage in which contact of some sort, visits and settlement of traders and clerics, leads to the breaking down of cultural barriers and the adoption of certain aspects, chiefly material, of Islamic culture, features like the wearing of Islamic amulets, ornaments and dress, and the acquisition of food and household habits; second, a stage which involves the assimilation of religious elements of Islamic culture- such as ritual prayer and recognition of certain categories of permitted and prohibited, making them during this second stage religious dualists; the third stage is the conscious rejection of old religious authority in favor of Islam.

H. T. Norris (1982) offers the best discussion of the genealogical origins of the Almoravids based on several Arab authors. His genealogical chart is based essentially on Ibn Abi Zar (d. 1315) and Ibn Idhari (1312). He stresses the importance of tradition, whether based on fact or not, in creating a sense of identity. Finally, he suggests that Lamtuna was not only a tribal name among the Saharans, but that it had another sense. It was, and still is, a caste name applied to nobility and to a military aristocracy. Vincent Lagardère (1978 and 1989) offers the most complete genealogical treatment of the Lamtuna clan of the Bani Turgut, the clan of Yahya and Abu Bakr Ibn Umar, of Yusuf Ibn Tashfin and his descendants.

The first major Muslim ruler among the Sanhaja may have been Muhammad, called Tarishna, of the Lamtuna tribe, who made the pilgrimage to Mecca in 411/1020 and acquired the idea of a jihad to justify his campaigns against the blacks to the south. When he was killed in 414/1023, succession passed to Yahya Ibn Ibrahim, who made the pilgrimage described at the beginning of this chapter. At that time, the process of conversion was in its second phase at best. The Berbers of North Africa converted first to the sect of Kharijism. Its tendency toward puritanism and austerity and its insistence on the independent, personal merits of the ruler were especially appealing to the Berbers.

The pilgrimage of Yahya Ibn Ibrahim likely began in 427/1036; at least that is the date accepted by most historians. That means he would have returned in 430/1038–1039. Ibn Abi Zar is the source for those dates. Ibn Khaldun (d. 1406) dates the pilgrimage in 440/1048–49. But al-Bakri (wr. 1068) and Ibn Idhari (wr. after 1312) mark the beginning of Ibn Yasin's jihad in the Sahara as 440/1048–49. If Ibn Khaldun's date were correct, Ibn Yasin would have had only a year or less to develop a following and mobilize a military offensive. Ibn Abi Zar's date, on the other hand, would have given him a full decade. *Kitab al-Istibsar* says that the adoption of Islam by the tribes of the desert was in the year 435/1043; that is within four years of Ibn Ibrahim's return from his pilgrimage with his new teacher.

H. T. Norris (1982) describes Abu Imran's political theory. Abd Allah Laroui (1979) suggests that Abu Imran was influenced by al-Baqillani's political theory of using Asharite law as the ideological basis for anti-Fatimid propaganda and saw a similar opportunity for Malikite Islam in the West, not only against the Shi'ites, but against Kharijites as well. After being expelled from Morocco by the Maghrawa rulers, it is not unlikely that Abu Imran felt more than a little resentment for the Maghrawa. The questions that Abu Imran put to Yahya Ibn Ibrahim, as recorded in the chronicles of Ibn Abi Zar and al-Nasiri al-Slawi (1894) suggest that his overly dramatic state of shock at Ibn Ibrahim's ignorance of the law might have had ulterior motives, that is, of spreading Malikite doctrine.

Al-Tadili (wr. 1221) is the source for the brief biographical sketch of Wajjaj Ibn Zalwi and the naming of his school *Dar al-Murabitin*.

The most complete picture that we have of Abd Allah Ibn Yasin is in the work of al-Bakri, who wrote his famous travelogue just after the Almoravids had begun their conquest of the Maghrib. They had not yet even begun to build their city at Marrakesh. Although al-Bakri never left Spain, his knowledge of the Maghrib and the Sudan was extensive. It was based on written and oral, historical, and contemporary sources. Al-Bakri was an Arab from Cordoba; he was not a Berber as were the Almoravids. We sense in him some resentment toward the conquerors. For instance, in the year that he writes this work, 460/1067–1068, a full decade after the Almoravids appeared in the Maghrib, al-Bakri writes, "The commander of the Almoravids until this day is Abu Bakr Ibn Umar, but their power is divided, not unified, and they stay in the desert." Yet he presents a total picture of Ibn Yasin, "warts and all," an uncompromising jurist of the Malikite school of law, a miracle worker, a fanatic and ascetic, a great lover of beautiful women, a military tactician

Commentary on Sources

and commander quite capable of victory, cruel and unforgiving, yet a saint revered by his followers long after his death. He certainly achieved a level of charisma equaled by very few individuals. The word that al-Bakri used to describe the quality that he had is *salah*, which means righteousness, or piety or godliness. It is al-Bakri who lists among Ibn Yasin's earliest goals, "the propagation of truth, suppression of injustice, and the abolition of illegal taxes."

The miracles of Ibn Yasin that al-Bakri recounts, like the liberties that he permitted himself while denying them to others, are part of Saharan culture and folklore. H. T. Norris (1971) tells us that similar stories appear in the biographies of other Saharan saints and are a tangible sign of their transcendental *baraka* or special status.

The severity with which Ibn Yasin punished those who transgressed the law is such that it seems exaggerated. Likely, it is. On the other hand, the use of the whip is one of the Almoravid practices that Ibn Tumart, the Almohad challenger, would later attack. Norris tells us that several medieval European illustrations depict a veiled Almoravid flailing a knotted strap.

Al-Bakri provides the most complete description of the capital of medieval Ghana. Again, the timing of his writing is important. He describes that capital shortly after the beginning of the Almoravid dynasty when the ruler of Ghana is not a Muslim, yet many Muslim merchants live there, and shortly before their alleged conquest of the city, a subject that is taken up in Chapter 8. The city that al-Bakri describes is more than likely Koumbi Saleh, about 150 miles southeast of Tegdaoust. What we know about that site comes from the archaeological investigations of A. Bonnel de Mézieres (1920), M. D. Lazartigues (1939), R. Mauny (1950–1954), and most recently a mission of the Institut Mauritanien under the direction of Serge Robert (1975–1981). The most recent archaeological publication describing the finds is that of Sophie Berthier (1997).

Qadi Iyad of Ceuta (d. 1149) offers us a biographical sketch of Ibn Yasin toward the end of the Almoravid regime. The Qadi was a convinced and militant Malikite, sympathetic to the Almoravids and, in fact, a leader of resistance to the Almohads in Ceuta. This sketch closely follows al-Bakri's description but adds a few interesting details. For instance, it is Qadi Iyad who calls our attention to the ignorance of Islam on the part of the Sanhaja in the western Sahara, saying that they do no more than profess the faith. He also identifies the interpreter Jawhar as the chief of the Bani Gudala and the one who discourses with Abu Imran. Contrary to the other Arabic sources, he omits any reference to

Ibn Ibrahim altogether. Norris offers as a plausible explanation that Jawhar served as an interpreter because of his superior knowledge of Arabic. Qadi Iyad focused on Jawhar's role because of his own interest in Malikite jurists.

Ibn Abi Zar's description also closely follows al-Bakri's, adding a few details. There is some confusion about the identity of Ibn Abi Zar, but we do know that his history was written in Fez in the early fourteenth century and reflects the historiographic genre of the Marinid dynasty, which accentuates the cumulative effect of a succession of dynasties on the formation of a single country. The link which attaches the Marinids to preceding dynasties is Moroccan soil—the country. Ibn Abi Zar's treatment of the Almoravids, then, underscores their role in the formation of Morocco as an independent geographic and political entity. Ibn Abi Zar places more emphasis than any other writer on the personal attachment between Ibn Yasin and his former teacher from Morocco, Wajjaj Ibn Zalwi. He says that it was Wajjaj himself who wrote to Ibn Yasin, imploring him to overtake Sijilmasa.

Ibn Idhari, writing at about the same time as Ibn Abi Zar, views the role of the nation more in a global context. He accentuates the unity of the Maghrib and Andalusia and emphasizes the influence of the Maghrib on the history of Andalusia, a view no longer acceptable to the Marinids, since their own experience was more limited than the preceding dynasties of the Almoravids and Almohads. He alone, for example, mentions Ibn Yasin's sojourn in Andalusia during the reign of the Taifa kings.

A puzzling turn of events is Ibn Yasin's departure or expulsion from the Bani Gudala and his subsequent move to the camp of the Bani Lamtuna. The change occurred shortly after the death of Ibn Ibrahim and the election of a new chief for the confederation. Following an accepted procedure for tribal election, Yahya Ibn Umar of the Bani Lamtuna was chosen. Norris (1972) tells us that Ibn Umar's mother was Safiya al-Gudaliya (of the Bani Gudala), and perhaps a sister of Yahya Ibn Ibrahim. That would be in keeping with the custom of matrilineal succession and intertribal marriages among the ruling elite.

Moroccan author Mukhtar al-Abbadi (1960) suggests that Ibn Yasin's endorsement of the Lamtuna candidate is the reason that he was exiled from his abode Arat-n-anna. Imposing some degree of egalitarianism among the elite of that town might also have contributed to Ibn Yasin's unpopularity. Norris (1982) discusses possible meanings of the word Arat-n-anna based on information from Saharan Berbers. The Berber word has been translated as "our camp of low pitched tents," or "our hollow place." Ibn Yasin fled to his former teacher at the *Dar al-Murabitin*. Upon his return to the Sahara, he waged jihad against those who opposed him. Both Ibn Abi Zar and Ibn Idhari say that it is at that point that he called his followers Almoravids (*al-Murabitun*). Whether it was because of their affiliation to the fraternity of Wajjaj in the Moroccan Sus or because of the establishment of a base (*ribat*) in Gudala territory in southern Mauritania is unclear from the Arabic sources and has been the subject of much discussion by scholars Paulo Farias (1968), A. Huici-Miranda (1959), and H. T. Norris (1986).

Almoravid is an Anglicized version of *al-Murabitun*. The root of that word is R__B__T__ which means "to bind, tie up, make fast." In form three, *rabata* means "to be lined up, posted, stationed (troops); to line up, take up positions; to move into fighting positions." The derivative *rabita* means "band; bond, tie; connection, link; confederation, union, league." Norris, in the glossary of his book, says that a *"Ribat* is a fortified post where horses were sometimes stabled, and the garrison which combined military duties with agriculture and pious and ascetic practices, geographically located on or near the frontier of *Dar al-Islam*. At times, however, this word had a metaphorical meaning and indicated a frame of mind, a spiritual resolve, or that which combined deep devotion to Islam, self sacrifice and the courage to face alone, or with a like group, those enemies which threatened the faith." Al-Bakri, Ibn Abi Zar, and Ibn Khaldun all described Ibn Yasin's withdrawal to a *ribat*. They do not, however, satisfactorily indicate where it was. Paolo Farias provides extensive discussion of its location.

Neither Qadi Iyad nor Ibn Idhari make mention of a *ribat* as such. The latter instead connects the name Almoravids with the valor of Ibn Yasin's followers in battle. The term "to be lined up, posted, stationed" could even refer specifically to the tightly linked battle formation described both by al-Bakri and Ibn Idhari. It could well be that the term Almoravid, as applied to this movement begun by Ibn Yasin, has a wide range of meanings; perhaps the meaning evolved as did the movement itself. In addition to the meanings discussed above, the term evoked a new meaning when the Almoravids carried their jihad against the Maghrawa of Sijilmasa and brought more reforms to the city than the residents might have wanted.

Al-Bakri is the source for the account of the Almoravid conquest of Awdaghust. Ibn al-Athir is the source for the appointment of Yusuf Ibn Tashfin as the first Almoravid governor of Sijilmasa, the springboard from which the Almoravids launched their campaign to control the rest of the Maghrib.

CHAPTER 2. GATEWAY OF THE SAHARA

Sijilmasa is located immediately to the west, just outside the city gate, of modern Rissani in the province of Errachidia. It is about 200 miles due south of Fez across the Middle and High Atlas mountains. The medieval city, at its largest stage, stretched along the east bank of the River Ziz between the village of al-Mansuriya at the north end and the village of Tabassamt nearly five miles down river. These limits have been determined on the basis of local oral tradition as well as research conducted by a joint Moroccan-American team under my direction sponsored by the Moroccan Institute for Archaeology and Middle Tennessee State University, and funded by grants from National Geographic, Earthwatch, the Social Sciences Research Council, the Max Van Berchem Foundation, and the Barakat Foundation.

Six seasons of excavation at Sijilmasa between 1988 and 1998 have succeeded in locating the very heart of the medieval city. We produced a detailed map of the central part of the site, the area where the central part of the medieval city is believed to be located and where most of the excavations have occurred. Those excavations revealed significant architecture with stone foundations and column bases in the area of what local tradition identified as the mosque. Trenches west of the mosque, dug during the 1994 season, revealed a bath complex with major canalization and what appears to be a hot water heater. Next to the bath is a public latrine. Both of these facilities are typically found near a mosque. In 1992, excavations along the SSE wall of the structure called "the mosque" exposed the foundation of the *mihrab* (prayer niche), several degrees off the correct orientation toward Mecca. Local inhabitants assured us that that was the case with many mosques built in Morocco during the middle ages, a fact corroborated by a study of the orientation of major mosques in Morocco by Michael Bonine (1991). The name of the mosque comes from the hagiography of al-Tadili (wr. 617), who identifies several scholars who taught in the mosque.

In 1994, further excavations in the mosque distinguished three levels of construction. At the third floor level beneath the surface, we observed two phases of construction, an original building and an expansion. The evidence suggests that the surface mosque was the renovation project of Sidi Mohammed Ben Abd Allah in the late eighteenth century. The mosque beneath that we believe to be the mosque built during the century following the collapse of the Merinid control of Sijilmasa. At the third floor level, to the right of the *mihrab*, we exposed two narrow trenches and wooden beams running perpendicular to the narrow trenches. We believe this to be the emplacement for the rails for a movable *minbar*, the only one to be found from that period in an archaeological context. The bulk of the evidence suggests that the expansion at this third level was the work of the Almohad dynasty, which controlled Sijilmasa from the mid-twelfth century to the late thirteenth century. The original structure at the third level, we believe, was occupied by the Almoravids and perhaps earlier dynasties, such as the late Midrarids and Maghrawa. Beneath that floor is evidence of occupation, dated by C-14, going back to the eight century, the earliest Midrarid period of Sijilmasa's history. During the 1996 season, a piece of plaster was found with the words *"wus'aha ... kasabat ... 'alayha ..."* words from the Koran II, 286. The entire verse reads *"la yukalifu Allahu nafsan illa wus'aha laha ma kasabat wa 'alayha ma'ktasabat,"* which translates as "On no soul doth God place a burden greater than it can bear. It gets every good that it earns, and it suffers every ill that it earns."

The geography team (Dale Lightfoot and James Miller) created a hypothetical map of medieval Sijilmasa, showing it as a large, elongated walled city surrounded by its *gamaman* (agricultural zone), and with a large market area to the west. Satellite imagery dramatized the finiteness of the water and agricultural resources and confirmed that the river Ziz, along the east bank of which Sijilmasa developed and thrived, was an artificial channel created by man during the Middle Ages (we now think during the reign of the Almoravids). In 1994, Tony Wilkinson refined the map of medieval Sijilmasa. We now know that Sijilmasa was not a single walled city. Souk Ben Akla, just outside of the wall of the *gamaman* on the west side of the city, turns out to be a self-contained urban entity, contemporary with and associated with medieval Sijilmasa. The distribution of surface finds at Souk Ben Akla, for example the high percentage of portable storage vessels compared to tableware, strongly suggests that it served as a staging area for the large caravans that crossed the Sahara. The central part of the city itself was not as large as we originally thought. It extended just under a mile from north to south with outlying occupation, probably individual villas that filled the elongated walled area to the north and south of the urban center.

The best description that we have of Sijilmasa contemporary to the Almoravids is that by al-Bakri. He provides not only a physical description of the city but also details of its history from its founding up to the conquest by the Almoravids. Other medieval Arabic sources provide additional important details. For example, al-Mas'udi (wr. 947) describes the central axis of the city as a half day's walk from north to south. Ibn Hawqal (wr. 988) tells us that Sijilmasa produced an annual revenue of 400,000 *dinar*s and estimates the entire Fatimid income for the Maghrib at 800,000 *dinar*s. Ibn Battuta (wr. 1355) says that every inhabitant of Sijilmasa had a house and a garden in the center of town, probably meaning within the city walls. Al-Umari (wr. 1337–1338) tells us of Sijilmasa's reputation for the production of dates, a reputation that the region of the Tafilalt still enjoys today.

In the late nineteenth century, an English journalist, W. B. Harris, wrote a journal of his travels in the region of the Tafilalt and provides descriptive passages of the environment and the ruins of the city as he saw them several hundred years after the decline of the city. Two standard articles on Sijilmasa have appeared in the twentieth century, one in the first edition of the *Encyclopedia of Islam* by G. S. Colin (1934) and a second article on Sijilmasa according to Arab authors by E. Mercier. Two young Moroccan scholars have produced doctoral dissertations on Sijilmasa, Mohamed El Mellouki (1985) and Lahcen Taouchickt (1989). The latter was especially useful in tracking down the names for the gates of the city as well as information on the limits of the city based on oral tradition. Mellouki gives us the name of the mosque based on the biographical sketch of Ibn al-Nahwi, established by al-Tadili and Ibn Maryam. Ibn al-Nahwi went to Sijilmasa to teach at the mosque during the reign of the Almoravid Ali Ibn Yusuf.

Raymond Mauny (1960) provides many details about the trans-Saharan caravan trade during the Middle Ages, about the routes traveled by merchants and the products exchanged in the trade. A more popular account of the trans-Saharan gold trade is provided by E. W. Bovill (1986), who cites several references to the use of blind guides in the western Sahara from medieval times through the nineteenth century. Leo Africanus, writing in the sixteenth century, also tells a story of a blind guide. The description of the silent trade during the Middle Ages is provided by al-Mas'udi. The first reference to the silent trade is by the classical Greek historian, Herodotus. There is also a reference as late as the fifteenth century in the writing of Ca da Mosto. So there must have been some continuity to this practice, or at least its legend, although not necessarily in the same location. Al-Umari tells the story of Mansa Musa, the king of Mali who became legendary for making a pilgrimage in C.E. 1334–1335. A myth associated with his pilgrimage is that he took with him 100 camels each carrying 300 pounds of gold in the form of millstones, the quantity of gold being so great that it caused inflation in the markets in Egypt. The best, concrete measure that we have of the volume of the trans-Saharan gold trade during the period in question is the production of gold coinage in North African and Andalusian mints. My analyses of gold coinage (1974 and 1980) suggest that the gold trade peaked during the late Almoravid period.

The slave trade is much more difficult to measure. The transportation of slaves across the Sahara on a regular basis is probably linked to the arrival of Islam. Al-Yaqubi, writing in the ninth century, is the first to mention it. Al-Bakri tells us of the specific culinary skills of black slave women in Awdaghust, who prepared *jawzinaqat* and *qata' if* and who sold for 100 *mithqal*s. That information, with slightly more detail is repeated by the anonymous author of *Kitab al-Istibsar* (wr. 1191); he adds *lawzinaqat* (almond cakes), *qahiriyyat*, *kunafat* (semolina with honey and butter), and *mushahhadat* (thin layered pastry) to the list of delicacies. Both Al-Bakri and the author of *Kitab al-Istibsar* tell us of the sexual exploits of the beautiful slave girls. The latter describes the purchase of slave girls to offer as prostitutes. S. D. Goitein (1967) suggests that a *funduq* was a place where one could meet, or was suspected to have met, with a woman of bad reputation, a *funduqiyya*. Al-Idrisi (wr. 1154) describes the incursions into the land of Lamlam to hunt for slaves destined for the markets in the Maghrib. He is also the writer who describes the merchants of Aghmat confiding their caravans to slaves. Ibn Idhari tells us that Yusuf Ibn Tashfin bought 2,000 slaves to serve in his new army. Leo Africanus, writing much later in the sixteenth century, describes the slave markets in the Dra'a Valley and in Sijilmasa.

Determining the volume of the trans-Saharan slave trade is near impossible. Ibn Battuta (wr. 1355) describes a single caravan going from Takedda to Touat as having 600 slaves. Al-Umari says that Mansa Musa took some 12,000 slaves with him on his pilgrimage. *Tarikh es-Soudan*'s figure of 500 is likely to be much closer to reality. At the figure of 500 to 600 slaves per caravan, if 35 to 40 caravans crossed the desert yearly, Raymond Mauny estimates that some 20,000 slaves were transported across the Sahara per year. More recently, Ralph Austen places the number of slaves taken across the Sahara during the medieval period at 6,000 per year or more.

The Geniza documents (Goitein, 1967) show the value of books in the Mediterranean world. They were the kind of property that constituted part of the wealth of a family, along with real estate, jewelry, and fine clothes. They became heirlooms and were used as collateral to obtain substantial loans. Al-Umari specifically refers to books on Malikite law coming from Cairo and being very expensive.

Three silver coins bearing the name Mas'ud Ibn Wanudin, the last Maghrawa ruler of Sijilmasa before the Almoravid conquest, were found at the site in 1988. Information on the earlier striking of coins by the Fatimids and the Umayyads comes from J. Devisse (1970). In a hoard of 32 *dinar*s (still unpublished), discovered in 1992 in Aqaba Jordan, 29 were struck in Sijilmasa during the late Umayyad period. The coinage of the Almoravids is described both by H. Hazard (1952), Hanna Kassis (1985), and R. Messier (1972 and 1980).

The conquest of Sijilmasa by the Almoravids is the most dramatic event in the city's history. It was the springboard from which the Almoravids launched their conquest of the rest of the Maghrib and Andalusia. The Almoravids brought Sijilmasa into a state that encompassed all of Morocco. Accordingly, the city changed from being the capital of an independent city-state, the capital of an autonomous Berber state, to a provincial capital, the center of a province within a much larger empire.

CHAPTER 3. FROM AGHMAT TO MARRAKECH

Ibn Hawqal (wr. 988) described Aghmat in the same breath with all of Ifriqiya, Fez, al-Andalus, and all of the Sus. Al-Bakri describes Aghmat as two cities, Aghmat Wurika and Aghmat Haylana. It is al-Idrisi (wr. 1154) who describes the wealth of the markets and the people of Aghmat. That geographer was a descendant of the Bani Hammud, former rulers of Malaga who were in turn an offshoot of the Idrisid founders of Fez. He wrote his book, often referred to as *Kitab Rujar*, for King Roger II of Sicily in the year 1154, thus within less than a decade after the collapse of the Almoravids. One of his principal sources of information is the work of al-Bakri, of which he repeats many of the details. He does update the information, though, to take into account historical changes over the preceding century. Aghmat, like other commercial centers, benefited from being within the larger economic system created by the Almoravids. Physical descriptions of Aghmat here and in later chapters are based on ongoing archaeological research begun in 2005 under my direction.

Of the conflict with the Barghwata, it is Ibn Abi Zar who gives the most detailed account, including the exact date of Ibn Yasin's death. Al-Bakri and Ibn Idhari confirm the year. Qadi Iyad gives the size of the Almoravid army. Several other sources—Ibn Khallikan (wr. 1274), Ibn Khaldun, and the anonymous author of the *Hulal al-Mawshiyya* (wr. 1381)—mention Ibn Yasin's death at the hands of the Barghwata. Of Abu Bakr's campaign against the Barghwata to avenge Ibn Yasin, we know almost no details. The fact that it is so briefly mentioned in the chronicles probably means that it had only limited success at best.

The role of Zaynab al-Nafzawiya seems only at first glance to be somewhat exaggerated. As H. T. Norris (1972) tells us, many of the stories told about Zaynab read like folktales. The imagery of subterranean dwellings, treasure, and protectors of uncanny powers are all characteristic of the *jinn*. Norris provides other examples of women playing key roles in the epic of the Bani Lamtuna: "These lettered Saharan princesses, Hawwa,' the free maid, the niece of Yusuf Ibn Tashfin, Tamima, the sister of Ali Ibn Yusuf, were personalities of charm and power." Both Ibn Idhari and the author of the *Hulal* say that Abu Bakr's authority in the Maghrib was established in the year 460/1068, the very year that they give for his marriage to Zaynab. Al-Bakri, writing one year before the marriage, says that the authority of the Almoravids is not yet established. Folklore notwithstanding, though, it seems clear that Zaynab was one of the keys to political power in the Maghrib, first for Abu Bakr and then for Yusuf Ibn Tashfin.

There is some confusion in the sources concerning the date of, as well as the person responsible for, the founding of Marrakech. Both Ibn Abi Zar and Ibn Khaldun date the founding of the city in 454/1062 and attribute the foundation to Yusuf Ibn Tashfin. In fact, both sources agree that this took place after Abu Bakr appointed Yusuf as his lieutenant in the Maghrib while he himself returned to the Sahara to quell a rebellion. Ibn Idhari and the anonymous author of the *Hulal* both agree on the date 463/1070 as the date for the founding of the city and on the role of Abu Bakr in choosing the site and laying the foundation before leaving for the Sahara in 1071. Al-Bakri, writing in 1067–1068, makes no reference whatsoever to Marrakech. Since al-Bakri is so thorough and detailed on all other matters, the fact that he omits any mention of Marrakech strongly suggests that the city was founded after he wrote, a suggestion that favors the date given by Ibn Idhari and the *Hulal*. The fact that Ibn Idhari describes in considerable detail the role of Abu Bakr in the founding of the city, plus the fact that the portion of the *Bayan* giving this account was discovered relatively recently (see A. Huici-Miranda, 1959) strengthen the argument for the later date. Several scholars who relatively recently have examined the issue rather closely favor the later date. See, for example the work of Paulo Farias (1967), Paul Semonin (1964), and G. Deverdun (1959). The latter is the most thorough modern study of the history, geography, art, and architecture of the city of Marrakech.

CHAPTER 4. THE SECOND FOUNDING OF FEZ

As early as C.E. 951, the Arab writer al-Istakhri, talking about the northern Maghrib, described Fez as "the principle city of this province." Ibn Hawqal, who visited Fez at about this same time, was impressed by the stone-paved streets and emphasized the commercial importance of the city by describing the variety of products available in the market. The people of Fez, he says, even unscrupulously trade with the heretical Barghwata. The most complete description of Fez that predates the Almoravids is that of Al-Bakri, who wrote just a year or so before the Almoravid conquest. He places Fez at the very hub of trade routes going to Oujda, Tangier, Ceuta, and Sijilmasa. He sizes the Qarawiyin Mosque at six bays. The Al-Andalus Mosque, he says, has only three bays. There are 300 mills in the city and 20 baths, compared to the 472 mills and 93 baths listed by Ibn Abi Zar. The source for Pope Sylvester II's study at the Qarawiyin is Moroccan author Abd al-Hady al-Tazi.

Accepting the later date of C.E. 1071 for the founding of Marrakech, as we suggested in Chapter 3, presents a different problem in chronology, that is, what to do with the series of events that Ibn Abi Zar and Ibn Khaldun chronicle in detail concerning Yusuf's campaign against the Zanata and the conquest of Fez. Those authors describe the events as taking place after the founding of Marrakech and Abu Bakr's return to the Sahara but date that long war with the Zanata as beginning in 455/1063 and culminating with the conquest of Fez in 462/1070. This date is from Ibn Abi Zar and repeated by Ibn Khaldun. Ibn Idhari and the anonymous author of the *Hulal*, on the other hand, say that Fez was taken by the Almoravids in 467/1074–1075.

Vincent Lagardère (1989) offers a lengthy discussion supporting the later date. Overall, he is very suspicious of the accuracy of Ibn Abi Zar, even though that author presents the most detailed account, actually two accounts, which Lagardère says are contradictory. I do not find Ibn Abi Zar's accounts contradictory. Rather they emphasize different events in the long complicated sequence. The biggest problem that I have with Lagardère's chronological framework is that it presents a gap of almost an entire decade in Almoravid history.

What we have, in the final analysis, are two conflicting chronologies. There is that of Ibn Abi Zar (wr. 1315), who offers a very detailed account of the Almoravid war against the Zanata culminating in the conquest of Fez. The imminent historian Ibn Khaldun (wr. 1374–78) adopts the same chronology. The second is that of Ibn Idhari (wr. 1312), who presents a shorter, more straightforward account (according to

Commentary on Sources

Lagardère) that is adopted by an anonymous author (wr, 1381). All four were historians who compiled information from earlier writers. We will probably never know for sure which sequence is true.

R. Le Tourneau (E.I.2, II, 818) is skeptical of any date before C.E. 1075 for the conquest of Fez. Le Tourneau's reasoning is that Yusuf conquered Fez after the founding of Marrakech, which most scholars now place in C.E. 1071. A plausible chronology that resolves the dilemma of the relationship between the founding of Marrakech and the conquest of Fez is that the entire campaign against the Zanata was sandwiched between the establishment of Marrakech as a fortified camp sometime in the 1060s and the beginning of the actual building of the city in C.E. 1070–1071, which will be discussed in Chapter 5.

The chronology in our narrative is admittedly based primarily on Ibn Abi Zar, who Hopkins and Levtzion (1981) caution might have manipulated chronology to present what he considered a more meaningful history. Maya Shatzmiller (1982), on the other hand, says that Ibn Abi Zar preserved "with vigor" the chronological order of his history of the various dynasties. Ibn Khaldun, the famous Arab historian who wrote his universal history in the late fourteenth century, felt comfortable copying Ibn Abi Zar's chronology in most instances. J. Bosch Vila (1956) has written a monograph on the Almoravids in Spanish in which he sorts through much of the confusion in chronology. Still, some problems persist in his analysis. He retains, for example, the earlier date of C.E. 1060 for the founding of Marrakech.

Concerning the date of the conquest of Fez, the author says that it is simply *too* confusing; though he does make some interesting observations concerning Yusuf's more or less successful strategy in this campaign to isolate the major cities by controlling the space between them.

The layout of what is called Fez al-Bali today was basically established by Yusuf Ibn Tashfin. Roger Le Tourneau (1961) suggests that most of the engineering of Fez's medieval waterworks date from the Almoravid period. The most detailed description of the water supply of medieval Fez appears in Ibn Abi Zar's writing more than 200 years after Yusuf's conquest of the city, but the description makes it clear that the water system had been operative for a long time.

Fez al-Jadid was built immediately to the west of Fez al-Bali in the late fifteenth century, and the Ville Nouvelle was built to the west of Fez al-Jadid by the French beginning in 1912. This pattern of westward expansion of the city was established when the Almoravids built their citadel to the west.

CHAPTER 5. THE URBAN NOMAD

What we know of Abu Bakr's return to the Sahara is mostly folkloristic. To be sure, authority among the Sanhaja depended directly upon the personal presence of rulers. In that context, Abu Bakr made more than one return trip to the Sahara to keep his authority alive there. Ibn al-Athir mentions such an expedition taking place just after Abu Bakr gained complete control over Sijilmasa and after he appointed Yusuf Ibn Tashfin governor. Another trip took place in C.E. January, 1071, after the founding of Marrakech and after Yusuf had conducted his successful campaign against Fez and was called back by Abu Bakr to serve as his deputy in the whole of the Maghrib. Again, there is some confusion over the date for this expedition.

Was it necessary for Abu Bakr to divorce his wife Zaynab before returning to the Sahara? If not necessary, it was at least practical. He knew that he would be gone for some time and that there was a certain amount of danger in going to quell a revolt in the desert. Divorcing his wife made it easier for her to come under the protection of another man. Before modern modes of transportation made travel easier, a person from West Africa or from the Maghrib making the pilgrimage to Mecca could be gone for as much as two years. And many pilgrims never returned at all. It was custom among Moroccans until recently to divorce one's wife before leaving on the pilgrimage. It was the same custom that Abu Bakr had observed. That Abu Bakr spent time in Sijilmasa making final preparations for his return underscores the importance of that desert port to the Almoravids' control over the Maghrib. It is here that the Almoravid military strength was split between Abu Bakr and Yusuf Ibn Tashfin. Ibn Abi Zar says that the army was split in half, Abu Bakr taking half with him to the Sahara and leaving the other half under Yusuf's command. Ibn Idhari, on the other hand, says that the split was two-thirds of the army returning to the Sahara and one-third remaining under Yusuf's command. In either case, the armies of each would have to be rebuilt. Abu Bakr was returning to the desert where he could recruit more Sanhaja tribesmen. Yusuf Ibn Tashfin would recruit more Sanhaja, to be sure, but he also had to rely on maintaining the allegiance of tribes in the Maghrib and upon local reinforcements. Both Ibn Abi Zar and Ibn Idhari provide details of Yusuf's military recruiting. Vincent Lagardère (1978–1979) has written an excellent article on the military organization of the Almoravids. The anonymous author of the *Hulal* undoubtedly exaggerates when he describes the abundant gifts that Yusuf offered to

Abu Bakr when they confronted each other upon Abu Bakr's return. Still, it must have taken a considerable fortune as well as a show of force to induce Abu Bakr to surrender half of his realm without a fight. Abu Bakr decided to retreat to the desert, ceding jurisdiction in the Maghrib to Yusuf. Abu Bakr led the Almoravid movement in the Sahara until his death in 480/1087. Abu Bakr's success in the Sahara was climaxed by his conquest, albeit short lived, of Ghana. Al-Zuhri, writing in the first half of the twelfth century and quoted by Paul Semonin (1964), says that "formerly the inhabitants [of Ghana] were infidels, but in the year 469/1076–77 they became good Muslims under the influence of the Lamtuna."

Yusuf, for his part, was sincere in his piety and was an ascetic in his own personal habits. He may not have been a visionary. On the contrary, when it came to political power and his desire to spread the rudimentary Malikism of the Almoravids, he was every bit the opportunist.

CHAPTER 6. WAR IN THE MAKHZAN

Moroccan historian Abdallah Laroui (1977) criticizes "colonial" historians, that is, historians that are European or European trained, of oversimplifying the structure of the Almoravid state by calling it tribal. It was tribal, but it was more than that. Authority of the state, as Yusuf Ibn Tashfin set it up, was twofold: military and religious. The army was made up of contingents of diverse origin, but positions of command, positions that invariably carried some administrative responsibility, were held mostly by members of Yusuf's confederation and most often from his own tribe. Religious authority was exercised by the *faqih*s (doctors of Malikite law).

Ibn Idhari is the only one of the medieval chroniclers who mentions the important episode of Ibrahim's challenge of Yusuf's authority. Hanna Kassis (1985) makes interesting observations about it, especially in reference to numismatic evidence. He refers to a coin struck in Sijilmasa in A.H. 453 bearing the name of Ali, the nephew of Abu Bakr, indicating that Ali was one of Yusuf's successors as governor of Sijilmasa. The fact that Ali was also bold enough to strike coins in Sijilmasa raises interesting questions about the unsettledness of the affairs of the nascent state in these early years. Governors of Sijilmasa were tempted to assume more authority than was intended.

The account of Yusuf's confrontation with Suqut al-Barghwati and Suqut's reference to the Almoravid drums comes from Ibn Abi Zar and

An-Nasri as-Salawi. Suqut is not the only opponent of the Almoravid military to express terror at the sound of the Almoravid drums.

Both Ibn Khaldun and An-Nasri as-Salawi tell us that Yusuf Ibn Tashfin consulted with the *faqih*s in Fez on the concept of jihad before he embarked on his campaign in Andalusia. We do not know exactly what the *faqih*s told him, other than that it was his duty to defend Islam against the infidel. In all likelihood, it was consistent with Malikite doctrine as it was taught in Western Islam. Ibn Abi Zayd al-Qayrawani (d. cir. C.E. 972) wrote in his *Risala* that jihad was a duty of divine institution, that Malikites should not initiate hostilities unless the enemy takes the offensive, and that they should offer the enemy three choices that Yusuf indeed offered to the king of Castile.

CHAPTER 7. JIHAD IN ANDALUSIA

The Muslim commander who conquered Spain was Tariq Ibn Ziyad. It was in the year 92/711 that Tariq left Tangier with an army of 9,000 Berbers and established a foothold on the rock that bears his name, *Jabal Tariq*, better known today as Gibraltar. According to legend, he burned the ships that carried him to Andalusia and told his followers that they were here to stay: "Whither can you fly? The enemy is before you and the sea behind you." Within three years an army of some 20,000 Arabs and Berbers conquered Spain and decided to stay. Although only one source, Ibn Idhari, mentions Ibn Yasin's sojourn in Spain before he went to preach to the Sanhaja in the Sahara, it is likely that Ibn Yasin did go there and that his own puritanical understanding of Islam was scandalized by life in the courts of the Taifa kings. That would explain why the Almoravids viewed the Andalusians to be too lax in their practice of religion. The philosophic speculation engaged by Andalusian scholars was more lax than the strict adherence to the Malikite law of the Almoravids.

The rulers of the Muslim states in southern Spain on the eve of the Almoravid invasion are called in Arabic, *Muluk al-Tawa'if*. The term usually used in English is Taifa kings. The most important ones included Badajoz, Toledo, Seville, Cordoba, Granada, Murcia, Denia, Valencia, and Zaragoza. But at times there were as many as 30 Taifa states. The number varied as more powerful ones absorbed weaker ones. David Wasserstein (1985) remains one of the foremost authorities on the Taifa kings.

The anonymous author of the *Hulal* identifies al-Mutawakkil Ibn al-Aftas, king of Badajoz, as the first to write to Yusuf asking for his help to fight the Christians in 474/1081–82. The Zirid king of Granada, Abd Allah, who kept detailed notes of his own reign and involvement in the *reconquista*, reports that his brother, the king of Malaga, was the first to invite the Almoravids to come to Andalusia giving him an edge in his rivalry with his brother in Granada, promising Yusuf a share of the spoils. The *Hulal* reports Mu'tamid's proverbial response to his son, expressing his preference to be a camel driver in the desert than a swineherd in Spain.

Ibn Abi Zar describes the Almoravid crossing itself. Yusuf's words sound overly dramatic. Still, there is little doubt that the Almoravids were convinced that they were fighting in God's cause and that he would grant them victory. Ibn Abi Zar says that the crossing took place on 15 *Rabi al-Awal*. But Huici-Miranda (1963) offers convincing arguments for a date one month later than the one given by Ibn Abi Zar—hence, 15 *Rabi al-thani*, 479/30 July, 1086. Shortly before the Battle of Zallaqa, Yusuf made a final offer to Alfonso VI to "convert, pay the *jizya*, or fight." These are the same three choices listed by Ibn Ziyad al-Qayrawani in his *Rihla*. Yusuf's long letter to Alfonso is reproduced both in the *Hulal* and by al-Maqqari (d. 1632), as is the debate over the choice of the day to begin the attack.

To document every detail of a battle of the magnitude of Zallaqa is a reporter's nightmare. There are many varying narratives of the course of the battle, each from a different vantage point. Specific details of the battle are remembered differently by each narrator. Just how many troops were engaged in the battle of Zallaqa on that day is hard to say. The numbers of a charging army always seem greater than they really are. The *Hulal* says that 300,000 Christians were killed, which is surely an exaggeration. His figure of 3,000 Muslim casualties is probably much closer to being realistic. All of the accounts say that Alfonso VI was wounded in battle. The *Hulal* and al-Maqqari describe the black slave pinning Alfonso VI's leg to the horse with his dagger. Al-Maqqari gives the figure of 500 of Alfonso's men who managed to escape; Ibn Abi Zar says that there were 100. As to the total number of forces engaged in battle, the sources give a wide range of estimates on both sides. Ibn Abi Zar estimates the size of the Christian army at 80,000 knights and 200,000 foot soldiers. He does not give a total number of the Muslim army but says that Da'ud Ibn Aisha left with an advance guard of 10,000 knights while the main army followed. Ibn al-Kardabus (twelfth century) cites the number of Christians at 60,000 and the number of Muslims at 12,000. Ibn al-Athir (d. 1233) gives the number 50,000 for Alfonso's army. Abd al-Wahhid al- Marrakushi (wr. 1224) lists the total number of Muslim troops at 20,000, of which 7,000 were mounted. Al-Himyari (wr. 1347) lists the Christian army at 40,000. The author adds that the Christians feel that the number is exaggerated, but that both sides agree that the Muslim forces were less numerous than the Christians. If the truth is somewhere in the middle of the various estimates, then the Christian army probably outnumbered the Muslims two to one, cir. 40,000 to 20,000. It is clear that both sides had misjudged the strength of the opposition.

Huici-Miranda (1963) discusses the various Muslim and Christian chronicles. He presents each of the principal narrations of all of the important phases of the battle as well as to the events leading up to it. He presents arguments supporting or refuting the different narratives. In a sense, Huici-Miranda does what al-Maqqari did in the sixteenth century, to present a summary of the chronicles trying to portray what he thought really happened as he waded through the conflicting reports. Although Huici-Miranda, as al-Maqqari, claims to be objective, I detect a national bias in the writing of both. This comment is not intended to deter the reader from examining Huici-Miranda's excellent summary and analysis.

Vincent Lagardère's monograph (*Le Vendredi de Zallaqa*, 1989) is the most recent, thorough discussion of the Battle of Zallaqa. As background, Lagardère summarizes much of the history of the dynasty both before and after this pivotal event. His intent is to highlight the significance of the Battle of Zallaqa as a focal point for Almoravid history. The earlier history of the dynasty led them logically to Zallaqa, to wage war against the Christian enemy, to defend the *Dar al-Islam*. What followed was the logical consequence—an unrelenting attempt to consolidate an empire that stretched from the Senegal River in Africa to the Ebro River in Spain.

CHAPTER 8. THE STATESMAN

The conquest of Ghana by the Almoravids is an issue of some debate. According to the *Kitab al-Jughrafiya* written by al-Zuhri in the first half of the twelfth century, the kingdom of Ghana accepted Islam in 469/1076–1077 due to the influence of Abu Bakr. David Conrad and Humphrey J. Fisher, in *The Conquest that Never Was* (1982), claim that Ghana was not conquered by the Almoravids. Their evidence is the absence of references to the conquest in sources other than al-Zuhri, whose statement, in their judgment, is inconclusive. On the other side of the argument is Sheryl L. Burkhalter, *Listening for Silences in Almoravid History: Another Reading of "The Conquest that Never Was"* (1992). She explains the "silences" of the medieval Arab authors who focus on the Almoravids in the Maghrib and Andalusia rather than in the Sahara and sub-Saharan regions by saying that, for those authors, the historically significant unit was the "state," and "the Almoravid state was the Maghrib and Spain as defined over and against, in the words of Ibn Khaldun, 'the various tribes of veil-wearers...who stayed in the desert [and] remained in their primitive state of dissension and divergence.'" Burkhalter suggests that the Almoravid who led the expedition to conquer Ghana was none other Abu Bakr's son Yahya.

Al-Tadili (wr. 1221) says that Abu Bakr engaged the services of Imam al-Hadrami to accompany him to the Sahara to teach and to administer justice among his people. That the imam had a considerable impact on the people in the desert is manifest in the oral traditions of the western Sahara. Paulo Farias (1967) describes several of these sources. Al-Tadili tells us that he died in 489/1096, a decade after the death of Abu Bakr. Farias suggests that during his last years the imam continued to teach and exert his religious influence upon the regions under Almoravid control.

Ibn Abi Zar provides the date for Abu Bakr's death. But the rich oral traditions of the area provide the details. Was Abu Bakr really killed by a blind bowman? Traditions in modern Senegal and Mauritania say that he was, and the Arab chronicler Ibn Abi Zar reports that he was killed by a poisoned arrow. The Senegalese traditions also tell us that before Abu Bakr left on his last campaign, he told the wife that he had married among the blacks that she was allowed to marry again, provided that her new husband was a pious man, a sincere convert to Islam who was able to read the Koran and performed the ablutions and the five prayers according to the law. Some of the descendants of this wife became leaders among their tribe. At the very least, Abu Bakr left a strong legacy in the western Sahara as a man of great *baraka*.

Three sources allude to Yusuf Ibn Tashfin's diplomacy with lands in the Sahara and beyond. *Kitab al-Istibsar* explicitly says that the king of Ghana sent a letter to Yusuf, but does not describe its content. Al-Maqqari mentions that Yusuf advised his son not to disturb the tribes in the desert. Yaqut, writing in the first quarter of the thirteenth century, says that the veiled people (the Sanhaja) acknowledged the superiority of the king of Zafun. He describes the king on his pilgrimage stopping to visit Marrakech. The Almoravid *Amir* met him on foot and led him into the palace while the visitor remained mounted on his horse. T. Lewicki (1971) suggests that this event happened in the second quarter of the twelfth century when the Almoravids were very much on the defensive against Ibn Tumart. The *Ta'rikh al-Sudan* is the source that tells us that Timbuctu was in fact a settlement of the Bani Massufa, who began to camp there around C.E. 1100, only thereafter to become the fabled city that it did.

The coinage of the Almoravids is described both by H. Hazard (1952) and R. Messier (1972, 1974, and 1980). The 1974 article discusses in detail the fineness of the coins and the purity of the ore from which the *dinar*s were struck. The 1980 article focuses on the volume of Almoravid currency in circulation and the opening of new mints. Articles by Duplessy (1956) and Misbach (1970) attest to the impact of Almoravid currency in Europe.

Ibn Abi Zayd al-Qayrawani, author of the most complete compendium of Malikite law available to the Almoravids, was born in Andalusia in 310/922–923. He spent most of his life and pursued his studies in Qayrawan, the fountainhead of Maghribi Malikism. Leon Bercher, in the introduction of his edition of the *Risala*, describes the work as a compendium of the doctrines, both dogmatic and legal, that conform to the *Sunna* of the Prophet as transmitted through the chain of Malikite legists. It is comparable to the better known work, the *Mukhtasar* of Khalil. But the latter was compiled in the fourteenth century and was not available to the Almoravids. Abu Muhammad Abd al-Wahid al-Marrakushi is very explicit in his criticism of Ali Ibn Yusuf for supporting the *faqih*s in their abandonment of the study of the Koran and *Hadith* in favor of the books of Malikite law.

"No illegal taxes" in an Islamic context means those taxes not sanctioned in the Koran. The problem with tax reform under Islamic law is that the tax structure is not that tightly defined in the Koran to begin with. The distinction between certain taxes, especially the land tax (*kharaj*), was much less clear in practice than it was in theory. Maghribi writers show little interest in the subject and restrict their remarks to conventional statements such as that "such-and-such a king, on his accession, abolished illegal taxes and imposed only those allowed by the *shari'a*." J. F. P. Hopkins, in his article, "Dariba," *Encyclopedia of Islam*, II, discusses the confusing question of taxation in Islam. In his *Medieval Muslim Government in Barbary*, he briefly describes policies of taxation of the Almoravids. His discussion is brief because that is all the medieval sources will permit.

As described in Chapter 2, Fatimid tax revenues in the Maghrib were considerable. They collected customs dues on the buying and selling of camels, sheep, and cattle, as well as customs on all the merchandise destined to or coming from Ifriqiya, Fez, Spain, the Sus, and Aghmat. Those taxes, in addition to the *zakat* and *kharaj* provided, according to Ibn Hawqal (wr. 988), were half of the revenue for the entire Fatimid state. Ibn Abdun, writing in the early twelfth century, describes the levies on commodities in Andalusian cities, as well as the agents responsible for collecting the taxes. The Almoravids promised "no illegal taxes" when they came to Andalusia as they had done in the Maghrib. Their popularity lasted only as long as their tax reform.

Yusuf Ibn Tashfin, like Abu Bakr before him, chose military commanders and governors from the association of various tribes among the Lamtuna, the Massufa, and the Gudala, but mainly from the branch of the Lamtuna known as the Bani Turgut. Ibn Idhari registers the myriad of parental ties among many of the Almoravid administrators, and Vincent Lagardère (1978) has graphically mapped these relationships in a very informative article.

Ibn Abd al-Malik al Murrâkushi, in his *al-dayl wa al-takmila*, provides the physical relationship among the mosque, the bridge across the *seguia*, and the main road of Aghmat. The Moroccan-American excavations under my direction (2004–2009) confirmed that information as well as descriptions of the palace and *hammam*.

CHAPTER 9. A WAR OF SIEGES WITH THE TAIFA KINGS

Ibn Abi Zar continues to provide the chronological framework for this chapter. The memoirs of Abd Allah, king of Granada, provide insights into the court intrigue that plagued the siege of Aledo and contributed to its ultimate failure. Abd Allah was a major participant in this series of events. His perspective is that of one of the Taifa kings who had solicited the military arm of the Almoravids but then grew leery of their presence and eventually fell victim to their conquest.

The anonymous author of the *Hulal* records Mu'tamid's crossing the straits and meeting with Yusuf Ibn Tashfin on the shores of the River Sebou. He provides us with Mu'tamid's solicitous words on jihad. The later chroniclers, al-Marrakushi and al-Maqqari, quote other sources, since lost, that add details for the events. Al-Marrakushi describes Yusuf's thoughts on the wealth of Spain, with Mu'tamid's disparaging words about the Almoravids and the verse that Ibn al-Labbana offered to console his king in exile. Al-Maqqari provides the details of Mu'tamid's defeat and exile as well as the verses that the exile composed in Aghmat.

It is testimony to Yusuf Ibn Tashfin's political savvy that he "legalized" his defeat of the Taifa kings by seeking a *fatwa* and having it sanctioned by highly respected legal scholars in the East. It is Ibn Khaldun who informs us of the *fatwa* and its approval by none other than al-Ghazzali. Equally astute was Yusuf's diplomatic mission to the Abbasid Caliph in Baghdad. Lévi-Provençal (1955) preserves the text of the petition along with the reply of the caliph and a description of the letter written by al-Mustansir's secretary Muhammad Ibn Muhammad Ibn Ghahir. Lévi-Provençal points out that the two ambassadors arrived in Baghdad as late as four years after their departure from Seville and that they remained in Baghdad for two years from 489/1096 to 491/1098 before they returned to Yusuf with the letter of investiture. The text of the Sevillian ambassadors mentions that during their stay in Baghdad, a *qadi* from the Maghrib also came to Baghdad after making the pilgrimage and informed them (the Sevillians) of the political situation of the Almoravid Amirate. It is Ibn al-Athir who informs us that Yusuf sent these ambassadors upon the suggestion of the *faqih*s. Numismatic evidence confirms what the envoys told the Caliph about Yusuf's minting policy. Most of the coins struck by the Almoravids bear the inscription "*al-imam*, Abd Allah, Amir al-mu'minin." A few coins of unknown date add "al-Abbasi."

CHAPTER 10. THE ALMORAVIDS CONFRONT EL CID

This chapter is not a history of El Cid. About that legend out of history much has already been written. An excellent appraisal of the role of Rodrigo Diaz, El Cid, was written by Richard Fletcher, *The Quest for El Cid* (1989). Fletcher identifies and describes the medieval sources for the history of El Cid. The most important ones on the Christian side are the *Historia Roderici*, a historical account, and the *Poema de Mio Cid*, an epic poem. On the Muslim side, there are also two medieval sources. Ibn Alqama a native of Valencia and who served as a bureaucrat in neighboring Denia, wrote the earliest account and called it "The clear exposition of the disastrous tragedy." Ibn Alqama (d. 1116) was a contemporary of the events that he describes, which include El Cid's capture of Valencia and his subsequent rule over the kingdom. As the title of his work implies, Ibn Alqama is hostile toward El Cid. He wrote from the point of view of someone on the losing side. The second source is that of Ibn Bassam (d. 1147), a native of Santarem in Portugal. He, too, was contemporary to the events he describes. He devotes only a few pages to El Cid at the end of his biographical account of Ibn Tahir, ruler of the Taifa kingdom of Murcia who settled in Valencia after he was deposed. Ibn Tahir survived El Cid's rule in Valencia with some difficulty. Fletcher also discusses "modern" historiography of El Cid. Over the centuries, El Cid became a legendary national hero in Spain. In 1849, Dutch Orientalist Reinhardt Dozy published an essay called "Le Cid d'apres de nouveaux documents," or "New light on El Cid." Dozy claimed to paint the portrait of a historical figure, rather than a legendary one. He described El Cid of history as a condottiere who was not humane, loyal, or patriotic. On the contrary, he broke promises, pillaged churches, and fought for whichever side would pay him money. Because he fought as much, if not more, on the Muslim side, Dozy described El Cid as "more Muslim than Catholic."

H. T. Norris (1982) addresses the legend of the "Amazons" in the Almoravid army, citing the *Primera Cronica General* of Alfonso X and L. P. Harvey's article in *The Journal of Semitic Studies*. The latter wrote: "I therefore think that King Bucar had a group of Touaregs in his army, and that because of their outlandish veiled garb these warriors smeared with indigo were mistaken by the Christians for negresses."

Menendez Pidal published *La España del Cid* in 1929 which sought, with considerable success, to restore El Cid's heroic reputation. Pidal does consider all of the sources but is hardly objective in his use of them. For Pidal, there is no distinction between El Cid of history and El Cid of legend.

Fletcher himself describes El Cid as a mercenary but adds that he uses "mercenary" as a neutral term that describes "one who serves for pay." He adds that El Cid made his living out of warfare; he was a professional soldier.

Rather than presenting a history of El Cid, this chapter hopes only to chronicle important events in the history of the Almoravids in Spain and to describe how they might have perceived El Cid. They were defeated more than once by the Christian mercenary. They knew enough of war and experienced the price of victory enough to respect El Cid for what he was. They also had to be frustrated by his presence in eastern Andalusia. He was the strongest opponent to their hegemony to date.

CHAPTER 11. ALI IBN YUSUF SETS HIS HOUSE IN ORDER

The physical description of Ali Ibn Yusuf comes from the work of Ibn Abi Zar. Consistent with his laudatory approach to the history of the Almoravids, Ibn Abi Zar portrays Ali favorably and specifically describes his reign as good government, modeled after that of his father. Much more critical of Ali's administration is Abu Muhammad Abd al-Wahid al-Marrakushi. The discrepancy between the two could possibly result from the fact that the first author has focused on the early part of Ali's career while the second is sensitive to conditions that became more problematic in the second half of Ali's reign. The figures for the wealth of the treasury that Ali Ibn Yusuf inherited are given by al-Nasiri al-Slawi (1894), whose chronicle is a composite of several of the medieval sources. The figures are probably hyperbolic, but all the sources underscore that the treasury was very rich.

The description of the new palace in Marrakech built by Ali is based on the work by Deverdun. His information about this structure is based, in turn, on archaeological work done by H. Terrasse and M. Jacques-Meunié. The size of the blocs in the corridor is 1.4 meters long by .6 meters wide. That Ali held audience here on a weekly basis is speculation on the part of Deverdun. Ali did, however, see himself as ruling in the fashion of an Andalusian monarch. "Going to the port" is an expression in Eastern Islam that refers to seeking an official audience with the sovereign.

Deverdun also summarizes the debate about the origin of *khettaras*, called *qanatir* in Spain and other parts of the Arab world. G. S. Colin argues that the system as it exists in Morocco originated in what the French call the "pré-Sahara," the steppes on the northern edge of the Sahara. There is no question that the system was introduced under Ali Ibn Yusuf, who surrounded himself with Andalusian scholars and engineers.

The date for the completion of the mosque is uncertain; dates given in medieval texts range from 514/1120–1121 to 527/1132. Deverdun favors the earlier date. The cost of the mosque is given by Ibn al-Qattan. The size was 120 by 80 meters. The minaret was 10 by 10 meters square, and if it was completed at a ratio consistent with what is standard, it would have been 30 meters high. The *minbar* is larger than most, at a height of 3.86 meters. The inlay is described as a symphony by Basset and Terrasse in *Sanctuaires et Forteresses almohades*. The fountain was 14.5 × 4.5 meters. The marble basin is in the *Madrasa* of Ali Ibn Yusuf. It is not certain from where the marble basin was imported; Ibn Abi Zar informs us of the one that Abd al- Malik installed in Fez. Nor is it certain that it was imported by Ali himself. Gaston Migeon (1926) claims that it was brought to Marrakech by the Almohads. Deverdun feels that that is not logical because it was not found in their mosque and the decoration is not consistent with their unitarian puritanism.

Idrisi (1866, 1879) informs us of the Almoravid decree forbidding Jews from living in the city or even staying overnight, allowing them only to do business and "specialized trades." On the other hand, S. D. Goitein provides evidence of Jews doing business in Marrakech from letters from the Cairo Geniza. Goitein concludes that there are no trades that are exclusively Jewish in this period, but there are some which are largely Jewish, for example gold and silver smiths, glass-makers, butchers, and textile workers. In Sijilmasa, al-Bakri says that Jews were the masons. Al-Wansharisi, in his *Mi'yar*, reports on the *faqih*s' ruling on the Almoravids' wearing of the veil. Al- Marrakushi criticizes Ali's heavy reliance upon the advice of the *faqih*s. He also provides us with Abu Ja'far's words that are so critical of the *faqih*s themselves. The incident surrounding Abu'l-Fadl Ibn al-Nahuwi's teaching in the Sijilmasa Mosque is reported by al-Tadili and by Ibn Maryam as quoted by Mellouki (1985).

Several sources describe the burning of the books. The chronicler Ibn Qattan identifies Ibn Hamdin as the *qadi* responsible for the *fatwa* and for initiating the book burning. The *Hulal* refers to "the first days of 503." Ibn Zayat al-Tadili and Ibn Maryam inform us of the dissident in Sijilmasa, Abu'l-Fadl Ibn al-Nahuwi.

The *katib*s were responsible for drafting official letters for the Almoravids. A considerable number of letters or fragments of letters that allegedly emanated from the Almoravid chancellery are quoted in the works of Ibn Bassam, al-Maqqari, Ibn Khaqan, and others. Ibn Abdun, before working for Ali Ibn Yusuf, worked as secretary for Syr Ibn Abu Bakr, after that Almoravid commander conquered the city of Seville. It was perhaps in that capacity that he wrote, or at least gained the knowledge to write, the handbook for market supervision, which falls under a genre known as *hisba*. Its purpose is to provide a code of behavior for the various trades in a Muslim city. Ibn Abdun's work goes beyond the narrow scope of urban trades and treats several urban institutions within the context of a single city that he knew very well, Seville. Rachid El Hour's articles (2000 and 2001) help define the offices of *qadi* and *hakim*, reinforcing the idea that the Almoravids relied heavily on local elites all while trying to maintain the legal system under their central control.

Professor S. D. Goitein describes the practice of Muslim law as personal rather than territorial to be the case within the world of the Cairo Geniza. Jews, like Muslims, were subject to laws determined by religious courts. Enforcement of the law was the state's responsibility. Lévi-Provençal (1949) feels that Ibn Abdun exaggerates the dependence on Andalusians to fill all of these important posts, especially in the position of the *sahib al-madina*. Yet there is no evidence of Almoravids filling that post on the local level. It seems logical that a local police chief could be effective, in most instances even more effective, especially if he is backed up by a strong garrison of Almoravids. Ibn Abdun describes the reaction of the Sevillians to the presence of the veiled Almoravid troops.

In his description of the city of Marrakech, the geographer Idrisi lists the items that were taxed during the reign of Ali, items that were supposed to be tax exempt under the Almoravids. It is clear in the work of Ibn Abdun that the customs duties that were commonplace under the Taifa kings were again being assessed and collected under Ali. Ibn Al-Athir tells us that Christian mercenaries collected the tax, which must have literally added insult to injury.

CHAPTER 12. ALI IBN YUSUF FACES MUSLIM AND CHRISTIAN CHALLENGERS

It is only in passing that Ibn Idhari mentions the fleet of 70 ships that Yusuf Ibn Tashfin dispatched to Palestine at the time of the First Crusade. It is an important reference, though, because it reinforces the notion that the Almoravids had become ideologically committed to waging jihad against Christians. The Eastern author who articulated the concept of jihad as a war against Christians is the Damascene jurist Ali Ibn Tahir al-Sulami. Hadia Dajani-Shakeel (1991) describes the evolution of the anti-crusading ideal among the Muslims of the East. Al-Marrakushi, who is generally critical of Ali's reign, does say that Ali, like his father, called his followers Al-Murabitin and continued to wage jihad against the infidel. Jihad had become the main focus of Almoravid foreign policy.

Ibn Abi Zar and the *Hulal* continue to be the main chroniclers of the Almoravid campaigns against the Christians. The former provides specific, even if exaggerated, numbers of participants. He says that Ali crossed the straits for the first time with an army of 100,000 soldiers and that there were 23,000 Christian casualties in the battle of Uclés. The *Hulal* provides most detail about the relations between the Almoravids and the Bani Hud of Zaragoza.

Ibn al-Khatib (d. 1374) is the main source of information about the maverick Saharan, Ibn Tifilwit. However, Ibn al-Khatib does not refer to him by that name. He calls him Abu Bakr Ibn Ibrahim *al-amir* Abu Yahya al-Massufi. It is Ibn Abi Zar and the *Hulal* who use the name Ibn Tifilwit. The clue that they are all three talking about the same person is the fact that the hero in all three accounts—Ibn Tifilwit of Ibn Abi Zar and the *Hulal* and *al-amir* al-Massufi of Ibn al-Khatib—held the governorship of Zaragoza from A.H. 508 and was killed in A.H. 510. The writers disagree on what post the hero held before his appointment to Zaragoza. Ibn Abi Zar and the *Hulal* both say that he came to Zaragoza from Murcia. Ibn al-Khatib says he came from Granada. It is actually quite possible that the Saharan warrior held all three posts one after the other. As mentioned earlier in the story, it was common practice for Ali Ibn Yusuf frequently to rotate the ablest and most trusted military commanders from his own tribe to respond to emergencies or simply to shore up his authority all over the empire. For example, the *Amir* appointed his own brother Tamim governor of Granada in A.H. 500. Three years later he sent Tamim to Tlemcen. Some time before A.H. 515 he sent his brother back to Granada. For a year and a few months in 515 and 516, he transferred Tamim to Seville before his last appointment in Cordoba.

Al-Marrakushi quotes Syr Ibn Abu Bakr's reference of the Christians as polytheists. He called them that undoubtedly because of the Christian doctrine of the Trinity. Both Ibn Khaldun and Ibn Kardabus inform us of the Almoravid occupation of the Baleares.

The principal chroniclers of the Almoravids' confrontation with Ibn Tumart are Ibn Abi Zar, al-Marrakushi, Ibn Khaldun, Ibn al-Qattan, and al-Baydhaq. The latter was an early and enthusiastic supporter of Ibn Tumart. His near-contemporary account of Ibn Tumart's activities heavily favors him over the Almoravids. Algerian author Rachid Bourouiba has written a very useful little book on Ibn Tumart in which he carefully summarizes all of the information gathered from the above sources, along with his own interpretation. For example, Bourouiba presents a detailed discussion of the issue of whether or not Ibn Tumart studied with al-Ghazzali. Bourouiba concludes that he did meet al-Ghazzali, as does R. Le Tourneau (1947). Ignaz Goldziher, on the other hand, does not think the two met. Bourouiba also describes the various accounts of the debate between Ibn Tumart and the *faqih*s in Marrakech. The most detailed account describing the debate itself is that of Ibn Abi Zar. The others state more succinctly that Ibn Tumart embarrassed the *faqih*s and that he was banished from Marrakech. It is Ibn al-Athir who reports that Ibn Tumart knocked the *Amir*'s sister from her horse.

Although not the exclusive cause, the ascendancy of the Almohads is directly related to the decline of the Almoravids. The construction of the walls of Marrakech is a material manifestation of the apparent strength of one becoming defensive against the growing strength of the other. Today, visitors cannot help but be impressed by the soundness of the military engineering that went into the Almoravids' construction of those gates which still stand today, especially *Bab el-Debbagh* on the east side of the city. That gate is a huge, square tower that requires three right angle turns through three sets of enormous wooden doors. The gates and the walls, although they have been restored many times over the centuries, are still essentially as they were at the time of Ali Ibn Yusuf. They are the most visible legacy of the Almoravids in the city that was their own creation.

CHAPTER 13. VOICES OF DISSENT

The discontented poet whose verse opens this chapter is Abu Bakr Ibn Baki. His verse was collected in an anthology called *Qala'id al-Iqyan*, compiled by al-Fath Ibn Haqan. Henri Pères presents the poem and describes the poet, the anthology, and its compiler in his work "La Poésie à Fez sous les Almoravids" (1934). Pères suggests that the stifling impact of the Almoravid censors on the intellectual life of the late eleventh and early twelfth centuries was not as black as the picture painted by Reinhart Dozy. Still, he shows that life was precarious for those intellectuals who openly or implicitly criticized the regime. Some criticized the regime anyway. Ibn Haqan introduces Ibn Baki's poem saying, "Ibn Baki said in his attacks against the Maghribis...."

The revolt in Cordoba and the events that provoked it are chronicled in greatest detail by Ibn al-Athir. The incident is also mentioned by the anonymous author of the *Hulal* and by Ibn al-Qattan. Ibn Abi Zar mentions Ibn Rushd's replacement as *qadi*, suggesting that the *Amir* initiated the dismissal. Ali Ibn Yusuf's response, personally leading an expedition, his fourth to Andalusia, seems rather drastic. But it also provided an opportunity to go through the motions of jihad, which had become a cornerstone of the ideological justification of his military hold on Andalusia. Since the Christian threat at that time was in the East of Andalusia rather than in the West where he was, it was a symbolic jihad.

The ongoing Almoravid-Almohad conflict is traced by the chroniclers Ibn Abi Zar, al-Marrakushi, Ibn Khaldun, Ibn al-Qattan, and al-Baydhaq. The latter, written by an Almohad sympathizer, is the most detailed but the least objective. There are disagreements between the chronicles as to the exact sequence of events. Even Jacinto Bosch Villa in his detailed account based on the sources concludes that "the period between Ibn Tumart's departure from Igiliz, his establishment at Tinmal up to the Almohad disaster of al-Buhayra in 1130 is confusing" (210). Al-Baydhaq provides the core of the narrative while the others temper the tone and fill in details. Regarding the first siege of Marrakech, for example, it is al-Marrakushi who reports on Abd al-Mu'min's message to Ali Ibn Yusuf and Ali's response before the battle. Ibn Khaldun and al-Zarkashi agree that it was Ali Ibn Yusuf himself who led the charge out of the Bab al-Aylan. The Ibn Humushk episode appears in the *Hulal*, which also mentions that the Almohads lost 40,000 men in this siege. This defeat was a major setback and amounted to the ruin of most of the *Mahdi*'s army. Finally, Ibn Al-Athir engages in a bit of interpretive reporting as he states that the victory of the Almoravids was the direct result of the aid sent by the governor of Sijilmasa.

Ibn Khaldun uses the term Seven Year's War to describe the campaign between the Atlas and the Mediterranean, culminating in the fall of Tlemcen. It is impossible to reconstruct the exact route of this campaign since the sources list different sites for encounters between the armies. There is consensus, though, that the armies did march along parallel routes, with each army following terrain favorable to its own style of warfare.

Ibn Khaldun identifies the Massufa nobles whom Ali Ibn Yusuf appointed to governorships in Andalusia. John Hunwick published an intriguing article (1980) suggesting that the Massufa were the key to the Almoravid connection from Timbuctu to Almeria. As evidence, he points to Andalusian tombstones in Gao along the bend in the Niger River, Ibn Battuta's and *Ta'rikh al-Sudan*'s references to the Massufa as founders of Timbuctu in 1100, *Kitab al-Istibsar*'s reference to Almoravid-style coins being struck in Warjala, al-Zuhri's mention of caravan traffic between Warjala and Gao, and finally the wealth in gold that Eastern Andalusia received in exchange for her luxury goods shipped south. In fact, the Almoravid mint in Almeria struck more gold coins than any other Almoravid mint, including Sijilmasa during the last 50 years of the dynasty's history. The role of the Bani Massufa in this connection is further suggested by Sheryl Burkhalter's identification of al-Zuhri's "Almoravids inhabiting the land between Sijilmasa and Warjala" as the Massufa.

Vincent Lagardère (1988), drawing on juridical documents of al-Wansarisi and the official history of the Almoravids of Ibn al-Sayrafi as reported by Ibn Idhari, as well as from *al-Hulal*, presents as complete a picture we have of the position of the Mozarab communities as the Almoravid jihad escalates under Ali Ibn Yusuf.

The most direct statement describing opposition to Ali's administration is al-Marrakushi's describing the softening of the Almoravid elite and neglect by the *Amir* himself beginning as early as the year 500/1106–1107. The earliest specific references to defections among Ali's ranks, though, occurred in 525/1131 with the flood of defections coming after the death of Ali in 537/1142 and especially after the fall of Tlemcen in 539/1145.

It is through Christian sources that we identify Sayf al-Dawla as the model for the defectors. The letter from Sayf al-Dawla's co-religionists comes from the *Crónica Adefonsi Imperatoris* in volume XXI of *España Sagrada*, which chronicles *El Batallador*'s campaigns against the Almoravids and provides another dimension to the Muslim histories of Andalusia. For a secondary Spanish perspective on the gradual loss of Spain by the Almoravids, see F. Codera (1899).

The *Crónica Adefonsi* is also the major primary source of information about the career of Reverter among the Almoravids. Ibn Khaldun calls him *al-Rubutayr* and praises his valor, whereas Ibn Baydhaq, respectful of Reverter's military prowess, is hostile toward "the villain (*al-shaqiy*) al-Abritayr" and is relieved at his death.

CHAPTER 14. THE CENTER CANNOT HOLD

Tashfin Ibn Ali spent all of his adult life waging war against the Christians in Andalusia or the Almohads in the Maghrib and became a legend for his courage in both Muslim and Christian sources. His courage is especially celebrated in a poem attributed to the historian Yahya Ibn Sayrafi of Granada and reproduced in the *Hulal*. He was the last effective Almoravid *Amir*. His reign lasted less than 26 months. Most of the Muslim chronicles—Ibn Abi Zar, Ibn Khaldun, Ibn Baydhaq, al-Maqqari—report his tragic death with only minor differences in detail. Conflict between Tashfin and the *sufi shaykhs* in Sijilmasa is reported in al-Tadili's *Tashawwuf*, in the biographies of Abu Abd Allah Muhammad Ibn Amr al-Asam and Abu Abd Allah al-Daqqaq, the two *shaykhs* who took refuge to Fez. The legend of al-Ghazzali's curse comes from the *Buyutat Fas al-Kubra* by Isma'il Ibn al-Ahmar, translated here by H. T. Norris (1982).

The chroniclers tell us that Tashfin was killed on 27 *Ramadan*, 539/23 March, 1145. Coins were still struck in his name during the following year, 540. F. Codera and H. Hazard suggest that the chroniclers are wrong about the date. A more likely explanation for the discrepancy, though, is that Ibrahim Ibn Tashfin's regime was not sufficiently strong to strike coins in its own name. Coins were actually struck in the name of the Bani Tashfin in some Andalusian cities for a few years after Tashfin's death, in Granada as late as A.H. 545. The Bani Ghaniya, the last of the Almoravids north of the Sahara, continued to strike coins in the Balearic Islands.

Bibliography

MEDIEVAL SOURCES

Abd al-Rahman al-Sa'di, *Ta'rikh al-Sudan*. Edited and translated by O. Houdas. Paris: Adrien-Maisonneuve, 1964.

Anonymous. *Kitab al-istibsar fi 'aja'ib al-amsar*. Edited by Sa'ad Zaghlul 'Abd al-Hamid. Alexandria: Jāmi'at al-Iskandarīyah, 1958.

———. *Al-Hulal al-mawshiyya fi dhikr al-Marrakushiya*. Edited by I. S. Allouche. Rabat: Impr. Économique, 1936; Spanish Translation by Ambrosio Huici-Miranda. *Coleccion de Chronicas Arabes de la Reconquista*. Tetuan: Editora Marroqui, 1952; edition by Suhail Zakar and Abd al-Qadir Zamamah. Casablanca: Dār al-Rashād al-Hadīdthah, 1979.

———. *Mafakhir al-Barbar, Fragments historiques sur les Berbères au moyen âge, extraits inédits d'un recueil anonyme compile en 712/1312 et intitulé: Kitab Mafakhir al-Barbar*. Arabic text edited with introduction by E. Lévi-Provençal. Rabat: F. Moncho, 1934.

al-Bakri, Ubayd Allah Ibn Abd al-Aziz. *Kitab al-masalik wa-'l-mamalik*. (Arabic Title) *Kitab al-mughrib fi dhikr bilad Ifriqiya wa-'l-Maghrib*. (French Title) *Description del'Afrique Septrionale*. Edited and translated by Baron MacGuckin de Slane. Paris: Librairie d'Amérique et d'Orient Adrien-Maisonneuve, 1965.

Himyari, Abd al-Mun'im. *Al-rawd al-mi'tar*. Edited and translated by E. Lévi-Provençal in *La Péninsule ibérique au moyen-âge d'après le Kitab ar-Rawd al-mi'tar d'Ibn 'Abd al-Mun'im al-Himyari*. Leiden: E. J. Brill, 1938.

Ibn Abdun. *Séville musulmane au début du XIIe siècle: le traité d'Ibn Abdun sur la vie urbaine et les corps de métiers*. Edited and translated by E. Lévi-Provençal. Paris: Librairie Orientale et Américaine G. P. Maisonneuve, 1947.

Ibn Abi Zar. *Kitab al-anis al-mutrib bi-rawd al-qirtas fi akhbar muluk al-Maghrib wa-tarikh madinat Fas.* Edited and translated by C. J. Tornberg. Uppsala: Litteris Academicis, 1846.

———. *Kitab al-anis al-mutrib bi-rawd al-qirtas fi akhbar muluk al-Maghrib wa-tarikh madinat Fas. Roudh el-kartas Histoire des souverains du Maghreb et annales de la ville de Fes.* Translated by A. Beaumier. Paris: L'Imprimerie Impériale, 1860.

Ibn al-Athir. *Al-Kamil fi'l-tarikh.* Translated by E. Fagnan. Algiers: Typographie Adolphe Jourdan, 1898; edited by C. J. Tornberg. Leiden and Uppsala: E. J. Brill, 1851–1876.

Ibn al-Khatib. *A'mal al-a'lam.* Edited by E. Lévi-Provençal as *Histoire de l'Espagne musulmane extraite du Kitab A'mal al-a'lam.* Rabat: Institut des Hautes Etudes Marocaines, 1934.

Ibn Battuta. *Tuhfat an-nuzzar fi ghara'ib al-amsar wa-'aja'ib al-asfar* (generally referred to as *Rihla*, "Travels"). Edited and translated by C. Demfremery and B. R. Sanguinetti. Paris: Imprimerie Nationale, 1893–1922.

Ibn Buluggin Ibn Badis, Abdallah. "Mémoires de 'Abd Allah B. Buluggin B. Badis, dernier roi ziride de Grenade." Arabic Text and Arab Translation. Edited and translated by Lévi-Provençal. *Al-Andalus* 3, 4, 6: Madrid (1935, 1936, 1941).

Ibn Hawqal, Abu 'l-Qasim al-Nasibi. *Kitab surat al-ard.* Beirut: Dār maktabat al-ayāh, 1964.

———. *Kitab surat al-ard.* Edited by J. H. Kramers. *Biblitheca Geographorum Arabicorum* II, 2nd ed. Leiden: E. J. Brill, 1938–1939.

Ibn Idhari al-Marrakushi, Abu 'l-Abbas Ahmad. *Kitab al-Bayan al-mughrib fi akhbar muluk al-Andalus wa 'l-Maghrib.* Edited by Ahsan Abbas. Beirut and London, 1967. "Un fragmento inedito de Ibn Idhari sobre los Almoravides." *Hesperis Tamuda* II (1961). *Kitab Al-Bayan al-mughrib fi akhbar muluk al-Andalus wa 'l-Maghrib.* Edited by Ambrosio Huici Miranda. Rabat.

Ibn al-Kardabūs, Abū Marwān 'Abd al-Malik. *Historia de al-Andalus.* (*Kitāb al-Iktifā'*). Madrid: Akal, 1986.

Ibn Khaldun, Abu Zayd 'Abd al-Rahman. *Al-Muqaddama.* Edited by M. Quatremère. Paris: Didot, 1858–1868.

———. *Al-Muqaddama.* English translation under the title *The Muqaddima, an Introduction to History.* Translated by Franz Rozenthal. New York: Pantheon Books, 1958.

———. *Kitab al-'Ibar wa diwan al-mubtada' wa 'l-khabar fi ayyam al-'arab wa 'l-'Ajam wa''l-Barbar.* French translation under the title *Histoire des Berbères et des dynasties musulmanes de l'Afrique septentrionale.* Edited and translated by Mac Guckin De Slane. Paris: Librairie Orientale Paul Geuthner, 1927; edition by Mac Guckin De Slane. Cairo: Bulaq, 1867.

Ibn Khallikan, Ahmad Ibn Muhammad. *Wafayat al-a'yan wa anba' abna' al-zaman*. English translation under the title *Ibn Khallikan's Biographical Dictionary*. Translated by MacGuckin De Slane. Paris, 1843–1871.

Ibn Maryam, Abu Abd Allah Ibn Muhammad Ibn Ahmad Al-Tilimsani. *Kitab al-bustan fi dhikri al-anbiya wa 'ulama bi Tilimsan*. Algiers: al-Matba'ah al-Tha'ālibīyah, 1908.

Ibn Tumart, Muhammad Ibn 'Abd Allah. *A'azzu ma yutlab*. As *Le livre de Mohammed Ibn Toumert*. Arabic text and translation by I. Goldziher. Algiers: P. Fontana, 1903.

al-Idrisi, Abu 'Abd Allah Muhammad Ibn Muhammad al-Sharif. *Nuzhat al-mushtaq fi ikhtiraq al-afaq*. Arabic text and French translation under the title *Description de l'Afrique et de l'Espagne par Edrisi*. Edited and translated by R. Dozy and M. J. De Goeje. Leiden: E. J. Brill, 1866.

Iyad, Ibn Musa al-Sabti. *Tartib al-madarik wa taqrib al-masalik li ma'rifat a'lam madhhab malik*. Edited by Ahmad Bakir Mahmud. Beirut: Maktabat al-Hayah, 1967.

al-Maqqari, Abu 'l-Abbas Ahmad Ibn Muhammad. *Nafh at-tib min ghusn al-Andalus ar-ratib wa dhikr waziriha lisan 'd-Din Ibn al-Khatib*. Edited by Ihsan Abbas. Beirut: Dār Sādir, 1968.

———. *Nafh at-tib min ghusn al-Andalus ar-ratib wa dhikr waziriha lisan 'd-Din Ibn Al-Khatib*. English Translation as *History of the Mohammedan Dynaties in Spain*. Translated by Pasqual de Gayangos. London: W. H. Allen, 1840–1843; edition as *Analectes sur l'histoire et la littérature des Arabes d'Espagne*. Edited by R. Dozy, G. Dugat, L. Krehl, and W. Wright. Leiden: E. J. Brill, 1855–61.

al-Marrakushi, Abu Muhammad Abd al-Wahid. *Kitab al-mu'jib fi talkhis akhbar al-Maghrib*. Cairo, 1963; French Translation as *Histoire des Almohades*. E. Fagnan. Algiers: Adolphe Jourdan, 1893.

al-Qayrawani, Ibn Abi Zayd. *Ar-Risala*. Arabic Text and French translation under the title *La Risala ou Epitre sur les élements du dogme et de la foi de l'Islam selon le rite malikite*. Edited and translated by Leon Bercher. Algiers: Editions populaire de l'armée, 1968.

al-Tadili, Abu Ya'qub Yusuf Ibn Yahya known as Ibn Zayat. *Kitab al-Tashawwuf ila rijal al-tassawuf*. Edited by Ahmed Toufiq. Rabat: Publication of the Faculty of Letters and Human Sciences, 1984.

al-Umari, Ibn Fadl Allah. *Masalik al-absar fi mamalik al-amsar*. Translated and annotated by Gaudefroy-Demombynes as *L'Afrique moins l'Egypte*. Paris: Geuthner, 1927.

Yaqut Ibn Abd Allah al-Hamawi. *Mu'jam al-buldan*. Edited by F. Wustenfeld. Leipzig: In Commission bei F. A. Brockhaus, 1866–1873.

Ya'qubi, Ahmad Ibn Abi Ibn Ja'far Ibn Wahb Ibn Wadih [al -]. *Kitab al-Buldan*. Edited by M. J. de Goeje. Leiden: E. J. Brill, 1892.

Zuhri, Abu Abd Allah Muhammad Ibn Abi Bakr [al -]. *Kitab al-jughrafiya*. Edited by Mahammad Hadj-Sadok in *Bulletin d'Études Orientales* XXI (1968): 1–194.

MODERN SOURCES

Abbadi, A. M. [al -]. "Dirasa hawla Kitab al-Hulal al-mawshiyya." *Titwan* 5 (1960): 139–158.

Amilhat, P. "Les Almoravides au Sahara." *Revue militaire de l'Afrique occidentale française* July 15 (1937): 1–3.

———. "Petite chronique des Id Ou Aich, heritiers guerriers des Almoravides Sahariens." *Revue des Études Islamiques* 11 (1937): 41–130.

Arbitol, M. "Juifs maghrébins et commerce trans-saharien du VIIIe au XVe siècle." *Le sol, la parole et l'écrit* 2 (1981): 561–577.

Benaboud, Muhammad and A. McKay. "The Authenticity of Alfonso VI's Letter to Yusuf b. Tashfin." *Al-Andalus* 43 (1978): 233–237.

Beraud-Villars, Jean Marcel Eugène. *Les Touaregs au pays du Cid: les invasions almoravides en Espagne*. Paris: Plon, 1946.

Bernard, J. "Le sel dans l'histoire." *Cahiers du centre de recherches africaines* 2 (1982).

Berthier, P. "En marge des sucreries marocaines: la maison de la plaine et la maison des oliviers à Chichaoua." *Hesperis-Tamuda* (1962): 75–77.

Bloom, Jonathan et al. *The Minbar from the Kutubiyya Mosque*. New York: Metropolitan Museum of Art; Madrid: Ediciones El Viso; Rabat: Ministry of Cultural Affairs, Kingdom of Morocco, 1998.

Bonine, M. E. "The sacred direction and city structure: a preliminary analysis of the Islamic cities of Morocco." *Muqarnas* 7, (1990): 50–72.

Boone, James, Emlyn Meyers, and Charles Redman. "Archaeological and Historical Approaches to Complex Societies: The Islamic States of Medieval Morocco." *American Anthropologist* 92 (1990): 630–646.

Bourouiba, Racihid. *Abd al-Mu'min, flambeau des Almohades*. Algiers: Société nationale d'édition et de diffusion, 1982.

———. *Ibn Tumart*. Algiers: Société nationale d'édition et de diffusion, 1982.

Bovill, E. W. *The Golden Trade of the Moors*. London: Oxford University Press, 1958.

Brett, Michael. "Islam and Trade in the Bilad Al-Sudan, Tenth–Eleventh Century A.D." *Journal of African History* 24 (1983): 431–440.

Briggs, L. C. *Tribes of the Sahara*. Cambridge, MA: Harvard University Press, 1960.

Brunschvig, R. "Al-Hulal al-maushiya." *Arabic and Islamic Studies in Honor of H. A. R. Gibb*. Edited by G. Makdisi (Leiden 1965): 147–155.

Bulliet, Richard W. *The Camel and the Wheel*. Cambridge, MA: Harvard University Press, 1975.

Burkhalter, Sheryl L. "Listening for Silences in Almoravid History: Another Reading of 'The Conquest that Never Was,'" *History in Africa* 19 (1992): 103–131.

Cahen, Claude. "L'or du Soudan avant les Almoravides, mythe ou réalite." *Le sol, la parole et l'écrit* 2 (1981): 539–545.

Cheikh, Abdel Wedoud Ould and Bernard Saison. "Vie(s) et mort(s) de al-Imam Al-Hadrami." *Arabica* 34 (1987): 48–79.

Coco, Julie. Caravans, Commerce, and Cities: A Preliminary Archaeological Study of Souk Ben Akla—A Medieval Moroccan Caravanserai and Marketplace. Murfreesboro: Masters Thesis at Middle Tennessee State University, 2000.

Codera, Francisco, *Decadencia y desparicion de los Almoravides en Espana*. Zaragoza: Tip. de Comas Hermanos, 1899.

Conrad, David and Humphrey J. Fisher. "The Conquest That Never Was: Ghana and the Almoravids, 1076. II. The Local Oral Sources." *History in Africa* 10 (1983): 53–78.

———. "The Conquest That Never Was: Ghana and the Almoravids, 1076. I. The External Arabic Sources." *History in Africa* 9 (1982): 21–59.

Crone, Patricia and Martin Hinds. *God's Caliph, Religious Authority in the First Centuries of Islam*. Cambridge, MA: Cambridge University Press, 1986.

Cuoq, Joseph M. *Recuil des sources arabes concernant l'Afrique occidentale du VIIIe au XVIe siècle*. Paris: Éditions du centre national de la recherche scientifique, 1975.

Dajani-Shakeel, Hadia. "A Reassessment of Some Medieval and Modern Perceptions of the Counter Crusade." *Jihad and Its Times*. Edited by Hadia Dajani-Shakeel and Ronald A. Messier. Ann Arbor, MI: Center for Near Eastern and North African Studies (1991), 41–70.

Deverdun, Gaston. *Marrakech des origines à 1912*. Rabat: Éditions techniques nord-africaines, 1959.

Devisse, Jean. "Routes de commerce et echanges en Afrique occidentale en relation avec la Méditerranée: un essai sur le commerce africain médiéval du XIe au XVIe siècle." *Revue d'histoire economique et sociale* 50 (1972): 42–73.

Dozy, R. *Recherches sur l'histoire et la littérature de l'Espagne pendant le moyen âge*. Leiden: E. J. Brill, 1881.

———. *Spanish Islam: A History of the Moslems in Spain*. London: Frank Cass, 1913.

Duplessy, J. "La circulation des monnaies arabes en Europe occidentale du VIIIe au VIIIe siècles," *Revue Numismatique* 18, Paris: Société d'édition "Les Belles Lettres" (1956): 101–163.

Farias, Paulo Fernando de Moraes. "The Almoravids: Some Questions Concerning the Character of the Movement during Its Periods of Closest Contact with the Sudan." *Bulletin de l'Institut Fondamental D'Afrique Noire* 29B (1968): 794–878.

Fierro, Maribel. "Christian Success and Muslim Fear in Andalusi Writings during the Almoravid and Almohad Periods." *Israel Oriental Studies* 17 (1997): 155–178.

Fili, Abdallah and Jean Pierre Van Staëvel. "Wa-wasalna 'ala barakat Allāh ila Igiliz: À propos de la localisation d'Igiliz-des-Harġa, le ḥiṣn du mahdī Ibn Tumart." *Al-Qanṭara: Revista de Estudios Árabes* 27, no. 1 (2006): 153–194.

Fisher, Humphrey J. "Early Arabic Sources and the Almoravid Conquest of Ghana." *Journal of African History* 23 (1982): 549–560.

Fletcher, Richard. *Moorish Spain*. New York: Henry Holt and Company, 1992.

———. *The Quest for El Cid*. Oxford: Oxford University Press, 1989.

Fromherz, Allen J. and Muhammad Ibn Tūmart al-Mahdī. "The Almohad Mecca. Locating Igli and the Cave of Ibn Tūmart." *Al-Qanṭara: Revista de Estudios Arabes* 26, no. 1 (2005): 175–190.

Gautier, Emile Félix. F. *Le passé de l'Afrique du nord, les siècles obscures*. Paris: Payot, 1952.

Gellner, Ernest. *Saints of the Atlas*. Chicago: University of Chicago Press, 1960.

———, and Charles Micaud. *Arabs and Berbers*. Lexington, MA: D.C. Heath and Co., 1972.

Glick, Thomas. *Islamic and Christian Spain in the Early Middle Ages*. Princeton, NJ: Princeton University Press, 1979.

Goitein, S. D. *A Mediterranean Society*. Five volumes. Berkley, Los Angeles and London: University of California Press, 1967–1988.

Guichard, Pierre. "Les Almoravides: perspectives d'ensemble." *Etats, sociétés et cultures du monde musulman médiéval Xè-XVè siècle* I, 151–167. Paris: Presses universitaires de France, 1995.

Harvey, L. P. "Nugeymath Turquiya: Primera cronica general, Chapter 956." *Journal of Semitic Studies*, XIII, no. 2 (1968): 232–241.

Hazard, H. W. *The Numismatic History of Late Medieval North Africa*. New York: The American Numismatic Society, 1952.

Heddouchi, Choukri. *The Medieval Coins of Sijilmasa, Morocco: A History of the Mint and its Minting Techniques*. Murfreesboro: Masters Thesis at Middle Tennessee State University, 1998.

Hopkins, J. F. P. *Medieval Muslim Government in Barbary*. London: Luzac, 1958.

Hour, Rachid el-. *La administración judicial almorávide en al-Andalus: élites, negociaciones y enfrentamientos*. Helsinki: Academia Scientiarum Fennica, 2006.

———. "Le sahib al-ahkam à l'épolque almoravide." *Al-Andalus—Maghreb* 8–9, no. 1, 2000–2001 (2001): 49–64.

———. "The Andalusian Qāḍī in the Almoravid Period: Political and Judicial Authority." *Studia Islamica* 90, (2000): 67–83.

Hrbek, Ivan and Jean Devisse. "The Almoravids." *UNESCO: General History of Africa* v. III, *Africa from the Seventh to the Eleventh Century*, ch. 13, London, Berkley, Paris: UNESCO, 1988.

Huici-Miranda, A. "El-rawd al-qirtas y los Almoravides—estudio critico." *Hesperis-Tamuda* 1, fasc. 3 (1960): 515–541.

———. "Un nuevo manuscrito de 'al-Bayan al-mughrib.' " *Al-Andalus* XXIV, fasc. 1 (1959): 63–84.

———. "La Salida de los Almoravides del desierto y el Reinado de Yusuf B. Tashfin." *Hesperis* 3e-4e trim (1959): 155–182.

Hunwick, John O. "Gao and the Almoravids: A Hypothesis." In *West African Culture Dynamics: Archaeological and Historical Perspectives*, edited by B. Swartz and R. Dumett, 413–430. The Hague and New York: Mouton, 1980.

Imauddin, S. M. *Muslim Spain 711–1492, a Sociological Study*. Leiden: E. J. Brill, 1981.

Jaques-Meunié, D. *Le Maroc saharien des origines à 1670*, 2 vols., Paris: Librairie Klincksieck, 1982.

Kassis, H. "Observations on the First Three Decades of Almoravid History (A.H. 450–480 = A.D. 1058–1088), a Numismatic Study." *Der Islam* (1985): 311–325.

La Chapelle, F. de. "Esquisse d'une histoire du Sahara occidental." *Hesperis* XI (1931): 35–95.

Lagardère, Vincent. "Communautés mozarabes et pouvoir almoravide," *Studia Islamica* 67 (1988): 99–119.

———. "Esquisse de l'organization des Murabitun à l'époque de Yusuf B. Tashfin (430/1039–500/1106)." *Revue de l'Occident musulman de la Méditerranée* 27 (1979): 99–114.

———. "Evolution de la notion de djihad à l'époque almoravide (1039–1147)." *Cahiers de civilization médiévale: Xe–XIIe siècles* 41 (1998): 3–16.

———. "La haute judicature à l'époque almoravide en al-Andalus." *Al-Qantara* VII (1986): 135–228.

———. "Le gouvernement des villes et la suprémacie des Banu Turgut au Maroc et en Andalus." *Revue de l'Occident musulman de la Méditerranée* 25 (1978): 49– 65.

———. "La tariqa et la révolte des Muridun en 539/1144 en Andalus." *Revue de l'Occident musulman de la Méditerranée* 35 (1983): 157–170.

———. *Les Almoravides*. Paris: L'Harmattan, 1989.

———. *Le Vendredi de Zallaqa*. Paris: L'Harmattan, 1989.

———. "L'unification du Malekisme oriental et occidental à Alexandrie: Abu Bakr At-Turtushi." *Revue de l'Occident musulman de la Méditerranée* 31 (1981): 47–62.

Lange, Dierk. "The Almoravid Expansion and the Downfall of Ghana." *Der Islam* 73, no. 2 (1996): 313–351.

———. "The Almoravids and the Islamicization of the Great States of West Africa." *Itinéraires d'Orient. Hommages à Claude Cahen*. Edited by Raoul Curiel and Rika Gyselen, 65–76. Paris: Groupe pour l'étude de la civilization du Moyen-Orient, 1994.
Langewiesche, William. *Sahara Unveiled*. New York: Pantheon Books, 1995.
Laroui, Abdallah. *The History of the Maghrib*. Princeton, NJ: Princeton University Press, 1977.
Le Tourneau, Roger. *Fez in the Age of the Marinides*. Translated by Besse Alberta Clement. Norman: University of Oklahoma Press, 1961.
———. *The Almohad Movement in North Africa*. Princeton, NJ: Princeton University Press, 1969.
Lévi-Provençal, E. "La 'Mora Zaida,' femme d'Alphonse VI, et leur fils, l'Infant Don Sancho." *Hesperis* XVIII (1934): 1–8.
———. "La toma de Valencia por El Cid, segun las fuentas musulmana y el original arage de la Cronica General de Espana." French Translation in *Islam d'Occident* (1948): 189–238.
———. "La Fondation de Marrakech (462/1070)." In *Mélanges d'histoire et d'archéologie de l'Occident musulman. Hommage à Georges Marçais*, II, 117–120. Algiers: Imprimerie Officielle, 1957.
———. "Observations sur le texte du Bayan d'Ibn 'Idhari." In *Mélanges Gaudefroy-Démombynes* III, 241–258. Cairo: Impr. de l'Institut français d'archéologie orientale, 1935–1945.
———. "Réflexions sur l'empire Almoravide au début du XIIe siècle." *Cinquantenaire de la Faculté des letters d'Alger (1881–1931)*, 307–320. Algiers: Société Historique Algérienne, 1932.
Levtzion, N. and J. F. P. Hopkins. *Corpus of Early Arabic Sources for West African History*. Cambridge, MA: Cambridge University Press, 1981.
———. "Abd Allah B. Yasin and the Almoravids." *Studies in West African History* I (London, Frank Cass, 1979): 78–112.
———. "The Almoravids in the Sahara and Bilad al-Sudan: A Study in Arab Historiography." *Jerusalem Studies in Arabic and Islam* 25 (2001): 133–152.
———. "Ibn Hawqal, the Cheque and Awdaghost." *Journal of African History* 9, no. 2 (1968): 223–233.
Lewicki, T. "L'exploitation et le commerce de l'or en Afrique de l'est et du sud-est au moyen âge d'après les sources arabes." *Folia Orientalia* 18 (1977): 167–186.
———. "Un état soudanais médiéval inconnu: le royaume de Zafun." *Cahiers d'Études Africaines* 11, no. 44 (1971): 501–525.
———. *West African Food*. London and New York: Cambridge University Press, 1974.
Lightfoot, D. R. and James A. Miller. "Sijilmassa: The Rise and Fall of a Walled Oasis in Medieval Morocco." *Annals of the Association of American Geographers* 86, no. 1 (1996): 78–101.

Marçais, Georges. *La Berberie musulmane et l'Orient au moyen âge.* Paris: Aubier, Éditions Montaigne, 1946.

———. "Notes sur les ribats en Berberie." In *Mélanges René Basset*, vol. II, 395–430. Paris: E. Leroux, 1923–1925.

Masonen, Pekka and Humphrey J. Fisher. "Not Quite Venus from the Waves: The Almoravid Conquest of Ghana in the Modern Historiography of Western Africa." *History in Africa* 23 (1996) 197–231.

Mauny, Raymond. *Tableau géographique de l'Ouest Africain au moyen âge.* Dakar: IFAN, 1961.

Mellouki, Mohamed el-. *Contribution à l'étude de l'histoire des villes médiévales du Maroc: Sigilmassa des origines à 668 (H)/1269 (J.C.)*, Aix-en-Provence: thèse du doctorat de 3e cycle, 1985.

Menendez-Pidal, R. *The Cid and His Spain.* English Translation by Harold Sunderland. London: J. Maury, 1934.

Messier, Ronald A. "Almoravids." *The Encyclopedia of Islam, 3rd ed.* Leiden: E. J. Brill, 2009, 75–80.

———. "The Almoravids, West African Gold, and the Gold Currency of the Mediterranean Basin." *Journal of the Economic and Social History of the Orient* 17 (1974): 31–47.

———. "The Almoravids and Holy War." *Jihad and Its Times.* Edited by Hadia Dajani-Shakeel and Ronald A. Messier, 15–29. Ann Arbor, MI: Center for Near Eastern and North African Studies, 1991.

———. "The Grand Mosque of Sijilmasa: The evolution of a structure from the Mosque of Ibn Abd Allah to the restoration of Sidi Mohammed ben Abdallah." In *L'architecture de terre en Méditerranée. Coordination: Mohammed Hammam / Al-miʻmār al-mabnī bi-'l-turāb fīḤawḍ al-Baḥr al-Mutawassiṭ, tansīq Muḥammad Ḥammām*, 287–296. Rabat: Université Mohammed V, Publications de la Faculté des Lettres et des Sciences Humaines, 1999.

———. "Quantitative Analysis of Almoravid Dinars." *Journal of the Economic and Social History of the Orient* 23 (1980): 104–120.

———. "Re-thinking the Almoravids, Re-thinking Ibn Khaldun." *Journal of North African Studies* 6, no. 1 (2001): 59–80.

———. "Sijilmasa: An archaeological Study—1992." *Bulletin d'Archéologie Marocaine/al-Nashra al-Athariya al-Maghribīya* 19 (2002): 257–292.

———. "Sijilmâsa: l'intermédiaire entre la Méditerranée et l'Ouest de l'Afrique." In *L'Occident musulman et l'Occident chrétien au moyen âge. Coord. Mohammed Hammam*, 181–196. Rabat: Publications de la Faculté des Lettres, 1995.

———. "The Transformation of Sijilmāsa." *Studi Maġrebini* 4 (2006): 247–257.

Messier, Ronald A. and Abdallah Fili. "La ville caravannière de Sijilmasa: du mythe historique à la realité archéologique." In *II congreso internacional la ciudad en al-Andalus y el Magreb. Coord. científica Antonio Torremocha*

Silva, Virgilio Martínez Enamorado, 501–510. Granada: Fundación El Legado Andalusí, 2002.

Mezzine, Larbi. *Le Tafilalt*. Rabat: Publications de la Faculté des Lettres, 1987.

Migeon, Gaston. *Les arts musulmans*. Paris: G. van Oest, 1926.

Miller, James A. "Trading Through Islam: The Interconnections of Sijilmasa, Ghana and the Almoravid Movement." *Journal of North African Studies* 6, no. 1 (2001): 29–58.

Monroe, J. T. "Hispano-Arabic Poetry during the Almoravid Period; Theory and Practice." *Viator* 4 (1973): 65–98.

Monteil, C. "L'ile d'Aoulil d'Idrisi." *Notes Africaines*, no. 48 (1950): 128–130.

———. "Problèmes du Soudan occidental, Juifs et Judaises." *Hesperis* XXXVIII (3e-4e trim. 1951): 265–298.

an-Nasri as-Salawi, Abu 'l-Abbas Ahmad Ibn Khalid. *Kitab al-Istiqsa li akhbar duwal al-maghrib al-aqsa*. French translation by G. S. Colin, *Archives Marocaines* XXXI. Paris: Librairie Orientaliste Paul Geuthner, 1925.

———. *Kitab al-Istiqsa li akhbar duwal al-Maghrib al-aqsa*. Edited by Ahmed Toufiq. Cassablanca: Manshūrāt Wizārat al-Thaqāfah wa-al-Ittiṣāl, 2001–2005.

Norris, H. T. *The Berbers in Arabic Literature*. London and New York: Longman, 1982.

———. "New Evidence on the Life of Abdullah B. Yasin and the Origins of the Almoravid Movement." *Journal of African History* XII, 2 (1971), 255–268.

———. *Saharan Myth and Saga*. Oxford: Clarendon Press, 1972.

Pères, H. "La poésie à Fes sous les Almoravides et les Almohades." *Hesperis* 18, fasc. I (1934): 9–40.

———. *La poésie adaloues en Arabe classique du XIe siècle*. Paris: Maisonneuve, 1953.

Sauvaget, J. "Les épitaphes royales de Gao." *Bulletin de l'Institut Fondamental de L'Afrique Noire* XII, no. 2 (1950): 418–440.

Semonin, P. "The Almoravid Movement in the Western Sudan, a Review of the Evidence." *Transactions of the Historical Society of Ghana* VII (1964): 42–59.

Shatzmiller, Maya. *L'historiographie mérinide*. Leiden: E. J. Brill, 1982.

Stern, S. M. "Two Anthologies of Muwashashah Poetry: Ibn al-Khatib's Jaysh al-tawshih and al-Safadi's tawshi' al-tawshih."*Arabica* II (September, 1955): 150–192.

Taouchikt, Lahcen. *Étude ethno-archéologique de la céramique du Tafilalet (Sijilmasa): état des questions*. Aix-en-Provence: Thèse du doctorat de 3e cycle, 1989.

al-Tazi, Abd al-Hady. *Jami' al-Qarawiyyin: al-masjid wa' l-jami'a bi madinat Fas*. Beirut: Dal al-Kitab al-Lubnani, 1972.

Terrasse, H. "Art almoravide et almohade." *Al Andalus* 26 (1961), 435–447.

———. "L'art de l'empire almoravide: Ses sources et son evolution." *Studia Islamica* 3 (1955): 25–34.
———. *Histoire du Maroc*. Casablanca: Editions Atlantides, 1952.
———. *La mosquée al-Qaraouiyin à Fes*. Paris: C. Klincksieck, 1968.
———. "Le role des Almoravides dans l'histoire de l'Occident." In *Mélanges d'histoire du moyen âge, dédiés à la mémoire de Louis Haphen*. Paris: Presses Universitaires de France, 1951.
Trimingham, J. S. *A History of Islam in West Africa*. London and New York: Oxford University Press, 1962.
———. *Islam in West Africa*. Oxford: Clarendon Press, 1959.
Vila, Jacinto Bosch. *Los Almoravides*. Tetuan: Editora Marroqui, 1956.
Wasserstein, David. *The Rise and Fall of the Party-Kings: Politics and Society in Islamic Spain 1002–1086*. Princeton, NJ: Princeton University Press, 1985.

Index

Note: Names appear in alphabetical order, disregarding the prefix "al-."
Page numbers followed by an "f" indicate figures.

Abbasid Revolution, 2
Abd al-Allah Mosque, 169
Abd al-Haqq, 142
Abd Allah Ibn Bassam, 128–29
Abd Allah Ibn Buluggin Ibn Badis, 179; Alfonso, king of Castile, alliance with, 101; charge of treason, 101; Ibn al-Khula, discrediting of, 97–98, 191; Ibn Tashfin, 97–98; jihad, 102; payoffs to Ibn Tashfin, 97; as prisoner, 102–3; Tamim, complaints against, 99
Abd Allah Ibn Mazdali, 137
Abd Allah Ibn Yasin, 3–9, 179; Almoravids, 84; armed warfare and, 9; as baraka, 9; as preacher, 4–5, 7f, 10, 84; Bani Gudala, 6, 10; Bani Lamtuna, 10; bride price, 8; Dar al-Murabitin teachings, 5; as iman, 38; Lamtuna, 84; as lawgiver, 8–9; Malikite reformism, 19; religious/politico-economic system, 16; Sijilmasa, 31
Abd Allah of Granda; caste of nobility, 10; charges of treason against, 101; disputes, 99, 101; introduction as a preacher, 4–5, 7; Malikite reformism of, 19; mosques of, 29; payoffs, 97; religious/politico-economic cohesion, 16; sieges, 102; teachings of, 84, *See also* Almoravids; Alfonso, king of Castile; Ibn Khulay'i
Abd al-Malik, 82, 106, 124, 211, 215
Abd al-Mu'min, 158–59
Abd al-Rahman Ibn al-Aftas, 77, 180, 207
Abu Abd Allah Ibn al-Hajj, 104
Abu Abd Allah Ibn Hamdin, 127, 215
Abu Bakr Ibn al-Arabi, 171
Abu Bake Ibn Baki, 134, 218
Abu Bakr Ibn Umar, 17; Aghmat, 41, 57; as Amir, 38, 51, 59; Barghwata campaign, 37–38; base, establishment of, 18–19; capital city, built by, 41–42; caravan routes, control over, 59; as commander of Almoravid army, 10–11, 17, 18–19, 179, 192; death of, 86–87f; as desert chief; 58–59; dinars, 34, 59; divorce of, 54; Ghana, inhabitants of, 86;

historical perspective, 191; Ibn Tashfin, concern over personal power of, 56–58; as Ibn Yasin's successor, 38; Ibrahim, son of, 63–64; legend of, 54; Maghrib, siege of, 35, 39, 54; Marrakech, base camp, 53; as nomadic tribeman, 39; political power, key to, 39; qasr (treasury-armory), 85; Qasr al-Hajar, 53; Shi'ites, 18; as successor to Ibn Yasin, 38; tribal government, 61; Zanata Berber war, 54–55, 57. *See also* Qasr al-Hajar; Zaynab al-nafzawiya

Abu Bakr Ibn Zaydun, 74

Abu Ghamr Ibn Azzun of Ronda, 171

Abu Hafs Umar, 142, 169

Abu Hamama, 105

Abu Hamid al-Ghazzal, 101, 180

Abu al-Hasan Yusuf, 142; Abu Imran al-Fasi, 1–4, 179; Almovadian campaign, 171, 173; al-Sahrawi, opposition to, 170; as Bani Gadmiwa commander, 143; as commander, 152; charismatic leadership of, 161; dike, building of, 167; Fez, siege of, 166–68; historical perspective, 219; Ibn Ghaniya, treaty with 164; Ibn Hud, preaching, 168–69; Ibrahim Ibn Tashfin, execution of, 168; immunity, exchange for, 167; Maghrib campaign, 159–60, 168–69; Marrakech campaign, 159, 219; piety of, 93; as successor to Ibn Tumart, 152; Tlemcen campaign, 161–62, 165; as warrior, 93

Abu'l-Abbas Ahmad Ibn al-Arif, 63

Abu'l-Fadl Ibn al-Nahuwi, 128–29

Abu'l-Hasan Baki Ibn Ahmad, 166

Abu'l-Qasim Ahmad Ibn Qasi, 163

Abu Ja'far, 127, 180, 215

Abu Marwan, 82, 128

Abu Umayya, 166

Abu al-Walid Ibn Rushd, 124, 147, 156

Africanus, Leo, 199

Aghmat, 35–42; Aghmat Wurika, 35; Almoravd assault, 35–39, 41; Almohavids campaign, 150–53; Andalusian monarchs, 106; Bab, 126; hammam (public bath), 92; Haylana, 35; historical perspective, 200–201; Ibn Yasin's preaching, 36–37; importance of, 35; Jews, 126; markets, 69; Marrakech, 59 mint, 35, 87; unity, 36–36, Wurika, 35

Aghmati, 183

Aghmatis (quarters), 88

Aguilar, 155

Ahl Tinmallal (people of Tinmal), 149–50

Aid al-fitr, 106

Aledo, siege of, 100

Alexandria, 140

Alfonso I of Aragon, 137

Alfonso of Castile, 96, 135, 163–64

Alfonso I. *See* El Batallador

Alfonso VI; 475/1082–83, 72–77; 479/1086, 76–77; al-Aftas of Badajoz, 71; army of, 79; Chimens, 118; Christian renegades, 73, 76; El Cid, relief force sent, 116; Jewish incident, 73; lamt, (broad shields), 73; Seville, battle of, 73, 76, 80–84; Taifa kings, 104–5; taxes, 72, 101; Toledo, 72–73; Uclés, 134; weaknesses of, 72; Zaragoza, siege of, 76, 101

Alfonso VII, 157

Ali Ibn Hammud, 64

Ali Ibn Tahir al-Sulami, 216

Ali Ibn Yusuf al-Massufi, 154

Ali Ibn Yusuf, 129–39, 166, 214–16

Almoravid army, 154

Almoravid rule, 170

Almoravids (al-Murabitun), 1–19; as Amir, 31, 34, 40, 96, 100; Andalusia jihad, 69–84; Andalusion kings, 97; arms storage, 53; army, 35, 37–38; Barghwata, 38; broad shields, 74, 76; cavalry, 13; Christian challengers, 133–44, 176; commercial network, 161; culture fusion, 178; destination, treatment at end of, 24 Diya al-Sawla Yahya, 67; doctrinal

Index 237

censorship, 163; drums of, 64–65, 82, 113–14; El Cid, 111–19; empire, 61, 178; fallen, reverence paid to, 17; Fez, 166; finance of, 16; folklore, 173–74; forced emigration, 133; gold mint, 88, 161; gold revenue, 175; historical perspective, 218–20 identity, 177; iman, 34; Islam, understanding of, 90; islamic reform, 1–19; Jews, 91; jihad, 1–19; Kurifala, 38; laws of, 18; legal advisors, 89; lesser jihad, 12; Maghrawa rulers, 30, 34; Maghrib, 67; Malikite Islam, 34, 89, 140; Meknes, state of rebellion, 63; mosques, 123; mujassimun, 140; Muslim challengers, 133–44; objectives, 175; orthodoxy, 31, 133, 177; prayer, leading of, 38; preaching of iman, 12; Qasr al-Hajar 53; as religious reformers, 31; Saharan authority, 53; saint of, 38; salt route, 32; Shaykhs, 13; Sijilmasa, raid on, 13, 16, 24; sikka (monetary issue), 88; taxes, 90–91, 132; Tlemcen, 161; trade control, 35; tribes, dominance of, 51; veils, face, 81, 108, 114, 118, 127; victories, 66; warrior tactics, 12–13, 114; Zaragoza, 136. *See also* Abd Allah Ibn Yasin; Ibn Uman; Ibn Yasin
Alvar Fanez; background of, 76, 81; death of, 117, 136; Seville, battle of, 80–81; Zallaqa, battle of, 94, 105, 117, 136, 179
aman, 183
Amir, 10
Amir al-Mu'minin, commander of the faithful, 91
Andalusia; Abd al-Mu'min, 168; Almohad campaign, 169. 193; Al-Sahrawi, 170
Andalusian campaign, 88; capital, 14; ginger roots, 26; Muslim kings, 66, qadi, 130, 170; Qadi Lyad, 193; regime, 45; siege of, 49, 66–67; Sunni, 1; Suqut al-Barghwati, 64; trade routes, 202; Umayyad dynasty, 1–3, 33, 4. *See also* Fez; Umayyads
Andalusia jihad, 69–84, 206–7; 475/1082–83, 72–73; 479/1086, 76–78; 479/30/1086, 78; Alfonso VI, Jewish incident, 75; drums, 82; Ibn Tashfin, 66; king of Seville, 73–74; maritime support, 74; Seville, 77–82; Taifa kings, 71–72; Zallaqa, 82; Zaragoza, 76. *See also* Ibn Tashfin; Syr Ibn Abu Baker, Umayyads
Aqaba Jordan, 200
Arabo-Andalusian aristocracy, 129
Aragon, 72
Arat-n-anna, 9
army units, 56;
asabiya (solidarity), 10, 38, 183
Asharite theology, 3
ashkari (clother), 58
Asr, 151
Asturia, 72
Atlas, 86
Austen, Ralph, 199
autodafe, 163
Awdaghust, 16
Awkazant, 6
ayt arba'in (notable assembly), 124
Azrou, 159

bab, 184
Bab Aghmat (Gate of the Southeast), 126
Bab Aylan, 126, 168
Bab al-Debbagh, 151
Bab Dukkala (Gate of the Northwest), 126, 168
Bab al-Faraj, 105
Bab Fez, 23
Bab al-Gharb (Gate of the West), 22
Bab al-Khamis (Gate of the North), 126
Bab al-Naffis (Gate of the southwest), 126
Bab al-Rih (Gate of the wind), 23
Bab al-Shari'a, 151
Bab al-Sharq (Gate of the East), 22
Badajoz, 136, 171
Baena, 155
Baghdad, 140
Balearic Islands, 136, 171–72

Balencia, 155
Bani Gadmiwa, 143
Bani Ganfisa, 143
Bani Gudala; aggression upon, 17; army, 177; iman, during prayers, 8; Jawhar Ibn Sakkun, conspiracy, 11; religious teachings, 8; Sanhaja confederation, break with, 17
Bani Hammud, 64
Bani Hargha, 143
Bani Hazmira, 37, 41
Bani Hintata, 142, 143
Bani Ifran, 5
Bani Igan, 159
Bani Lamta, 184
Bani Lamtuna; army units, 56; Bani Gudala aggression upon, 17; Bani Massufa dispute, 161–62; caravan routes, control of, 59; caste of nobility, 10; chief of, 10; defeat, by Bani Lamtuna, 17; description of, 5–7; dispute, 161; homes, first, 6; as horsemen and cameleers, 13; permanent housing, 53; polytheism, 9; power, administration of, 19; spoils of victory, 12; veils, 6; women in, 201; Wurika, daily life in, 42. *See also* Almoravids, jihad; Syr Ibn Abu Bakr
Bani Lukay, 159
Bani Maghrawa, 3, 13; expelled for criticizing injustice, 3; Islam culture, 4; tribal disunity and sectarianism, 3
Bani Makkud, 159
Bani Masmuda, 41
Bani Massufa 12; Ali Ibn Yusuf al-Massufi, 154; Bani Lamtuna dispute, 161; conflicts between tribes, 12; description of, 5–7; disputes, 161–62; historical perspective, 220; religious practices, 12; tribal confederation, 86, 161
Bani Sarta, 17
Bani Tarja, 17
Bani Yifran, 48
baraka (man with powers given by God), 9

Barakat Foundation, 196
Barghwata, 184; campaign against, 37–38; captives, 64; as heretics, 37; historical perspective, 200 Koran, 37; Muslims, 37; opponents, 67; Salib Ibn Tarif, 37; Zanata Berber tribe, 5
Barn Tarja, 17
Beja, 171
Ben Shalib, 72–73
Beraud-Villars, J., 189
Berbers; al-Aftas of Badajoz, 71; alliances, 2; Al-Qadir, 73; Andalusian nobility, contempt for, 100, 108; Arab, ethnic differences, 69–70; Awdaghust, 16; description of, 129; Dhu' al-Nun of Toledo, 71; disunity, 174; Historical perspective, 200, 206; horses, 27, 85; Ibn Zalwi, 4; Jabal Tariq, 69; Kharijism sect, 29, 191; Koran, 37; Maghrawa, 30, 33 Maghrib, 56, 124; Masmuda, 37, 85; as merchants, 23; North Africa, 175; political instability, 174; reform theology, 142; resistance to centralized authority, 29; sociological analysis, 190; Takrart, 66; Takrur, 17; Toledo, 73; as traders, 23; as vassals, 71; warfare style, 12; Zanata, 5, 15, 43, 45, 54, 61; Zirids of Granada, 71. *See also* Sanhaja Berbers; specific types
berni dates, 27
Berraz Ibn Muhammad al-Massufi, 161, 164, 171
Bilad al Makhzan (land of the storehouse), 61
Bilad al-Sudan (Land of the Blacks), 5, 21
Bishop of Lescar, 158
Book of Malikite law. *See* Muwatta
Borja, 139
Bourouiba, Rachid, 217–18
burnoose, 57
Burkhalter, Sheryl L., 209
Cabra, 155
Calatayud, siege of, 139
caliph, 184

Caliph Abd al-Rahman II, 131
caravans; camels, 27; description of, 21, 24; destination, treatment at end of, 24; as food providers; 6 funduqs, (caravansaries), 23, 26; gold trade, 32, 219; protection to, 6–7, 13, 21, 32; rarities sold, 26; risks, 24; routes, 21, 24, 26, 31–33, 39, 59, 198; salt, 32; servants, 23; Sijilmasa, 14, 21, 26, 31–32; slaves, 23, 25–26, 199; Souk Ben Akla, 197; Taghaza, 32
caravansaries. *See* Funduqs
caste of nobility, 10
Castile, 72
Ceuta; Algeciras, 78; Cordoba, 71; siege of, 66; tribute collection, 72
Champion of the Cause, 133
Chimene, 118, 179
Christian campaign, 158, 163–64
Christians; Abd Allah, alliance with, 101; of Aledo, 79, 96–100; Almoravids, last major battle, 157–58; of Andalusia, 77; armor of, 81; combined army, 137; holy days, 89; Ibn al-Hajj, ambush of, 135; justifiable war, with Saracens, 79–82; Mutawakkil, collusion with, 115; poll tax, 67, 132; power, balance of, 76; surrender terms, 80; Uclés, siege of, 134; Zaragoza, siege of, 139
Colin, G. S., 198
Commander of the Muslims, 133
conflicts between tribes, 12;
Conrad, David, 208
Cordoba, 14, 28, 44, 71, 147
Cueca, 134
Cutanda, 139

Damnat, 159
dar al-darb (the mint), 34
Dar al-imara (governmental palace), 19
Dar al-Islam (Muslim realm), 69, 84, 108, 184
Dar al-Murabitin, 2–5, 11, 18, 31, 59, 176
Dar al-Saff (the mint), 86, 184

Da'ud Ibn Aisha, 81, 112–13, 116–17, 180, 207
Day, 159
Dbu al-Qa'da (month), 136, 139
Defender of the Faith, 133
Deverdun, G., 214–15
Devisse, J., 189
Dhu al-Hijja (May-June), 169
Dhu' al-Nun of Toledo, 71
Dhu' al-Sabbah, 156
Diaz de Vivar, Rodrigo. *See* El Cid
dinars (gold coins), 25, 28. 87–88, 119, 153–54, 161, 184
dirham, 91, 184
dissent, voices of, 145–60; Abu Bake Ibn Baki, 134; Aloravids, 145; attacks against Almoravids, 150–52; Bani Massufa nobles, 154; Christian tax collectors, 150; defense of the plains, 152–53; dinars, production of, 153–54; Fez, 166; illegal taxes, 145; jihad against Andalusia Christians, 153, 154–55; last major battle against Christians, 157–59; Marrakech, 147, 150–52, 150; moral reform, 145; religious, 29; riot of 515/1121, 146–47; seven-year campaign, 130–31; siege of Cordoba, 147; Tinmal inhabitants, 149–50; vocal expansion of, 145. *See also* Abd al-Mu'min; Alfonso VIII; Abd al-Wahid Ibn Rushd; al-Fallaki; El Batallador; Ibn Tumart; Tashfin Ibn Ali; Reverter; Sayf al-Dawla Ibn Hud
Diya al-Dawla Yahya, 65–67
Djabal al-Dhahab (Mountain of Gold), 86
Draa, 18, 33, 184
du Bearn, 157
du Languedoc, 157

Earthwatch, 196
Ebro River, 139
Ecija, 155
El Batallador; as commander; Cordoba, 155–58; 519/1125, 155; Calatayud, siege of, 137–39; Granada, 155;

Murcia, 155; Reconquista, 147; Toledo, 139; Tudela, fall of, 139; Zaragoza, siege of, 76, 101, 139
El Cid (Rodrigo Diaz de Vivar), 111–19, 181; Almenara, siege of, 117; Al-Qadir, 111–12; background of, 96; Chimene, 118; death of, 118; historical perspective, 212–14; military genius of, 116; Musta'in, Taifa King of Zaragoza, support of, 96; *Song of My Cid*, 116; tribute, collection of, 111, 112–13, 117–18; Valencia, siege of, 114–17
Evora, 136

al-Fallaki, 159
faqihs; Andalusian, 101; Ibn Rashik's trial, 98; Malikite, 89, 127, 141–42; reliance on, 176; religious legalists, 49; Taifa kings, 71
Fatimids, 1; background, 3; establishment, 2–3; expansionism, 33; Ifriqiya, 1, 33; Shi'itye, 1, 4; Umayyads, 33
Fatimids of Ifriqiya (modern Tunisia); antipropaganda, 3, 192; Egypt, move to, 3; expansionism, 33; gold trade, 2; historical perspective, 198, 200, 211; ideological appeal of, 3; Sanhaja Berbers alliance, 2; Shi'ite, 4, 33; Sijilmasa, control of, 33; taxes, 33; Umayyads of Andalusia, 33; Zirids, 4
fatwa (legal opinion), 11, 101–2
Fazaz Valley, 47, 63
Fernando I, 72
Fez, 43–51; Aghmat Wurika, 35; Aghmat, 25; Almoravid resistance, 43–44; Arab, 15; Berbers, 23; blockade of, 47–49; caravans, 21, 24–25; Christians, 104; commercial importance of, 35; control of countryside, 46, 48, 56; cultural center for Moroccan trade 44; custom taxes, 33; daily life of, 2–23; direct assault of, 48–49; dissent in, 166–67; economic and intellectual importance, 28, 166; fall of, 47, 49, 171; faqihs of, 77, 140; founder of, 65; gold mint, 153; gold trade 16; historical perspective, 202–3; Idris II, 44; Idrissid rulers, 35; investments of, 27; jihad, 77; Lamtuna, 145; loss in campaign, 47; Magrrawa, 3, 5; markets of, 69; Marrakech, 124–25; Massufa, 145; as medicine men, 26; Meknes, lords of, 45; merchants; monumental fountain, 124; Moulouya, key route to, 33; olive presses, 126; opponents to rulers of, 45–47; permanent positions of, 126; potters of, 50; products offered by, 26–28; Qarawiyin Mosque, 49, 69, 167f, 169f; rebellion, 122–23; repair of damage to, 49; routes traveled by, 197; second founding of, 43–51 siege of, 166; slaves, 25–26; as sought after prize, 45; spice, 26; taxes, 90; treatment at destination, 24; Umar Ibn Sulayman, 65. *See also* Ibn Tashfin; traders
Fez al-Bali, 203
Fez al-Jadid, 203
fiqh, 184
Fisher, Humphrey J., 208
al-fitr (ending fast of Ramadan), 155
Fletcher, Richard, 190
funduqiyya (a woman), 26, 184
funduqs (caravansaries), 23

Galicia, 72
gamamin (agricultural zone), 22, 185
Gao, 86
Garcia Ordoñez, 134
Garrur al-Hashimi, 97, 99, 106
Gaston de Bearn, 158
Gazula, 185
Gellner, Ernest, 190
Geniza documents, 199
Ghana, 15–16
Goiein, S. D., 216
Gold; trade, 24–25
Grand Mosque, 19, 130–31

Index   241

habus, (religious endowment), 166, 185
haddith, 89
al-hadi (he who guides), 168
hadith (traditions of Prophet) 3–4, 185
al-Hajib, 111, 180
hajib (chamberlain), 185
hakim (secondary judge), 130, 185
Hammam of Aghmat, 92f
Harakat, Ibrahim, 189
Hart, David M., 190
Hasham (military corps and bodyguard), 156–57, 185
Herodotus, 198
High Atlas, 35, 39, 41–42, 61
hisba (manual for marketplace supervision), 185
Hrbek, I., 189
Hudayr Ibn Wasnu, 105
huerta (belt of irrigated land), 185
Huesca, 135
hurras (agents), 90

Ibn Abdun, 129–30
Ibn Abi Zar, 173, 175, 191, 192, 194
Ibn al-Aftas, al-Mutawakkil, 181; as prisoner, 115; buying protection from Yusuf Ibn, 115, 180; Christian collusion, 115; Cordoba, 71; Granada, 77; death of 115; Historical background, 207; Yusuf Ibn Tashfin, loyal follower of, 74, 103
Ibn Alqama, 212–13
Ibn al-Athir, 195
Ibn Barrajan, 128
Ibn al-Faraj, 105, 111–13, 180
Ibn Ghaniya, 158
Ibn al-Hajj, Abu Abd Allah Muhammad, 83, 93, 104, 117, 135–37, 180
Ibn Hawqal, 190
Ibn Hud, Musta'in, 94, 96, 111, 135, 180
Ibn Idhari, 191–92
Ibn Iyad, 158
Ibn al-Kalas, 154–55
Ibn Khaldun; Almoravids, 173–78; chronicle of the Almoravids, 173–74; desert versus the city, 177; dynastic weaknesses, 177
Ibn al-Khulay, 97–98

Ibn al-Khulay'I, 97–98, 101, 180
Ibn Qasi of Silves, 171
Ibn Qasira, 129
Ibn Rashik, king of Murcia, 94, 180; Almorvids, 98–99; as aman, 98; Mu'tamid, opposition to, 98–99; playing both sides in conflict, 98; Taifa kings, dispute with, 98–99; trial, 98–99
Ibn Rushd, 88, 130
Ibn Sakkun, 4, 11, 180
Ibn Tashfin, 102; Almoravids, curse upon, 163, 221; faqihs, denouncement by, 127–28; science of jurisprudence, 127; works burned, 128, 140, 163
Ibn Tifilwit, Abu Bakr Ibn Ibrahim, 136–37, 217, 180
Ibn Tuli, 45
Ibn Tumart, 225; Almoravids, criticism of, 140; army units, 143; arrest of, 142–43; background, 140; Bani Hargha, 143; as censor of mores, 140; death of, 152; historical perspective, 193, 210, 217–18, 219; as Mahdi, 147–48; Malikite faqihs, rebuke of, 141–42; Marrakech fortifications, 143–44; preaching of, 140–41, 142, 148; taxes, 148; Tinmal, settlement in, 148–50
Ibn Wuhayb, Malik, 124, 141–42, 180
Ibn Zalwi, 4; Ibrahim Ibn Tashfin Ibn Ali, 180; as Amir, 165; decrees of, 165; ineffectiveness of, 168
Id al-Fitr (feast, breaking the fast of Ramadan), 140
Idris II, 44–45
Ifriqiya (Tunisia and Algeria), 185
Igiliz, 140, 143
Ihya Ulum al-Din (revival of religious science), 128
Ijtihad (independent judgment), 89, 185
Imad al-Dawla Ibn Hud, 135, 157
iman, 3, 7, 11, 12, 29
Iman (Muslim prayer leader), 185
Iman al-Hadrami, 86, 209
Iman al-Mahdi (the Guided One), 142–43, 147

al-iman Mas'ud, 14
imports, 29
Isa Ibn Yazis al-Aswad, 30
Ishaq, 172
Ishaq Ibn Ali, 165, 168, 172, 180
Ishaq Ibn Ali Ibn Yusuf, 168
Islam culture, 4; Islamic law; fatwa (formal legal opinion), 184; remarriage, 54; tax structure, 210
Islamic reform; Almoravid, conquest of, 195; genealogical origins, 191; Ghana, 193; historical perspective, 191–96; Muslim rulers, 191–93; political theories, 192
Italukan Ibn Talakatin, 10

Ja'far Ibn Jahhaf, 112, 180
Jabal Lamtuna, 17
Jabal Tariq (Gibraltar), 69
Jaen, 164
Jahada (jihad root) 5
jahiliya ward, 37
jami' (Friday mosque), 185
Jami' Ibn Abd Allah, 29
Jami' Ibn Adb Allah mosque, 29
Jawhar, 193–94
Jawhar Ibn Sakkun, 4, 11, 180
jawzinaqat (sugared nuts), 26
Jewish incident, 72–73; Alfonso VI, surrender letter, 73–74; as poet, 75f; Ben Shalib, 72; siege of the capital, 73
jihad (holy war), 12, 185
jinn (supernatural spirits), 39–40
jizya (poll tax paid), 67, 91, 132, 185
jubbas, 58
Jumada al-Ula (November), 115, 151

al-kanbitur, 111, 116, 117
kasba (fortress or citadel), 185
katib (secretary or scribe), 185
Khaldun, Ibn, 189–90
khanjar (dagger), 82
kharaj (land tax), 90, 132, 185
Kharijite Muslims, 3
Kharijite sect; allegiance owed, 3; attitude toward central authority, 29; Bani Gudala, 8; Berber tribes, 2, 29; as diplomats, 16; extremists, 30; Ibadi school of, 86; iman, 8; instruction of, 8; Maghrawa Berbers, orthodoxy, 30; Maghrawa of Fez, 3; moral strictness, 30; Shi'ite, 3, 18
khettara, 185
khettqiblara, 123
khurras (tax assessor), 185
khutba prayer, 171
King Bucar, 213
King of Granada. *See* Abd Allah Ibn Buluggin Ibn Badis
King of Seville. *See* Mu'tamid Bin Abad
King Roger II of Sicily, 200
Koran, 3, 30; as allegory, 141; Barghwata, 32; customs dues, 90; edicts, 108; infidels, 30; Jihad, 78; maghram (illegal taxes), 186; ma'una (tax or aid during war), 186; paid reciters of, 16; science, 141; taxes, 5, 14, 18, 97, 102, 121, 132, 175, 176; wives, 8
Koumbi Saleh, 193
kufic (Arabic script), 124, 185
Kutubiya Mosque, 169

Lagardére, Vincent, 189, 191, 202, 208
Lahcen Taouchickt, 198
lamt (Arican Oryx skin shields), 13, 74, 185
Lamtuna, 186
Langewiesche, William, 178
Laqut Ibn Yousus Ibn ali al-Maghrawi, 36, 40–41, 66
Laqut Ibn Yusuf Ibn Ali al-Maghrawi, 36
law of the land, 18, 59
Leon, 72
Lisbon, 136
litham (veil), 127, 129, 177, 186
Luques, 155

madhhab (person subject to the law of his denomination), 130, 186
madrasa (theological university), 186
Magallon, 139
maghram (illegal taxes), 132, 186
Maghrawas, 33–34, 186

Index

Maghraws of Fez; heretics, 3; independence, 14; rulers, execution of, 15; as vassals, 14
Maghrib (West), 1, 186
al-Maghrib al-Aqsa, 44
Mahalla, 116
Mahdi (guided one), 186
Mahdiya, 88
Maimum Ibn Yaddar al-Lamtuni, 164;
Majjun Ibn al-Hajj, 83
Makhzan war, 61–57; 467/1074 siege, 66–67; 472/1079 siege, 65–66; 473/1081 siege, 66; 477/1084 siege, 67; Bani Hammud, 64; Bilad al Makhzan, 61; Diya al-Sawla Yahya, 66–67; garrisons, 62; historical perspective, 205–206; law and order, maintenance, 62; Sijilmasa, 62–63; Suqut al-Barghwati, 64–65; Taza Gap, 65; tribal government, 61; Tlemcen, 65; Umar Ibn Sulyaman, 65. *See* Ibn Tashfin
Malaga, 133
Malik Ibn Wuhayb, 124, 141–42, 180
Malikite Muslim law, 3
Malikite scholars, 3–4
Mallen, 139
maridin (insurgents), 186
Maridin revolt, 163, 171
Marrakech, 62; 472/1079, base camp, 65; Aghmat, 35–42; Almoravid warriors, 127; Amir Abu Bakr, base, 51; aristocracy, 85; Bilad al Makhzan (land of the storehouse), 61; book burnings, of al-Ghazzali, 128; dinars, 87–88, 119; emissaries, 72; evolution of, 91–92, 122–23, 125–27 expansion of, 59; fall of, 172; faqihs, payment to, 127; fortifications and power base, 59, 85; ideology, 85; imperial capital, 85; Jews, 126; Khettara (gravity-fed, water transportation system), 123; merchant businesses, 59, 125; mint, 153; mosque, 55–56, 85; olives, 126; palace, construction, 123; political and law center, 125; qadi, 82; qasr, 85, 121; Qubba, 124–25f; siege of, 150–52; Sufi Ibn al-Arif, execution, 128; Suq (market place), 127 taxes, 150; walled fortification, surrounding, 141–42, 144; war in. *See also* Ali Ibn Yusuf; Yusuf Ibn Tashin
Marrakech qubba, 124–25
al-Marrakushi, 174
Mas'ud bin Wanudin, last ruler of Sijilmasa, 14f–15
Masjid al-siqaya, 123
Masmuda, 186
Massufa, 186
Mauny, Raymond, 199
Max Van Berchem Foundation, 196
Mazdali Ibn Tilankan, 63, 66, 122, 136, 181
Mecca, 140, 186
Meknes, 43
ma'una (special war tax), 91, 186
merchants; bartering, 29; book, buying, 28; Friday mosque, 29; goods, 27–28; holy days, 29 Mali, 28; profits, reinvestment of, 27; success of, 27–28
Mertola, 163, 171
Middle Atlas Mountains, 43, 45, 62
mihrab, 167
minbar (iman preacher), 124, 142, 186
Mohamed El Mellouki, 198
Moroccan Institute for Archaeology and Middle Tennessee State University, 196
Moulay Idris, 43, 44, 65
Moulouya River, 56
Mozarabs, 133, 154–55
Mu'ammil, 102, 103, 181
Mu'ansir Ibn Ziri, 46–48
Mu'tadd, 95, 106, 181
Mu'tamid Bin Abad, King of Seville, 181; Aledo, siege of, 97; Andalusian war, 66, 77–78, 79, 80–82, 104; authority, handling of, 83; Castilian knights, raids on, 95, 96; historical perspective, 207, 211–12; Ibn Rashik, king of Murcia Ibn Rashik, quarrel with, 98–99;

Murcia, inhabitants complaints, 99; naval support, offer to Ibn Tashfin, 66; palaces of, 83; war preparations, 96; Zallaqa, battle of, 80–82
Mu'tasim Ibn Samadah, 101, 181
Mu'tasim, the king of Almeria, 99; boastfulness of, 99–100; in exile, 106–7 Ibn Tashfin, victory over Granda, 102; Seville, campaign, 105–7
Mubasir Nasir al-Dawla, 136
muezzin (man who calls to prayer), 31, 186
muhajirun (emigrants), 150
Muhammad, Prophet, 1
Muhammad Abd al-Hady Shu'ayrah, 189
Muhammad Ibn Abd Allah Ibn Hud, 168
Muhammad Ibn al-Hajj, 117, 135–37, 180
Muhammad Ibn Maimun, 164–65
Muharram (month), 73, 121, 139
Muhtasib, 131
al-Mu'izz, 89, 181
mujassimun (anthropomorphism), 40
Muluk al-Tawa'if (Taifa kings), 12
Murabits (gold coin struck by Almoravid state), 88
Murcians, 96, 99–100
muruqah (amir qualities), 55
mushrif (provost), 167
Muslims; African, 154; amir, 101; Bani Masmuda, 177; black guard, 82; books of law, 142; custom dues, non-Muslim, 90–91; dissent of, 2, 30; God, interpretation of, 140–41, 177; heretical, 77; holy days, 80; hostilities, initiation of, 67; inhabitants of Ghana, 86 jihad, 78–82, 102; land, non-Muslim owned, 90; Maghrawa rulers, 30; Maghribian, 176; Spain, 72; tawhid (absolute unity of God), 140; tribute, paying, 80, 112; unity among, 93; Valencia, 116; victory over Christians, 134; Zaragoza, 111. *See also* Alfonso VI; El Cid

al-muwahidun, 142
Muwatta (book of Malikite law), 8, 31, 186

Nafis River, 150
al-Nasiri al-Slawi, 192
Nassif Valley, 41
National Geographic, 196
Navarre, 72
Niebla, 163, 171
Nomads, 53–59; Bani Masmuda, 41; Berbers, 23; camel supply, 13–14; historical perspective, 204–5; homes of, 5–6; livestock, 27; pastoralists, 5, 13; protection service, 32; resources and services of, 14; seminomadic, 42; steppes, 65, 89. *See also* Abu Bakr
Norris, H. T., 191, 192, 193, 194, 201

Oporto, 136
Oran, 164, 165

Plain of the burnoose, 57, 63
poll tax, 67, 90–91, 132
Pope Sylvester II, 45
Pope Urban II, 133
prayer, call to, 31

qadi (judge), 74, 98, 131, 186
Qadi Iyad of Ceuta, 193, 200
al-Qadir, 72–73, 94, 111
Qal'at al-Mahdi, 45, 64
Qarawiyin Mosque, 45, 49–50, 167f
Qasba Bou Jaloud, 50–51
Qasim Ibn Abd al-Rahman, 48
qasr (treasure-armory), 53, 85, 186
Qasr al-Hajar (fortified repository), 53
Qasr al-Kabir, 159
qata'if (honey doughnuts), 26
Qayrawan, 2–4
qibla (direction toward Mecca), 31, 123, 186
Qubba, 124
Qubba al-Murabitin, 125f
qusur (sing. qsar), 22, 187

Index

Rabi al-thani (August), 55, 67, 78, 122
Rajab (month), 37, 106, 135
rak'a (prostration), 8, 31, 187
Ramadan (March), 37, 102, 103, 116, 142
Ramadan, feast of, 152
Raymond Berenger III, 137
Razi, 78, 106
Recemund of Elvira, 190
reconquista, 66, 72, 72, 135, 139, 147
Regaya River, 150
religious practices, 12
religious reformers, 31; Malikite, 19; Almoravids, 31, 45, 176–77; symbols of, 169. *See also* Ibn Tumat; Ibn Yasin
religious scholars (ulama), 3
ribat (fortified post), 11, 163, 187
Ribat Massa, 168
Risala (Malikite law compendium), 89–90
River Fez, 43
River Sebou, 211
River Ziz, 26, 43
riyad (garden), 123, 187
Rosenthal, Franz, 190
Rueda, 135

Safar (March), 155
Safiya al-Gudaliya, 194
Sahara Desert; Almoravid authority, 53, 175–77; Amir, 86; architecture of the, 178; Awdaghust, 15; Bani Gudala, 5; Bani Lamtuna, 5; Bani Massufa, 5; Berbers, 100; chiefs of the, 4, 86; cultural fusion, 178; customs of inhabitants, 88, 141; dates (fruit) produced in the, 28; desert warrior tactics, 19, 129; ethos, impact on inhabitants, 178; folklore, 10, 174; gold trafficking, 153, 161; historical perspective, 196–200; jihad in the, 77; Land of the Blacks, 6, 13, 21, 24; Maghrib, 6, 58; military governor, 129; nomadic encampments, 42; rebellion in the, 17–18; safe passage through, 13, 86; salt, source of, 32–33; Sanhaja confederation of tribes, 1, 4–9, 32, 53–54, 132, 137; Sijilmasa, 21, 24, 169; Sus al-Asqsa, 4; Taghaza, 32; teachers sent to, 4–5, 7, 174; territorial control of, 53–54, 59; trading centers, 23; Trans-Saharan trade, 2, 16–17, 21, 35; traveling through, 6; tribes of, 5, 7, 36, 177 178. *See also* Ibn Yasin
Sahara Unveiled, 178
sahib al-madina (chief of police), 131, 187
al-Sahrawi, 170
salah (piety), 187
salat al-hawf (prayer of fear), 155
Salé, 168, 170
Sancho Ramirez, 134, 135
Sanhaja, 187
Sanhaja Berbers, 2
Sanhaja nomads; Arat-n-anna, 9; Bani Hammad, 162; Bani Massufa, 66, 153; Bani Ziri, 3; baraka, 6; Berbers, 13, 14, 34, 129; bride price, 8; camel's milk, 55; clothing, 6; co-confederationists, 154, 176; commanders, 88; concubines, 8; confederation, 5; daily life, 6–7, 9; divorce, 8; dues, levied, 7; Fatimids, 2; garrisons, command of, 62; historical perspective, 191, 193, 204, 206; law of Islma, 7; male elite, 6; monogamy, 8; nourishment, 6; protection, selling of, 6; saints of, 8; solidarity, 10, 53–54; succession, 122; tribal aristocracy, 177; wives, legal, 8. *See also* Sanhaja
Santa Maria, 139
Santarem, 136
Sebou River, 45
Seddrai Ibn Wazir of Beja and Badajoz, 171
seguias (man-made canals), 35
sieges; 467/1074, 66–67; 472/1079, 65–66; 473/1081, 66; 477/1084, 67; Aledo, 97, 100; Calatayud, 137–39; Fez, 166–68; Maghrib, 35, 39; tactics, 97; Taifa kings, 211–12; Uclés, 134; Valencia, 114–17; Zaragoza, 76, 101, 139

Seljuk Truks, 3
Semegal River, 174
Seven Years' War, 159, 219
al-Shakir li'llah ("one who gives thanks to God"), 33
Sha'ban (January), 55, 86, 118, 171
al-shaqiy (villain), 154
Shari'a (law of Islam), 187
shashiyar (shawls), 58
Shaykh (a chief of a tribe), 187
Shaykh Haddad, 64
shaykhs, 13, 39, 41, 53, 61, 121, 167
Shi'ites, 1, 18
Sidi Mohammed Ben Abd Allah, 196
Sijilmasa; Agadir, 65; Aghmat Haylana, 35; Aghmat Wurika, 35; Andalusian, 69; Arab, 23; Awdaghust, 24; bargaining, 29; camels, 27; caravans, 24, 31; citadel, 19; control of, 24; daily life, 21; date production, 27; dates, 27; description of, 21–24; folk lore, 24–25; food staples, 28; Ghana, 16, 24–25; housing, 49; Isa Ibn Yazis al-Aswad, 30; Islam, introduction of, 4; itinerants, 49; Jami' Ibn Adb Allah mosque, 29; legends, 24; manufactured items, 26–28, 69, 88; Marrakech, 59, 125; merchants, 24–25, 27–28; Morocco, 88; Mosque of Ali, 136; Muslim, 193; nomads, 27; pasturage, 31; peddlers, 29; products, trade rarities, 26, 28; prosperity of, 24; Qarawiyin Mosque, 45, 50; religious dissent, 29–30; salt trading, 32; scholars and students, 28; Seville, 83; silent trade, 25; slave trade, 25–26; spices, 26, 83; Sunni Islam, 30; Suq Ben Aqla, 23; taxes, 90; traders; 23–25 tribes of, 12; water, 31; weights and measures, 131; wine, 145, 174
Sikka (striking of coinage), 87–88, 187
Silves, 171
Social Sciences Research Council, 196
Song of My Cid, 116
Souk Ben Akla, 197
spoils of victory, 12

sufis (mystics), 29, 163, 187
Sufriya, 30
Sufriya Kharijite, 30
Sunna (traditions of the Prophet), 1, 3, 11, 99, 127, 187
Suq (market place), 187
Suq Attarin (market of the spice merchants), 50
Suq Ben Aqla, 23
Suqut al-Barghwati, 181; Almoravid drums, 205–6; governor of Tangier, 47; as slave, 47, 64; Yusuf Ibn Tashfin, confrontation with, 205
Sura (Koran chapter), 31, 187
Sus, 62, 187
Syr Ibn Abu Bakr, 181; Andalusian war, 103–6; Badajoz. King Mutawakki, 115; death of, 135–46; Ibn Raskik, 98; linage, 64; Meknes, 88–89; polytheists, Christians as, 217; Santarem, victory of, 136; Seville, battle of, 81–82

Tadjra, 159
Tadla, 62
Tadmkka, 86
Tagat, 86
Taghaza, city of salt, 32–33
Taifa, 187
Taifa kings; Albarracin, 96; Aldeo, 112; Almoravids, 76, 98, 100, 111; al-Qadir, last ruler, 72, 113; Andalusia Muslim, 174; Bani Hud of Zaragoza, 71; Castilian force, 95; Christian reconquista, 76; cooperation among, 74; Cordoba delegates, 74; disputes among, 99; Ibn Tifilwit, 137; jihad, 72; misdeeds of, 101; Murcia, 112; Mu'tamid bin Abbad of Seville, 71, 129; Mutawakkil, 129; mutual mistrust among, 94; political cohesion, lack of, 71; religious laxity, 71; religious scholars, 89; Seville, 104; sieges, 93, 95, 98, 100, 103; 467/1074; taxes, 97; Toledo, fall of, 72; tribute, 80; Valencia, 72;

Zaragoza, 135. *See also* Alfonso VI; Ibn al-Khulay; Ibn Rashik; Musta'im; Mu'tamid of Seville; Yusuf Ibn Tashfin; Rodrigo Diaz de Vivar (El Cid)
Taifa war, 112; Alvar Fanez, 117; El Cid, 116–17; historical perspective, 207; Valencia campaign, 113, 116–17
Tajo River, 156
Takrart (outpost), 66
Talrart, 165
Tamasna, 62
Tamdult, 17
Tamim, Muhammad Ibn, 181; Aghmat, retreat to, 150; Andalusian jihad, 134; brother, dispute with, 99; capture of, 99; Ceuta, siege of, 66; as commander, 89. 134, 150; as general, 56; as governor, 62, 147; as minister of state, 89; Suqut al-Barghwati, execution of, 67; Uclés, siege of, 134; Zaynab, 121
Tangier, 47, 64–65
Tansift River, 41
taqlid (blind adoption), 89, 187
Tarazona, 139
Tarudant, 18, 159
Tashfin Ibn Ali, 181; battles of, 158–60; geneaological background, 156; historical perspective, 220–21
tawhid (belief in the unity of God), 140, 142, 187
taxes, 67, 90–91, 132, 186
Taza Gap, 44, 89
Tebferilla, 17
Tetouan, 159
Tinmal (white), 149
Toldeo; Alfonso VI, 72–73, 76, 82, 207–8; Almoravids, confront, 159; Andalusian campaign, 157; as Amir, 161; campaign against, 73; as Christian tributaries, 72; Christian campaign, 155–56; command, removal from, 156; death of Reverter, 164; decrees of, 163; defeat of, 159; fall of, 71; Granada, defense of, 155; hasham, 156–57; historical perspective, 217, 220–21; legend of, 157; Mozarabs, 154, 158; Oran campaign, 171; Tetouan, occupation, 159; Timal, battle of, 158–59; Tlemcen, 161–62
traders, 25–26, 86, 161. *See also* merchants
Trimingham, J. S., 191
Tunisia, 88
al-Turtushi, 3, 102
Two Rocks, 162

ulama (religious scholars), 3, 140, 167
Ulama of Sijilmasa, 13
al-Umari, 198, 199
Umar Ibn Dayyan, 150
Umar Ibn Sulayman, 56, 65, 88–89
Umayyads; Cordoba, 33, 44, 70–71; establishment, 1–2; gold, 2; Malikite law, 45; Qarawiyin Mosque, 45; Sijilmasa, 33; Sunni, 1; trade center, control of, 33; ushr (tithe), 188; Zanata confederation, 2–3

Valley of the Law, 159
veil, wearing of, 127, 129, 177, 186
Vila, Bosch, 189
vizier (state administrator), 188
Volubulis, 43

Wadi al-Kabir river, 83
Wajjaj Ibn Zalwi, 4–5, 11, 181, 192, 194
Wawayzagt, 159
Wurika, daily life in, 42
wusta, 71

Xeres, 171

Yahya Ibn Abu Bakr al-Sahrawi, 166, 167, 170
Yahya Ibn al-Aziz, 162
Yahya Ibn Ghaniya, Muhammad, 156, 180; Almoravid rule, 170; Balearic Islands, 171–72; Berraz Ibn Muhammad, 164; Christian

campaign, 158, 163–64; as governor of Cordoba, 154; Jaen, 164; Maimum Ibn Yaddar al-Lamtuni, 164
Yahya Ibn Ibrahim; camel loads, dues upon, 6–7; chief of the Sanhaja, 1; death of, 10; historical perspective, 191–92 pilgrimage, 4; Saharan confederation, 4; Zanata, free agents, 3
Yahya Ibn Ishaq, 161
Yahya Ibn Takaght, 161
Yahya Ibn Umar, 165; as Amir, 165; Bani Gudala conflict, 17; Berber alliance, 17; as chief, 10, 53–54; death of, 17; fatal mistake of, 17; Gudala nobility, 11; Ibn Yasin's teachings, 10; ideological platform, 176; mother, 10; retreat of, 11
Yahya Ibn Yaghmur, 164
Yaqut, the geographer, 178
al-Yasa Ibn Abu 'l-Qasim, 29

Yusuf Ibn Ahmad al-Batrugi of Niebla, 171
Yusuf Ibn Makhluf, 169–70

Za River, 164
zakat (alms), 12, 12, 188
Zanata Berber, lack of unity, 5
Zanata confederation, 2
Zaragoza, 76, 135, 137
Zawi Ibn Ziri, 70
Zaynab al-Nafzawiya, 188; Aghmat, 92, 107; ambitions, 57; as concubine, 40; divorce of, 54, 204; education, 39; Laqut Ibn Yousus Ibn ali al-Maghrawi, 40; legend of, 40–41; marriages, 40–41, 54–55; physical description, 38–39f; political influence of, 55; role of, 201; sons of, 89, 121; as widow, 40. *See also* Abu Bakr Ibn Umar, 39
Zirids of Granada, 3–4, 71
Zuhr, 151

About the Author

Ronald A. Messier is professor emeritus of history at Middle Tennessee State University (MTSU), where, from 1972 to 2004, he was professor of Islamic history and historical archaeology. From 1992 to 2008, he was also a senior lecturer at Vanderbilt University. He directed the excavation of the ancient city of Sijilmasa, the city in southeastern Morocco that served as a springboard for the Almoravid advance into the Maghrib. He is currently directing a new archaeology project, the medieval city of Aghmat, which served as the Almoravid capital before they built their new capital of Marrakech.